C000244274

Escape from Stalag Luft III

I find him a born raconteur. His escapes, his operations as a Spitfire pilot, his experiences as a prisoner of war, and his incredible escape crossing the Pyrenees – all are described in a breathtaking manner which made me read his book through in one sitting. I have seldom read a book which shows such sincerity and modesty.

Dr L. de Jong
Department of Documentation
Ministry of Defence of The Netherlands

Squadron Leader Bram Vanderstock, 1945

Escape from Stalag Luft III

The True Story of my Successful Great Escape

Bram Vanderstok

Foreword by Robert Vanderstok

Preface by Simon Pearson

Greenhill Books

Escape from Stalag Luft III: The True Story of my Successful Great Escape

Greenhill Books

Greenhill Books, c/o Pen & Sword Books Ltd,
47 Church Street, Barnsley, South Yorkshire, S70 2AS, England
For more information on our books, please visit
www.greenhillbooks.com, email contact@greenhillbooks.com
or write to us at the above address.

PUBLISHING HISTORY
The memoir of Bram Vanderstok was first published in 1983 in Dutch by De Haan/
Unieboek bv., Bussum. It was translated and published in English by Pictorial Histories
Publishing Co, Montana, USA in 1987. This revised edition has a new foreword by
Robert Vanderstok, a new preface by Simon Pearson and a new plates section.

CIP data records for this title are available from the British Library

ISBN 978-1-78438-434-0

Typeset and designed by JCS Publishing Services Ltd
Typeset in 12pt Minion Pro

Printed and bound in in Great Britain by TJ International Ltd

Contents

Foreword

Robert Vanderstok

The admonition, 'For you the war is over!', is a recognizable phrase
from many a Hollywood movie. While the line has become camp,
the meaning is certainly one that every captured pilot was made to
understand. Their incarceration in the 'escape-proof' Stalag Luft III
prisoner of war facility was designed to invalidate and incapacitate these
warriors from continuing their military missions. Of course, the British
and European RAF pilots of the North Compound of Stalag Luft III
had ideas that differed greatly from their jailers. They were still active
service members and they had a role, indeed an obligation, to escape
and harass their captors. That they would succeed in this effort to plan a
'great escape' and thereby redirect Nazi resources and personnel to such
a great extent would surprise historians for decades after the event. That
event, now termed 'The Great Escape', has been filmed, documented and
written about by numerous authors and military historians.

While the initial plan was to break out some 200 plus men,
circumstances reduced that number to less than half. Still, this was no
small feat and the impact it created within the Nazi war machine was
palpable. Hitler's initial reaction was to shoot all escapees as a message to
all others still held. Others in his high command convinced him to lower
that number to only half of the recaptured airmen.

Remarkably, seventy-six men succeeded in exiting the tunnel 'Harry'
on that cold winter night in March 1944. Equally remarkable is the
German's efficiency in recapturing seventy-three. And sadly, fifty of those
seventy-three were shot. Or more accurately – murdered. Twenty-three
were returned to various camps (seventeen returned to Stalag Luft III,

four were sent to Sachsenhausen and two to Colditz Castle). Rounding out the statistics, only three escapees made a 'home run' to Great Britain.

This is the story of one of those home runners – my father, Bram (Bob) Vanderstok.

———

Before and after the war, my father was a medical student. Coincident to his studies, he had learned to fly as a reserve officer in the Royal Netherlands Air Force. His dream of becoming a physician was obviously interrupted by that small, life-changing event we now call World War II. He could never have anticipated the disruption to his life and his country in the days and months ahead.

The invasion of Holland took place in May 1940. The Dutch were no match for the German *Blitzkrieg* and capitulated after a mere five days. To young men like my father, the new dynamic of living in an occupied homeland became unbearable and challenging at the same time. He was determined to get to England, the only Allied territory in Western Europe still able to resist the Hitler juggernaut.

While most remember my father as a successful escapee from the infamous Stalag Luft III camp, in fact he made numerous attempts to escape occupied Holland. He ultimately succeeded, in 1941, by travelling in the hold of the freighter *St Cergue*, sailing under a Swiss flag. The many Dutch nationals who succeeded in escaping their German overlords and reaching England were called *Engelandvaarders*. There was great pride in being an *Engelandvaarder*. It meant your resistance to the Nazis would remain proactive.

With the Dutch royal family ensconced in Great Britain, my father, who had come to know HRH Prince Bernhard, discussed how he could best serve his country. He was already a flyer and the RAF readily took him on as a pilot officer. He excelled at flying and in short order established himself as an ace. Those moments of glory were short-lived. On 12 April 1942 this Spitfire fighter pilot was shot down over France.

He was captured and brought to the prisoner of war camp Stalag Luft III, in Sagan, Germany, near the town of Breslau. His memory of the camp was 'that it was not all that bad'. What he didn't know was that his two brothers, who had remained in the Netherlands and engaged in espionage, had also been caught. Unlike him, they had been transferred to concentration camps and perished in those camps.

As chronicled in the many stories about Stalag Luft III, airmen were quickly drafted into the escape effort. Skills were assessed and assignments made. Individual contributions and propensity for success dictated one's escape number. My father was number eighteen out of the tunnel.

The effort to organize a major escape was somewhat akin to managing a large corporation in that the multiple pieces of the puzzle needed to fit together perfectly. Unlike a corporation, the 'Big X' organization had to maintain strict secrecy. Digging a hole was easy enough. Dispersing the excavated dirt, shoring the ceiling and walls, piping in vented air, electrifying the tunnel and hiding the tunnel entrances made the task more challenging. Securing documents as templates for false documents was doable, but painstakingly forging precision documents with implements as small as paint brushes with two brush hairs took extraordinary patience and durability.

After months of work, the escape was finally set for the night of 24 March 1944.

While many escapees travelled in pairs, my father felt that a solo journey would be the safest for him. The story herein details that journey. It is frightening, today, to read his 'arrest' warrant in the *Sonderausgabe zum Deutschen Kriminalpolizeiblatt* (Special Edition of the German Criminal Police Bulletin) subsequent to his escape. His parents' home in Holland was under constant surveillance. His father was brutalized in the interrogations conducted by the Gestapo.

The postscript to the story is that he successfully completed his escape, returning to England within four months. He returned to service, was given command of the 322 Spitfire Squadron and flew for the rest of the war. At the conclusion of the war he and his squadron were repatriated to the Netherlands.

Most importantly, my father achieved his dream of becoming a physician and emigrating to the United States. His children knew him as a physician, not a military man. And it was years before we came to learn his true and complete record. He received an honorary OBE (Order of the British Empire) from Great Britain, the French Croix de Guerre and the Dutch Distinguished Flying Cross twice. He went on to become the Netherlands' most decorated military officer. He was offered the post of Chief of Air Defence on the Dutch General Staff, a position delivering a most promising military future. None of these accolades or career opportunities swayed him from his larger goal of becoming a doctor in America.

The story of 'The Great Escape' has taken on a certain timelessness, even as many wars and conflicts have preceded and succeeded this event. Most participants in this event have long passed on, but for their families there is much pride. It is with such pride that we present his story.

Preface

Simon Pearson

Three quarters of a century after seventy-six Allied officers broke out of Stalag Luft III in eastern Germany in March 1944, the story of one of those men still resonates strongly with the glorious spirit of their endeavour and the wretched pain of their sacrifice.

He was the Dutchman Bram Vanderstok, better known today as Bob Vanderstok, author of this book and the eighteenth man out of the 350-foot tunnel known as 'Harry', which was immortalized in the Hollywood film *The Great Escape*. Perhaps more importantly he was one of three men who managed to get back to Britain, making it the most successful escape of the war involving RAF officers.

The breakout was just one skirmish in Bob Vanderstok's multi-faceted battle against the Nazis, in which he was driven by the events he witnessed and the knowledge of what the Germans had done to his country and his family. And late in his life, he bore testimony against Hitler's regime with this biography, which was written from memory and published in 1987, long after the years when he had taken lives in combat and then dedicated himself to the preservation of life as a physician and surgeon.

By the time the war ended in May 1945, Vanderstok had confronted the Nazis in many guises: as a fighter pilot in two air forces; as an 'intelligence officer' trying to organize the Dutch resistance; as a belligerent prisoner of war confronting the Germans in their own backyard; and, once back in Britain, as a member of the Allied forces liberating Europe.

First and foremost, though, he was a proud patriot, a son of the House of Orange who developed strong connections with his country's royal family. The reader can almost hear his Dutch accent in the English translation.

But while his courage and single-mindedness brought him victories – he ended the war as a fighter 'ace' and the most decorated Dutch airman in history – every step in Bob Vanderstok's war was blighted by tragedy, even in his moments of triumph.

When the Germans invaded Holland in 1940, Vanderstok was a fighter pilot with the Dutch air force, and made several 'kills', but the country was quickly overrun.

When he decided to become an *Engelandvaarder* – one of the Dutch men and women who chose to resume the fight alongside British forces – he made a remarkable escape in the hold of a boat, where he had to put up with all sorts of privations. Worse still, he became all too aware of the plight of his own people and the collaborators in their midst.

When he finally reached the safety of Spain after escaping from Stalag Luft III, his sense of absolute elation – his moment of triumph – was dispelled with the news that fifty of the officers who escaped with him had been murdered on Hitler's orders.

Worse still, the news was delivered by a high-ranking British official, a Mr Street, who told Vanderstok, 'We are extremely proud of you. A beautiful job.' And then had to admit that his own son, Denys, was among the RAF officers shot by the Gestapo. It must have been an unbelievably difficult moment for both men. But that is the nature of this book. It rattles with honesty, delight – and pain.

Vanderstok paints a rich picture of cosmopolitan London, the restaurants and underground clubs where the Dutch *Engelandvaarders* gathered, the joy of shopping at Austin Reed in Regent Street, not to mention the forbidden fruits of the wartime capital. As he writes with obvious delight more than forty years later: 'Girls? Everywhere, and with enthusiasm on their side. The general evaluation of the English girls had been that they were slightly cool, a little snooty, and a little Victorian. But … at night, they're all right!'

He also gives a graphic account of air combat, being shot down and the distress and discomfort of his first days as a prisoner.

He makes one statement about being incarcerated that stands out above all others made in the many books about the motivation of the prisoners at Stalag Luft III. As he writes of his experiences in the camp, where there were many fellow Dutchmen: 'X was an escape organization and also caused as much damage to the enemy as possible in every other way. German morale sank, and we were able to use more guards than ever before [for gaining information and supplies]. We still were fighting a war!'

That was just what was intended by Roger Bushell, 'Big X', the leader of the Great Escape, and more than any other man involved in the enterprise, a kindred spirit of Bob Vanderstok. The prisoners in the huge camp just outside the town of Sagan carried on the fight by all means possible.

Primarily a forger, Vanderstok was involved in virtually every theatre of operation in the camp, a mission that was breathtaking in its ambition and scope, and involved about 600 men, an army of elite Allied serviceman engaged behind enemy lines. Bushell ordered the building of three tunnels – the legendary Tom, Dick and Harry – so that, if one were discovered, they could fall back on the other two. The shafts were deep and the tunnels robust, shored up with wooden boards pillaged from beds and panelling, lit by electric lights and air-conditioned. They are still used today as case studies on engineering courses.

At the same time the prisoners turned Stalag Luft III into an outpost of British intelligence, gathering information on industrial data, military manoeuvres and German secret weapons, which was sent to London in coded letters.

While the escape committee intended to get 200 men out of the camp, the overriding goal was not to get prisoners back to Britain, which they knew was unrealistic, but to aid the Allied war effort. As Vanderstok wrote more than forty years later, the senior officers 'agreed that most escapees would have very little chance of making it to a neutral country, and even less of a chance of reaching England. Two or three pilots in the huge organization of the Allied forces would hardly make any difference at all, but a mass escape from Stalag Luft III would be an event of major importance.'

He was right. Within twenty-four hours the escape was the subject of heated exchanges at Hitler's headquarters in Bavaria; and just a few days later it was in Winston Churchill's in-tray.

Unusual among the men who broke out of Stalag Luft III, Vanderstok travelled alone – relying on his own skills and instincts – just as he would for the rest of his life, and he succeeded in returning to Britain.

He rejoined his band of Dutch patriots in England, and flew again with the RAF, but he started to turn his back on the past, a lost world in which he had revelled as a child in faraway parts of the Dutch empire, part of a happy, thriving family, a young man who learned to handle a boat on the Zuider Zee, excelled at ice hockey and entered medical school.

Vanderstok lost not only fifty comrades from Stalag Luft III, but bore the suffering of his father, who was tortured by the Gestapo after the escape from Stalag Luft III, and his two brothers, who died in the Nazi concentration camps.

Instead of helping to rebuild the country that he worked so hard to liberate, he turned down the opportunity to lead the post-war Dutch air force, and left for a new life in America.

Vanderstok was proud of his role in defeating the Nazis, and strong anti-Nazi sentiments remained with him for the rest of his life. So did the solitude and his single-mindedness. As his son Robert acknowledged: 'Great men often have great flaws. But those flaws are hard to express in an autobiography … one element in his character is that he kept a distance in all his relationships. In the context of the war, this is understandable, but that distance remained with him throughout his life. On the one hand it saved him, on the other it diminished him. Everyone was kept at arm's length. Showing vulnerability was not part of his character.'

But there was a rich dividend too. 'Getting shot out of the air is not necessarily heroic, but it is pretty unique,' said Robert. 'And escaping from a POW camp is utterly unique. Few of us can put that on our résumé. For us, our father is as much a hero for his work as a doctor as he is in flying his Spitfire. But it's not heroics that are central to the story. Rather, it's the uniqueness of his story which is of the greatest importance to us, his family – and unique stories can be inspirational.'

Introduction

When I was asked to put my experiences during World War II on paper, I thought of two possibilities. Because of the fact that there is so much literature about the war, I first considered describing the adventures and circumstances in the form of a novel. On second thoughts, although the novel form would offer more dramatic liberties, it would be impossible for the reader to distinguish reality from fantasy. For me, the book is of importance because it is a part of my life. It actually happened to me. For this reason, I decided to write it as a documentary, whereby only true facts are described, exactly the way I lived through them.

It was not my intention to simply give a chronological account of what happened in the war in the air during those years from 1940 to 1945. For this, one should read the works of Churchill, Eisenhower and those historians who give the complete survey of the war in Europe, including all those events that had nothing to do with me. This book tells of episodes and events as they were related to me, and as I and my family personally experienced them.

Many persons are involved in any war, and certainly in a war like World War II. It is, of course, impossible to mention all the people who were part of the happenings of those days in that theatre of war, but I have also left out names on purpose; names of persons related to events of an extremely unpleasant or degrading nature have been left out. This does not change the truth of the facts and it would only tear old wounds wide open without benefit to anyone, or to the course of history.

The book *The Great Escape* by Paul Brickhill, which was made into a film of the same name, gave a very good and truthful description of life and events at Stalag Luft III. Yet many personal experiences could not, of course, be included in Brickhill's work because some of those involved could never tell their stories; they were killed.

I am one of those lucky ones who survived the war, and I can remember my emotional experiences, and those of my friends, as if they had happened yesterday. For many of us the horror, the injustice, and the cruelty can never be forgotten or forgiven; but I have tried to write without too much bitterness. I believe I can, now, after forty years. It is no secret that not all people were heroes during the war, and that in those days we saw the weaknesses of many of our brethren, sometimes friends, sometimes even family members.

When Paul Brickhill wrote *The Great Escape*, he asked my permission to write about my part of the escape, which I of course granted whole-heartedly. In turn, he gave me permission to use parts of his book in case I would ever write my own story. The drawing of the tunnel in Stalag Luft III is from his book; most photographic pictures are my own.

This book has been dedicated to the Dutch fighter pilots of World War II – my friends, my pilots who so rightfully earned the military Williams Order for the Dutch Air Corps, as it was called in those days. The Royal Dutch Air Force of today was created after the war. Except for those five days in May 1940, there was no Dutch Air Corps or Dutch Air Force. All Dutch pilots were attached to units of the British Royal Air Force or British Royal Navy. Also, the 322 Dutch Spitfire Squadron was a regular RAF squadron, though almost all pilots were Dutch.

Escape from Stalag Luft III originally was written in the Dutch language. After much publicity, I was repeatedly asked to translate the book into English, which in some instances is almost impossible. Every language has its idioms and slang expressions which do not quite translate into another language. How would one say the Yiddish *mazzel*, the German *überhaupt*, or the Dutch *lellebel* in English? There was even a considerable difference between the English we spoke then in London and the English we speak today in the United States.

The English version of *Escape from Stalag Luft III* is slightly different from the original Dutch version, but the documentary nature of the work has not been changed. The text still reflects true adventures, as they happened to me personally. Some names have been changed, and some passages of the original script which had been scratched have been re-inserted.

Bram (Bob) Vanderstok
1 January 1985

Vanderstok's Escape Route from Stalag Luft III

Location of Stalag Luft III

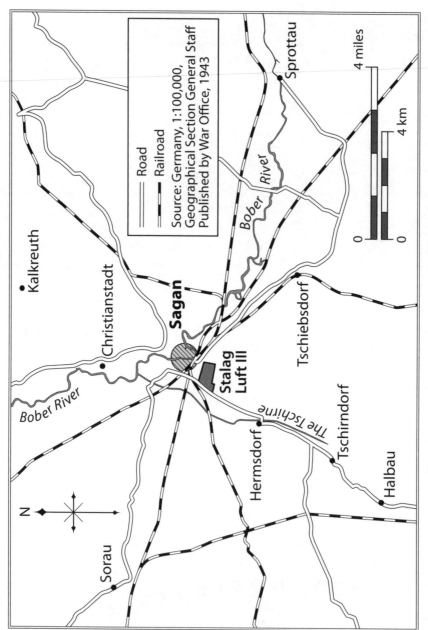

Transport Links around Sagan and Stalag Luft III

Stalag Luft III

Hut key
A Russian barracks
B Red X parcels store
C Book censorship
D Clothing
E Dentist
F Russian barracks
G Theatre
H Church

Shower block
Sick bay
Cells
Coal shed
VORLAGER
C E
A B D F

Cook house
Sports field
Lat.
Fire pool
Lat.
East Compound

G
H
Fire
Pool
Cook house
Sports field
Centre Compound

Kommandantur

Woods
Guard room

Harry
Sick bay
Cells
Coal shed
Parcels store
Electrical building
Guard room
VORLAGER
Coal shed

Fire pool
Cook house
Theatre
Shower block
Sports field
Dick
Tom
North Compound

South Compound
Woods

West Compound

N

Shot Down over France

It was 7:30 in the morning on 12 April 1942. Royal Air Force Squadron 41 was being briefed by Squadron Leader Peter Hugo for the operations of the day. The German radar stations were active along the entire coast, from Brest to Den Helder, in the north of Holland, but it was known that the reliability of the German radar left much to be desired. For instance, the Germans could not pick up fast-flying aircraft below a thousand feet, except at very short distances, and then too late to scramble their own fighters.

Therefore, it was possible to approach the French coast before the flak was ready to receive us. Naturally, it was important to know where the German fighters came from, their strength, and how much time it would take them to respond to our tactics. These were the reasons that we carried out the so-called sweeps, to get the Luftwaffe up in the air. Our own high-flying reconnaissance Spits gathered photographic intelligence, and our own radar on the south coast of England could follow the reactions of Herman Goering's fighter squadrons.

There had to be a reason before the Germans would respond in great force. They knew that a sweep of a few fighters over France would be relatively harmless; their flak could shoot at them and there was no need to use the Luftwaffe in strength. For this reason, we staged such sweeps with a great number of Spits and Hurricanes, which on German radar screens would appear as a major bomber force.

At 7:55, we sat in our Spitfires under absolute radio silence from pilots and control towers. At 7:57, Squadron Leader Hugo gave the hand signal to start our engines. Twelve Rolls-Royce Merlin engines thundered into action; checklists were done in seconds, blocks were removed, and Spits began taxiing to the leeward side of the grass field. At 7:59 Peter (Hugo) was with Red Section – ready to scramble, cockpit canopy still open, checking on his boys. A hand went up, canopies were closed, and at 8:00 a.m. Red Section took off, immediately followed by Blue and Yellow Sections.

In command of Yellow Section, I set my gyro-compass just before takeoff and followed Peter on his right. We had written our code word of the day on the palms of our hands so it could be wiped off with a little spit in case of …

The Spit roared into action and I felt myself pushed against the back of the seat. Wheels were up almost immediately after they left the ground, and then I adjusted the pitch of the prop. Next, I put the cannons and machine guns in firing position.

We kept a close but comfortable formation, on a course of 110 degrees, and climbed to an altitude of 10,000 feet, 'angels ten', as we called it. After a while, we saw another Spitfire squadron, and another one, and several more a little higher. Halfway across the English Channel, the sky was full of Spitfires and Hurricanes. I knew there were twenty-five squadrons assigned for today's sweep over France. In my thoughts, I counted: twenty-five times twelve. Well, that meant three hundred fighters, each with two cannons and four heavy machine guns. Six hundred cannons and twelve hundred machine guns were quite a deadly force to reckon with. We carried no bombs and no external fuel tanks this time, so speed and manoeuvrability were ideal. We maintained absolute radio silence.

When we passed the French coast, we heard the first radio message from our own ground control station. We were to change course and head for Target A. This message was expected because we knew there were no ground targets for us. But for the Germans, who tried to decipher such radio messages, it sounded like a bombing run on a certain target. For us, it was the signal to widen our formation into so-called battle formation. This meant we flew about two hundred feet apart, freeing our eyes to look around.

At this point the Germans could see us, and started shooting with their heavy flak. I saw the black smoke puffs of the exploding ammunition at our altitude which meant they were shooting at us. One of those black clouds came rather close, however, and I ordered my flight to take evasive action:

'This is Jackknife Yellow Leader, Yellow Section 30 degrees to the right.' After a few seconds we repeated the turn to the left to join Red and Blue again. I felt a slight shaking, as if flying through an air pocket.

The flak was not very effective because we were such small targets. And due to our speed and frequent course changes, we were also difficult targets. The altitude of our operation, between seven thousand and ten thousand feet, was too high for their light flak and somewhat low for the heavy anti-aircraft guns, due to speed-angle problems. We veered to the north, and for some time we were not bothered by flak, but other squadrons reported heavy anti-aircraft shooting. From my viewpoint, I saw an area to my left which was literally dotted with the deadly, little black cloud-puffs.

Ground Control back in England gave a short message: 'Jackknife, this is Olympic. Bandits scrambling.' That was what we were waiting for. The Luftwaffe came into action and the Germans began sending up their fighters, exactly what headquarters at home had planned and hoped for.

We heard a few other squadron commanders giving orders, indicating that they had already seen 'bandits'. Soon I also saw some formations of three or five Focke-Wulf Fw.190s – little black dots, about three miles off our starboard side – but nothing happened other than more radio talk. Because of that, some squadrons were shifted to other radio channels. It was 8:30 a.m., and the sun was still very much in the eastern, cloudless sky. In the west, I could just see the white cliffs of Dover just across the narrow part of the English Channel.

At that time, each of our Spits already had a 'bubble canopy'. This Plexiglas contraption over the cockpit gave the pilot a slightly better field of vision than the older types. The windshield was made of laminated glass, of a plate at least two inches in thickness. Not only did this provide a nice, bullet-proof piece of protection right in front of your head, but it was made with optical precision so that it formed an integral part of the gunsight. A small, lighted cross was projected, as if suspended in air, apparently two hundred yards in front of the plane, at the point of highest concentration of the bullets of our machine guns.

It was not easy to hit a fast-moving and turning target with bullets fired from a fast-moving and turning airplane. Furthermore, bullets are ballistic projectiles, so they travel in a curve toward the ground. It takes the bullet a little while to reach its target and, during this little while, the target moves at a speed of some 300 miles per hour. These five factors make it a certainty that you will miss your target if you pull the trigger while keeping the little cross on the enemy plane.

With a good carpenter's eye and a lot of practice for corrective angles, a very good marksman could score about 2 per cent hits. In the Dutch Air Force such a sharpshooter was said to have 'shoes with points'. If you kick somebody with pointed shoes, it hurts. Some of us even had two pointed shoes painted on the fuselage as a warning: 'Watch it, these shoes can hurt you.'

'This is Jackknife Leader. Bandits four o'clock above.'

All heads of Squadron 41 turned to the right and looked up. Indeed, there they were, nine Focke-Wulf Fw.190s flying in three, loose V-formations of three, about one mile to the right and behind us. From our ground station 'Olympic', back in England, we heard, 'Jackknife, cockerel crowing. Bandits on your starboard.'

We instantly flicked a little switch. Within seconds came, 'Jackknife, cockerel out,' and we complied.

The *cockerel* was a very secret little electronic gadget. It produced a small deviation at the top of the radar blip, on the screens of the boys at home in the operations room. Our radar operators picked up not only German fighters on their screens, but also our own. Because of this very ingenious little bit of electronic wizardry, they knew who was friend and who was foe. This way we were warned when enemy units would come a little too close.

But in spite of this very important information, a fighter pilot, out of habit, constantly looks around, above and below himself. Looking back was not possible, and the wing blocked out some of the view down, but for that we had a tactical system that worked if everybody did his job as he should, a difficult task in combat.

The RAF believed in the 'buddy system' – always stay in pairs. A squadron was usually made up of flights, and each flight consisted of four fighters. The squadron commander was 'number one' of the Red flight, and the Blue and Yellow flights had the two flight commanders as their 'number ones'. The others followed in succession – Red two, Red three, and Red four – and the same with the other two flights. 'One' and 'two' were buddies, as were 'three' and 'four'.

Buddies were never to leave each other. The number two and four buddies would fly behind and slightly to one side of their leader, so we could always see our buddies. Also, our buddies would not fly in the turbulence of the ones in front of them. Number twos and number fours covered the space behind the flights next to them. Number ones and number threes could concentrate on right, left, ahead, and above.

I flew as number one of Yellow flight, at the starboard side of Peter Hugo, our South African squadron commander. Out of the corner of our eyes, we watched our own places in order to keep the general formation intact. On the other side, we kept an eye on those 'bandits'. It was a matter of wait and see; we actually did not fly an aggressive mission.

Probably blinded by the sun, or whatever, nobody had seen the Focke-Wulf Fw.190 that pulled up right in front of me, not more than a hundred yards away.

The radio crackled in my ears, 'Jackknife Yellow Leader, bandits attacking.'

It happened fast, in spite of all eyes looking and everyone expecting to see the German pilots attacking. We knew there were bandits at four o'clock above and yet they jumped us, unseen. The Focke-Wulf pilot was fast in his dive, but because he pulled up, he lost his speed and for just a moment remained hanging in front of me.

I reduced throttle and only had to make a very small correction to get the German exactly in the middle of the gunsight. This was such an unusual situation that I opened with cannons and machine guns at the same time. After the first burst, of about three seconds, I gave a short order, 'Jackknife Yellow, attack.'

The Focke-Wulf was still in front of me and I saw a thin stream of white smoke coming from its fuselage. That meant that I had hit his gasoline tank – or was it a condensation trail? – but he was still an ideal target. Again I opened fire, this time with the cannons only. It might be better

5

to save my other ammunition, you never knew. The Focke-Wulf jerked to the right and made a complete roll, leaving a white and black trail of gasoline and oil.

On the radio I heard, 'Good shot, Van!' Van was, at that time, my nickname.

With a smile I said, 'Jackknife Yellow, form up again. Join the squadron,' and I looked behind at my number two. No number two; where in the hell was my number two?

'Oh, my God,' I thought, 'the attack must have been on him and he may have been hit.' I barked, 'Jackknife Yellow Two, where are you?'

There was no answer, but after a few seconds I recognized the voice of 'Dutch' (Peter Hugo's nickname), our squadron commander. 'Jackknife Yellow Leader, your number two is over here with me.'

'Jesus Christ,' I muttered. 'You will hear from me, buster.'

But I had no time for such thoughts or mutterings. A second Focke-Wulf came from the right, straight at me. I pushed my nose down, throttle wide open, made a hard roll to the right and pulled up. Again I saw the German, now to my left and just a little ahead of me. Again I had a target exactly in the right place. But with my head turning from left to right, I saw yet another Focke-Wulf to the left, well below me. Now, I made my mistake. The bandit in front of me was such an ideal target that I aimed and pumped him full of 20-mm, armour-piercing bullets. Part of the tail flew off and the rest of the machine went down in a jerking spin.

In the excitement of the moment, I had forgotten that I had no number two – I was not covered from the rear! This was the most essential factor of air-combat tactics. Immediately after I realized my situation, I heard a sharp click somewhere in the back of my Spitfire and … there was the other Focke-Wulf firing at me. I saw his tracer bullets and again I heard that clicking noise in the back of my fuselage. The rudder vibrated, but I could still steer the machine during the dogfight that followed.

The rudder began to vibrate much more and I was losing altitude in my left turn. The German was now behind me, and I could see him use his 20-mm bullets. At the next moment came a loud explosion, and it was clear that he had hit me to the point where I had become a lame duck. I was hit and my Spit couldn't fly anymore, but ailerons and elevator still worked.

Planing through the air at seven thousand feet, 'angels seven', there wasn't much else I could do. I thought a moment. But then reality came back:

'For God's sake, don't go off in a daze, do something! If you continue like this the German will, no doubt, come back and blast you with another full load.'

Fortunately, that did not happen. A belly-landing? Without a rudder, probably without flaps? No, that would not be the right solution. Bail out? Well, that seemed to be the only choice. First, disconnect the electric wires and the oxygen tube. Second, undo the straps, but only the seat straps, not your parachute straps. Next, your hand in the grip of the rip cord and just climb out of the cockpit.

At the top of the canopy there was a little rubber ball, the emergency release, and I pulled the thing with a positive jerk. The canopy flew off and I found myself in an open cockpit, going some 350 miles per hour. Just climbing out of the cockpit was entirely impossible, and I did not want to pull up to an almost-stall with that Focke-Wulf Fw.190 still next to me. The Spit could still be steered a little, the elevator still worked. Black oil came into the cockpit and I could smell gasoline. An explosion or fire is not something to wait for, so I made a forward loop by kicking the stick to the front as hard as I could. Instantly, I was in the air.

It was a strange feeling. My thoughts were crystal clear, my right hand firmly on the rip cord handle, and I remembered the classroom instructions on parachute jumping: 'When you are in the air, free from your plane, count to ten and pull the rip cord.' I began … 'one, two, three …' Then, 'What the hell?' I saw no Focke-Wulf, I saw no Spitfire – forget that counting – 'seven, nine, ten', pull. The beautiful, white, Irving parachute opened with a slap and I just hung in the air, at 'angels six'.

Not quite. Parachute straps go over your shoulders and between your legs, and they should be as tight as possible, according to regulations. The Spitfire cockpit is small and body movements are somewhat restricted, so very tight straps are uncomfortable. My straps had been loose, so I could move my shoulders and look around better. The seat belts must be tight, of course, in case of 'negative-g', but two sets of very tight straps were too much. So when the parachute opened, I got a hard direct hit between my legs, an unpleasant part of the male body for hits.

There was a blue sky, a bright sun, and I could see the cliffs of Dover across the Channel, some seventy miles to the west. And, far away, a number of small black dots, my squadron and the others going home. Below were wheat fields, grass fields, a small village, and a few country roads; it all looked very peaceful and quiet. Was that land under me a place so involved in a terrible and brutal war?

I looked around and nothing seemed to happen. I actually had a feeling that I wasn't going down at all. I simply stayed in mid-air – vertical air movement? Suddenly I heard engine noise and a Focke-Wulf Fw.190 passed me with incredible speed. My first thought – 'Would he fire on a man hanging from a parachute?' But then I saw him wiggle his wings before he disappeared in the distance.

After a while I saw that I had been going down, and that I seemed to go faster and faster. My landing point was clearly in front of me, right on top of a church steeple! A church steeple, of all things. That was certainly the last place you want to come down with your parachute. Imagine the possibility of being speared on the sharp steeple and making history in such an hilarious manner.

Back in flight school days, we had learned that one could steer a parachute, at least a little, by pulling a handful of strings on one side. The chute would then veer to that side. I pulled about ten strings with my right hand, because I wanted to miss that church. The whole damn parachute all but collapsed, and I very quickly let go again. Instantly the silk ballooned open and I got my *second* hit between the legs. But I was well away from the church, and I landed in a small courtyard of a farm.

The farmer and his wife rushed toward me, as if offering help in case I was injured, but said nothing. Nervously, I said, in my best French,

'S'il vous plaît, mes amis, aidez-moi, où sont les maquis? Je suis un aviateur anglais. L'église peut-être, vite, aidez-moi.' Total silence.

I tried it in English, 'Help me, quick! I am an English pilot, get me to the underground people.'

At this time a German squad entered the courtyard. With machine guns pointed at me, I was made a prisoner. The farmer now started to talk to his wife, '*Lien, de moffen waren al op het erf…*' 'Lien, the Germans already were in the yard.'

By God, that was pure Dutch, my mother language. I did not know that the people in this northern little corner of France still spoke Flemish, which is very much the same as Dutch.

Whatever the language, I understood that I had been coming down with a large white parachute on a bright sunny day, and that everybody had seen me landing in that courtyard. Chances of escape would be nil and any attempt at this time would have resulted in shooting. Calmly, I gave my handgun to the German *Feldwebel*. Then I noticed that my parachute straps were still locked on me. The Germans were polite, but kept their guns trained on me and ordered me to take my shoes off. I was then escorted to an open army vehicle. With a German soldier on each side of me we drove off, to … well, where to?

They took me to an airfield and I saw at least forty Focke-Wulf Fw.190s parked under trees, with the usual camouflage nets and some small buildings. The *Feldwebel* ordered me to get out and enter a building, which turned out to be the officers' mess of this small base. Several German pilots looked at me as if I were a monkey in a zoo, and then I was introduced to a lieutenant:

'*Leutnant Hanselhoff, ich habe Sie abgeschossen* – 'I have shot you down.' I had little desire to say anything at all, and he went on in an unpleasant tone, 'How many victories do you have?'

'Six,' I said.

'*Ach so, ein Anfänger,* a beginner,' Hanselhoff said. 'But you shot down two of ours; we lost one pilot. Get out!' He continued in German and I was escorted out to the car again. 'A beginner?' Nobody had ever called me that.

We went to a headquarters in a nearby town, a big house with stairs and a row of regular prison cells on the second floor. They pushed me into one of these and locked the door. No interrogation, no food, no water, no shoes. There was a small window high on the wall, too high to reach, and a bed with a mattress. Nothing else.

I just sat on the bed, trying to think about all that had happened in the last few hours. Reality came without further talk; I was a prisoner of war. Automatically, I reached for a packet of cigarettes in my breast pocket. There were no cigarettes. Instead, my escape kit was there, fully intact. Night came and I heard the noise of bombers and anti-aircraft guns. I just sat there, too tired to sleep, wondering what would happen to me next.

The next morning I was given a mug of water and a piece of bread, and I was allowed to use the toilet. With a short, *'Heraus, bitte'*, I was taken to a car again. *Heraus, bitte* means 'come out, please'. I had not expected the word 'please'. Frankly, I had expected a kick in the butt. This time the car took me to a railway station where I saw a long train full of prisoners of war, waiting for departure. After two hours the train started to move.

The Trip to my Youth

The train was a combination of the old-fashioned, third-class passenger cars and open freight cars – with German guards, heavily armed with rifles, pistols, hand grenades, tommy guns, and machine guns mounted on tripods. The train compartments were each filled with twenty prisoners, with a number of guards in the corridors. In contrast with the relatively polite reception I received at the German air base, the attitude now was quite different.

Shouting, pushing, and kicking seemed to be the order of the day. Many of the prisoners sat on benches or on the floor, tending their cuts and bruises from German rifle butts and boots. None of us were allowed to wear shoes, we were dirty, and the windows were closed. Even a request to go to the rest room was quickly and roughly refused:

'Absolutely not, *Schweinhund*. If you want to shit, just do it in your pants.' A rifle butt made it clear we had better be very obedient.

The trip by train lasted two days and two nights, sitting in the overcrowded compartment. Occasionally, a guard entered with a bucket of water and a cup. Everybody was allowed to drink the stale water, and twice during the entire journey we were given two large pieces of sourdough bread, which we divided among our companions. The windows remained closed but the door to the corridor was open, allowing at least a little air to come in. The stench was almost unbearable when some of the *Kriegies,* prisoners of war, vomited or could not hold their other natural functions.

The first few hours I thought of escaping. I could take a guard by surprise (after all, I still had my pocket knife) and then quickly change into his uniform. I could easily smash the window and jump out (during the night, for instance), in a tunnel when the train would go slowly. But these thoughts disappeared quickly.

The glass of train windows is thick and strong, and I had no shoes or anything else with which to smash windows. The train did not travel at a great speed but still it went too fast for human bones. Attack a German guard? Come on, they were standing in pairs, they were armed, they would not come into the compartments, they had shoes on, they had fingers on the triggers of their guns. Come on, dreamer, forget it.

Escaping from the train became an absurd thought and I began to think about other things. Where would they take us? A concentration camp? A military prisoner of war camp with official rules according to the Geneva Convention? Of course nobody knew, and it made no sense to think about it. There was nothing I could do but simply wait and see what would develop.

I began to daydream about my life, and how probably one bullet or one little manoeuvre in my Spit had changed the entire course of my existence. This was something I had not planned on and not expected, in spite of my knowledge of the chances of survival for a fighter pilot. A South African pilot with a dirty bandage on his head could not 'hold it' any longer, he had to go. He put his head through the door opening and called the guard in the corridor. Instantly he was hit, and the wound started bleeding again.

I said in German, 'Herr Lieutenant, the man is sick. He has diarrhoea. Please.'

The German, not a lieutenant at all, softened slightly and said, 'Out of ze vindow.'

A second guard appeared in the doorway, with his finger on the trigger of his tommy gun, and the first guard entered the compartment to open the window. The poor South African pulled his pants down and, with the help of two of us, tried to sit in the window with his behind halfway outside. Then he let go the full load, which blew and splattered all through our compartment.

Two others asked for the same privilege but the guard said, 'No, too much *schweinerei*', and closed the window. One of our boys tried once more, 'Please, sir', but he was roughly pushed back on his seat with a short *'Nein'*. The stench became worse.

I could understand part of the conversation between the guards. The 'shit situation' was the same in all the other compartments and very unpleasant for the German guards, as well. An officer, followed by a *Feldwebel*, walked through the corridor and gave short commands, always answered by, *'Jawohl, Herr Leutnant. Heil Hitler.'*

An hour later, the train stopped somewhere in the middle of open terrain and through the windows we saw a group of soldiers set up machine guns on tripods. Six machine guns were in a semicircle, and the rest of the circle was completed with branches or shrubs which were stuck into the ground. Between the machine guns were other guards with rifles in their hands and hand grenades on their belts. Those canisters with their handles, yes, we knew what they were. No, this was unthinkable. Not even German soldiers would murder a bunch of unarmed prisoners of war in cold blood.

But why, then, that preparation? Soon we knew why. Through the window, we saw a group of about fifty POWs being marched out to the circle and almost immediately all trousers went down. So that was the reason for the stop, the stink became too bad for the Germans themselves. After a few groups had done their poop, the lieutenant came to our door and yelled, *'Raus, scheissen!'* Translation into English was entirely unnecessary. Our group went out to shit.

The South African with the bloody bandage started to vomit again. With both hands on his stomach, he walked to the edge of the circle. Instantly a machine gun rattled and bullets splattered in the mud in front of his feet. His face white as a sheet, he looked where the bullets came from and then collapsed. Trousers went up. There was no toilet paper, of course. We carried our friend back to our compartment. He was not hit but the warning was clear. We took our places in the stinking train car. No one talked. I heard the Germans complain monotonously, *Schweinerei*, or *Jawohl, Herr Leutnant*. When the last group was back in the train we moved on again, destination unknown.

Now I realized what was happening. My hands trembled, which was something very foreign to me. I had never felt much fear, even when

Germans would approach me with guns and bullets, but now I realized that those bullets of the Focke-Wulf were aimed at me – to kill – and that these guards would shoot to kill.

Being shot at was not a new experience for me, but being hit and *shot down* was something nasty. Having my life saved by means of a parachute was also a little more stunning than the everyday glamour of the life of a fighter pilot. Although I was not physically hurt, the emotional shock was bigger than I would have liked to admit. Was the war finished for me? That was an unacceptable thought. What about my medical studies which I had started before the war? And if, yes, if I ever became a doctor, would I practise in a Germanized Holland?

We just sat in the stinking train with blank expressions on our faces. Nobody spoke, and after my thoughts about by own future, which seemed to have taken such an abrupt change of course, my memories took me back to the days of my youth and the beautiful and fantastic life in our family. At that moment, I realized more than ever the love and affection of our Vanderstok family.

My father, Cornelis Vanderstok, had made a career in the Shell Oil Company as an engineer from the University of Delft. My mother, Annie Snethlage Vanderstok, was an exceptional person with artistic talents and a classical education. The three sons – Felix, myself, and Hans – were born in Indonesia (at that time the Dutch East Indies), and one girl, Ankie, was born in Holland. My place of birth, Pladjoe, Sumatra, I do not remember. But Balikpapan on Borneo, where Hans was born, came clearly to my mind.

The house was built on poles to provide some protection against snakes and crocodiles, and opposite was the company soccer field. My father was on the soccer team. Every Sunday there was the *Wajang* show, a performance of puppet shadows projected on a screen, accompanied by the typical gong-music of a gamelan orchestra. I was five years old, but I remember how, about once a month, we were put on the kitchen table with a sheet pinned around us for the Chinese barber to snip at our hair.

The house had an outhouse, one of those boards with a hole and a lid, placed over a small ditch which ran to the river. The outhouse made a lifetime impression on me because one day, when my father lifted the lid, he looked straight into the eyes of a crocodile. He ran back to the house to get his shotgun and then fired a shot through the hole. In a flash, the monster ran to the river and disappeared.

Shell Oil transferred us back to Holland. On a freighter with passenger accommodation we travelled from Soerabaja, on Java, to Rotterdam, a voyage which took a month. We were on the Indian Ocean when I saw all the passengers hurry to the port side of the promenade deck, shouting something like, 'There she blows,' so I also ran to the railing and saw nothing.

'Did you the see the whale, Bobbie?' With a red face I said, 'yes', and even today I feel embarrassed. A few days later we were in the Suez Canal and again everybody ran to the side and shouted, 'There, there.' Again I ran, and again, being only three feet tall, I saw nothing but legs and skirts of other passengers. 'Did you see the camels, Bobbie?'

In Port Said, a magician came on board and he produced live little chicks – from my mother's purse, from under my hat, from everywhere – and finally pulled a little dog out of a basket we knew was empty. The next day, in the Mediterranean, my father pulled a dead chick out of his pocket.

The arrival in Rotterdam was also very clear in my memory, as was the beautiful, red brick house just outside The Hague. The three little boys, who at this time spoke better Malay than Dutch, were now real Hollanders for the first time. This meant that I had to go to school. But little Bram, or Bob, as I was called, already showed a sense of independent decision-making and simply said, 'No, I don't want to go to school.'

And no team of mothers or teachers could make me take one step toward that classroom. My mother had to take me home, where she promptly called my father at the Shell headquarters in The Hague. I had to answer the telephone myself, and within half an hour I was sitting in the first grade classroom. I have never revealed what my father said over the telephone.

In 1927, we went to Curaçao in the Dutch West Indies, where my father was appointed managing director of the then-largest oil refinery in the world. Living in the company house, we had a life of swimming, sailing, water polo, fishing, and hiking in the special atmosphere of the Caribbean. We caught sharks, lobsters, and, as members of the Sea Scouts, we had our own little island in the huge harbour – the Schottegat.

Every morning a company launch took us to school in Willemstad. There were two huge wrecks of three-masted ships in the bay, which we explored and searched for imaginary treasure. Under the guidance of my mother we created a large shell collection, with scientific names and all. It was life in Paradise, with parents who understood what we had.

After two years in Curaçao, my older brother Felix and I were sent back to Holland for further education. When I was fourteen, we returned to the family for an extended vacation of three months in Curaçao. Paradise had not stopped yet.

For a moment, when the train slowed down, I came back to reality. The guards had allowed the window to be slid down a few inches, which gave us some relief from the stench, but then I sank back into my thoughts again.

In Holland, with many friends, we established an ice hockey club. During Christmas vacations we went to St Moritz in Switzerland to play hockey and ski. I remembered the international ski jumping competitions, sitting in the bleachers, next to Charlie Chaplin. Strange that such thoughts would come up in such detail. The wonderful events during that episode of my life must have made a deep impression on me, a memory spectacle that cannot be erased.

After high school in Holland, my parents sent me to the Lyceum Alpinum in Switzerland, a junior college-level boarding school where the spoken language was German. The difficult academic demands of the school were extremely well combined with a programme of sports – ice hockey and skiing in winter and tennis, field hockey, cricket, swimming and gymnastics at other times.

The school was in Zuoz, a village in the Engadin which was the heart of Switzerland's winter sports and a gathering place for tourists from the entire world. It was here that I was bitten by the ice hockey bug; it became my major sport for the next eight years. Every day I skated and practised on the fabulous ice rinks of the school, skating faster and faster, shooting the puck harder every day.

What did all this dreaming have to do with the abominable situation of the moment? Instead of musing about my fabulous youth, my incredible parents, my brothers and sister, wouldn't it be much better to start thinking about the present situation – the stinking train, the wounded South African pilot? The reality was, however, that there was nothing any of us could do at this time. During these hours of unpleasant emptiness, the memories overwhelmed the reality.

In 1934 I graduated from Zuoz, and in the almost-hypnotic stream of thoughts, I even remembered the questions of the oral exam in mathematics:

'Herr Vanderstok, would you please describe the spheres of Dandelin?' (Those two fitting balls in a cone.) And then, in French, 'Monsieur Vanderstok, let us talk about Jean Jacques Rousseau, please.'

In physics, oh yes, the thickness and length of the wires in a transformer? It all came back to me. A bad one also.

I had never been very good in history and had never scored much more than a questionable passing mark on report cards. There was a break for me during these final exams. In the Dutch and German languages, my name in spelled van der Stok, with a capital 'S'. That is very late in the alphabet, and I was one of the last students to be examined. I noticed that the professor from Zürich used our history book. Tomorrow would be my turn for this oral exam and the next subject had to be Napoleon the Third. That evening I read the chapter again and again, and the next morning I entered the room where the professor and my own very nervous teacher were sitting at a table.

Expecting a disaster, the teacher asked with a trembling voice, 'Herr Vanderstok, please tell me something about Napoleon the Third.' His mouth fell open when I produced a smooth and fluent story of the life of Napoleon the Third.

'*Ausgezeichnet*, Herr Vanderstok! Very, very good!' my history teacher exclaimed, and looked at the professor who nodded in agreement. What a delightful memory. Passing the final exam provided me with an entrance qualification to any medical school in Holland. That summer I went sailing with Felix on the fabulous lakes near Leiden and the Zuider Zee, still a wide, open sea.

The train stopped again, probably somewhere in Luxembourg, and again the guards formed a half-circle with their machine guns on tripods. This time, guards with Luger pistols in their hands completed the circle. The place was at the edge of a wooded area and the Germans simply did not take any chances. A Polish pilot, who was in great need and thought that he could just make it to the 'shit circle', ran from the train to the marked area. The German officer shot twice, and our Polish friend fell to the ground screaming.

Instantly, all prisoners stood still with their hands up in the air. The officer ordered, '*Loss, scheissen*.' Trousers went down and the much-needed procedure continued. The Polish pilot was hit in his left foot and a German guard clumsily dressed the wound with a bandage from a first-aid kit. His friends carried him back to the train car. The rough reminder made me realize that shooting at a prisoner who appears to be running away is probably something our own troops would also do. If I had been in the lieutenant's shoes, I might have done the same thing.

Shoes? Strange, that word shoes. None of us had shoes and escaping by just running away, without shoes, might cause a problem even after an initial success. Walking around without shoes draws attention. Actually, it was rather clever of those Germans to have everybody take his shoes off. Would my brothers Felix and Hans be walking around in shoes? Or would they be wearing shoes with points, so they could hit the Germans hard enough to hurt them?

The train went on slowly and stank more than ever. This time it was my turn to sit on the floor, and I once again sank into the details of my youth.

With some friends from Zuoz, we had rented a real fishing boat in Spakenburg, a small village on the Zuider Zee. Before we went to sea, we gave the *Botter* a good going-over with water, soap and a FLIT spray, much to the surprise of the onlooking fishermen who could not quite believe that these skinny city boys could handle this boat. One of them, dressed in Sunday costume, including wooden shoes, came aboard and with one easy movement pulled up the big lee-board.

'You see, young man, that is how we do that,' he said with a smile, and stepped ashore again.

Without a word I took the thick Manila rope in my hand, put one foot on the gunwale and pulled the lee-board up with one hand. 'Is this the way you did that?'

The men on the shore laughed and joked in their Spakenburg dialect and we were considered OK. We sailed to Harderwijk, Hoorn, Urk, Marken, and Volendam. Then I remembered the shallows east of Marken where we struck ground and had to wait four hours for the tide to lift us off.

In September 1934, I entered medical school and became a member of the Student Fraternity, LSC. My hair was cut off and I had to go through the greenhorn initiation. A silly teasing period but it was tradition, so, well, not too bad. I played the saxophone and they put me on a mooring buoy in a harbour; I had to play there all day. There was a good side to this novitiate, called *groentijd*. Together, we novices endured the aggressive teasing of the older students and we got to know each other well, a process often resulting in lifetime friendships and the feeling of belonging to a worthy group. Fraternity brothers were our most honourable and trustworthy friends until the war destroyed those values.

The train stopped several more times, as more prisoners became sick and vomited on the floor. They apologized for making such a pigsty of the compartment but they could not help it, and for that matter, we could not do anything about it either. The German soldiers also were tired and didn't get much more than water and bread. The only difference was a piece of sausage occasionally, and probably some diluted beer whenever the train stopped at a station.

Every time the officer passed, they jumped up and shouted, 'Heil Hitler.' The lieutenant, also dead-tired, would respond,

'Sit, but don't sleep. Two hours to go. *Gott sei dank!*'

A few hours later we stopped at a large railway station, where a new group of guards was waiting on the platform. Our guards marched off. The officer handed a big yellow envelope to the new officer-in-charge, a *Hauptmann* – 'captain' – with the familiar salute, 'Heil Hitler!' accompanied by a clicking of heels and austere faces. An enormous load of shoes was thrown onto the platform, and some of the prisoners were ordered to pick them up and hand them to us in the compartments. It was obviously impossible to find your own shoes so we just took whatever looked more or less like our size.

I could count that there were about 180 prisoners on the train. About ten of them had to be carried or were in need of support. The Polish pilot with the bullet wound in his foot had somehow got hold of a broom, which he had transformed into a primitive crutch. He could walk by himself, and apparently the Germans allowed him to use it. I stood next to him and offered my shoulder because it looked as if we would have to walk some distance.

'*Djen dobri*,' said the Pole. 'No need, I can manage. Perhaps help some of the others.'

I replied, 'Bravo Polski,' and I believe I smiled.

'*Aufstehen!* Get up! *Marchieren!*' the German captain shouted. Several guards repeated: '*Marchieren! Loss, loss!*'

Our entire group slowly rose and started to march to the square in front of the railway station, where a number of old-fashioned streetcars were waiting. There were twice the number of guards, but I do not believe any of us had plans to escape, under these circumstances. We were tired, we were carrying our wounded comrades, and the emotional shock of the sudden change from combat pilot to prisoner of war had taken its toll.

The trams were comfortable, compared to the filthy train compartments, and we could breathe fresh air for a change. They took us through hilly countryside to a place perhaps half an hour outside the city. Nobody knew where we were. The streetcars stopped close to a group of buildings and I could read a sign: '*DULAG LUFT*'

Loud shouting again, '*Raus, Raus! Marchieren!*' We walked to our first prisoner of war camp – the receiving and interrogation unit for prisoners of the Luftwaffe, at Oberursel.

From Medschool to Dogfight

Dulag Luft was a receiving camp just outside Frankfurt, on the Main River. Without any show of military discipline, the pitiful group of prisoners marched through the gates. Small red-, white-, and black-painted sentry boxes were at the entrance, and a double, eight-foot fence of barbed wire surrounded the compound. The guards were now all Luftwaffe personnel, with the distinctive yellow patches on the lapels of their uniforms.

They counted us, '*dreiundfünfzig, vierundfünfzig …*'

Very soon I discovered that this was only a temporary place, but it was a tremendous relief to walk around and be among English-speaking colleagues and comrades. It felt good to use our own RAF customs and manners. There was an English senior officer, a wing commander with the equivalent rank of a lieutenant colonel in the Dutch military.

The camp was a complex of six wooden barracks, a sort of central warehouse, a kitchen, and a reception hall. All the prisoners I saw were Allied air crews – pilots, observers, bombardiers, navigators, radio operators, and gunners – and all belonging to the various nationalities of the Allied forces. There was a small sports field, about half the size of a football field, and around the whole setup ran two rows of barbed wire fence, with rolls of barbed wire in between. At the corners of the camp there were watchtowers, equipped with searchlights and machine guns mounted on tripods, and manned by German Air Force soldiers.

The sudden quiet, the fact of not feeling surrounded by enemy soldiers with their fingers on the triggers of their weapons, gave me a strange and almost relaxed sensation. Wing Commander Jones came to me with outstretched hands and a smile. He introduced himself and then conducted a sort of tour to the showers and the warehouse, where we each could get new clothes, socks, shoes, a toothbrush, soap, and a towel. We each were assigned a wooden bunk with mattress, a pillow, and two blankets.

'Wings' Jones, already two years a prisoner himself, was, compared to most of us, an older man – of about forty. He happened to know 'Dutch' Hugo, my squadron commander, quite well. We immediately felt like old friends.

Smiling, I left the warehouse with all my new gear under my arm, and a sergeant took me to a room in one of the barracks. The room had three double bunks, a table with two benches, and a stove in a corner. Each of us had a locker, and each barracks building had one room equipped with washbasins and cold-water showers. The cold showers shook me out of the apparent peacefulness. I still had my escape kit, which I had been hiding under my dirty garrison cap when we entered the camp.

'Just a minute, my friend,' I said to myself. 'There is obviously a great difference between the train and this relatively comfortable camp. But …'

As an officer, it was not only my duty to try to escape, it was also my wish. I soon learned that prisoners of war were called *Kriegies*, a colloquialism derived from the German *Kriegsgefangen*.

After getting acquainted with my cell buddies (although it was not a real cell but more a room), I walked along the barbed wire to the sports field, and examined the fence inch by inch. I tried to find weak spots, dead angles for the watchtowers. What would I need to get through this double barrier? Then I walked to the entrance gate. How and when was it opened, who could pass, did they have to show a pass or did they use a password?

The big gate was opened for supply and garbage trucks only. Individuals walked through a small gate at the side. The Germans showed a piece of paper every time they went through. One by one, some of us were escorted to a building outside the camp and would return after an hour or so, obviously for interrogation. Then I noticed a small building, just outside the gate, with large cages on one side. I could see at least four big German shepherds.

In the afternoon, about four o'clock, there was an inspection called *appel*. We had to line up on the sports field in four rows. Guards posted themselves at four corners and a *Feldwebel* counted the number of *Kriegies*; I think about four hundred.

After the count, which was done twice a day, we each received our meal, which consisted of a watery soup of potatoes and carrots with a large bone somewhere in the huge pan. All of this was distributed by our own people. It was at this time that I learned about the food parcels sent to us by the American Red Cross. Not only were these parcels a heavenly contribution to the barely adequate meals the Germans provided, but they would later play an important role in the activities of all POW camps.

The next morning, I went to our senior officer and told him I still had my escape kit fully intact and I wanted to escape. I knew this part of Germany quite well and I spoke German fluently; Dutch was my mother language and Holland was not too far from here. In Holland I would be able to get help, and I was physically in good shape. Squadron Leader Jones looked me straight in the eye, and with a sympathetic smile he said,

'Van, I know how you feel, but think and plan a little longer before you act. We don't want to lose fellows like you.'

My first thought was something like, 'Oh, oh, this man has been here too long. Can't expect much help from him.'

Fortunately, that was only a momentary thought, because very soon it became clear that he was right. The Germans were no small boys at this game. *Kriegies* from Dulag Luft had tried to escape many times, but nobody ever made it. It was almost impossible to escape from this relatively small camp without being shot at or having a big police dog cornering you within minutes. For hours and hours I walked along the barbed wire, thinking, observing and trying to create a plan. But again and again I had to admit that escaping from here was impractical, if not impossible.

A feeling of desperation came over me, but not for long. The incredible change from the glamorous and dangerous work with the Spits, furloughs in London, dawn patrols, sweeps, the safe return from missions and then the waiting at readiness again – it was all so different from my present situation, sitting in a closed camp, just thinking.

The next day my name was on the list of prisoners to be interrogated by German intelligence. I said to myself, 'Do not forget, name, rank and number and nothing else.'

But I knew about military interrogations with bright lights in your eyes, hitting in the face, injections, wood splinters under your nails, kicking, and so on, although I had not seen anybody return with signs of such treatment. A German guard calmly escorted me to one of the bigger buildings outside the camp, to a simple room upstairs where a *Hauptmann* sat behind a desk. He offered me a chair and gestured to the guard to leave us alone.

In fluent English, he started, 'Good morning, Captain Vanderstok. This is a routine interrogation without any strings attached. Please sit down and make yourself comfortable.'

I said something like, '*Dankeschön*', and sat down on the chair in front of him. No bright lights, no other Germans in the room, no orders, no arrogance.

'Well,' the *Hauptmann* said, 'did you ever get over the shock of being shot down? Would you prefer to speak in the German language?'

'English is OK. Whatever you like,' I replied. Immediately, I noticed that the *Hauptmann* apparently knew that I could converse in either one of these languages. Everything was quite different from what I had expected.

'Captain Vanderstok,' he continued, 'I see a look of surprise on your face, but, and this is no secret, I have your papers in front of me. And ... let's see ... you are a Dutchman, escaped to England?'

I said nothing and he continued, 'Well, you don't have to tell me that. I believe it is somewhere in these papers. Twenty-three years of age, your RAF number is 4468321 AN, and your name is "Bram". But we also have you under the name "Bob", how is that?'

'"Bob" is a nickname and "Bram" is my real name,' I said.

The *Hauptmann* went on, '*Ach so*, and your squadron was number 41, Squadron Leader Hugo, and your base was Westhampnett near Tangmere. Oh yes, shot down over St Omer by one of our Focke-Wulf Fw.190s, and you were on a sweep to get our fighters up in the air. Do you have anything to add to this report?'

No wonder I had a look of surprise on my face, and all I could say was, *'Deutsche Gründlichkeit'* – 'German thoroughness'. And I must admit, I could not suppress a moment of laughing.

The *Hauptmann* also laughed, and asked if I were wounded. When I said that I was not hurt, he continued, 'Medical student at the University of Utrecht, two brothers, a sister in Switzerland, parents live in The Hague in Holland. Are your parents in good health?'

I said, 'As far as I know, the whole family is in good health, but of course, very much concerned by the circumstances of the war.'

'That is understandable. Do you happen to know the telephone number of your parents in The Hague?'

I knew the number very well and gave it to him, after which he picked up the phone and said, *'Geben Sie mir Den Haag, Holland, 792251 bitte.'* After a few minutes he said, 'Herr Vanderstok, this is *Hauptmann* Schmidt of the German Luftwaffe. Your son Bram was shot down over France but he is healthy and he is not wounded. For him the war has ended, of course; he will be a prisoner of war.'

After a while he said, *'Ja, ja, bestimmt,* he is right here, next to me,' and he gave me the telephone.

'Père,' I said in Dutch, 'this is Bob. I am fine … not wounded, just a prisoner of war. And, at least so far, they have treated me reasonably well.'

'Das ist genug,' the *Hauptmann* said, and took the horn in his own hands again. Then he ended the call. I could not believe my ears because it was so totally different from what I had expected. Perhaps there were some human Germans after all.

Hauptmann Schmidt went on, 'I actually have no further questions. For military information, I do not need you. In this respect, we probably know more than you anyway. One more question, do you know Wing Commander Stanford Tuck?'

'Of course,' I said, 'every fighter pilot knows who Bob Tuck is.'

'Ach so, then Bob Tuck and Stanford Tuck is the same person?'

'Shit,' I told myself. Clever little fellow, that *Hauptmann*. 'Well, that was a clever question,' I said, 'but I actually believe that the entire Luftwaffe knows who Bob Tuck is, just as much as we all know who *Oberstflieger* Adolf Galland is. Both are exceptional fighter pilots.'

25

The German officer grinned and said, 'Very true … you may go back to the camp. But, before I forget, where are your brothers Felix and Hans?'

At that moment my friendliness cooled, and I said, 'I do not know where they are, I have been out of Holland more than a year now.'

'Your family is anti-German,' Schmidt said, 'and those brothers of yours are playing a very dangerous game. It would be better for those boys to sit out the war.' Then he pushed a buzzer and the guard took me back to the camp. I had experienced the surprise of my life.

On my way back to the compound, I took a very good look at the dog cages and tried to discover what kind of a pass the German showed at the gate, but he was not about to let me see it. I inspected the barbed wire once again, and became even more convinced that escaping through the wire would not be very possible. After a few days, I realized I was coming back to the same thoughts all the time and my thinking made no progress at all.

I forced myself, almost by self-hypnotic concentration, to start thinking along other lines. My brains needed a good bath, which is something you can only do yourself, by pure willpower; then direct your thoughts positively in another direction. Every time my thoughts tried to find weak spots in the barbed wire fence, I forced myself to change my mental computer in order to make room for new, fresh, and realistic planning.

It was difficult to do this. How could I wash my own brains, sitting in an escape-proof little prison camp that did not provide the figurative detergent so essential to cleanse my own brains? But I found my soap in older memories, memories of the years before 10 May 1940, beautiful years of happiness and fun. This self-invented therapy should not be too difficult, considering the fabulous days of my youth.

After graduation from junior college in Switzerland, I registered at the University of Leiden and rented a room. My father had given me a beautiful microscope and I was ready to go in for the real job and become a doctor. At home I was always considered the 'little doctor' if anybody needed a bandage, or minor care of a scratch or so on. I would wash the little abrasion, put tincture of iodine on the wound, and then dress it with a bandage.

At twelve years of age, I already said, 'This will burn just a little but hold on, it will disinfect the wound.'

I still say something like that when I give my patients an injection. During the initiation days in the fraternity, I missed most lectures. Except for zoology, they were all subjects which were not specifically medical – such as mathematics, physics, inorganic chemistry – like college basic sciences, but on a much higher level. Histology was at least something where we had to use our microscopes.

The study programme of the first year was almost entirely non-medical and much more demanding than I had ever anticipated. I talked to older students, and began to realize that the medical degree required far more than my youthful image of this profession had led me to imagine. At the same time, I had to adjust to the new phase of my life in a fraternity, my new friends, and the various activities of student organizations, which included sports and the traditional doings of Dutch students. These things I liked and I signed up for varsity rowing.

Life at the Club Minerva became more important than the dull lectures in mathematics and physics. Friendships with my fraternity brothers deepened; they became companions I took home on weekends to my parents' home in The Hague. These were the same kind of people who were my father's best friends, also fraternity brothers from the University of Delft. My brother Felix, also a student at Delft, had a very similar group of friends who also visited the house frequently. Now I was a student myself, enjoying the same traditional delights except for one thing. I thought they should just eliminate those difficult (in my opinion, non-medical) lectures in the first year of med school.

It became clear that, at eighteen, I was not ready for independent study at the university level. Soon I was so far behind that I felt embarrassed to attend classes; it was too apparent that I had missed 90 per cent of the lectures. I had 'no time' to study and, to make things worse, I happened to be in my best ice hockey years and regularly played with the national team in places like Amsterdam, Paris, Berlin, Hamburg, and Brussels.

Those were years of glory and the memory of those events was, for the moment, the best therapy for my turbulent thoughts.

World championships in Switzerland, our names in the newspapers, win or lose; it was a life of fun and glory. With ice hockey you can really get things out of your system by playing a hard and aggressive game.

You can play away the bothersome thoughts of not studying, and even feel good afterward. It became an accepted excuse for postponing my duties as a medical student: 'Oh well, one year just for ice hockey, that's no crime, I'll catch up later.'

But when the hockey season was over, it was doubly difficult to return to my studies; the rowing season had started. Well, this year was shot anyway so why not! Let's go rowing.

For all practical purposes, I had given up my first year of medicine. But I had not told my father yet. 'Père', as we called him, had only talked about it very casually. He knew, of course, but then he was also a little proud when he looked at all those athletic medals and trophies.

After the rowing season came summer vacation, and I went sailing again. But now I had so much more life experience, and a grown-up student would throw himself 100 per cent into his professional ambition. It did not happen. I played better ice hockey than ever, and the little doctor-to-be could not read more than ten minutes of a chemistry book without being distracted by the thought of shooting the puck high and hard into the upper corner of the net. It became inevitable; one day my father called me in for a serious talk.

Much to his distress, I said something about professional hockey in Canada, but then he took over. Calmly he told me that my sporting talents were obvious, but that as a profession ice hockey might be questionable. Especially in a small country where no professional hockey existed. Also, how long did I think I could play such a hard, physical game? And what would I do when the adding years slowed my physical abilities?

He saw that my willpower, though strongly present in sports, was not ready for the intellectual discipline of academic study. He talked about his own military service, many years ago. Felix was in officers' training in the artillery reserve and would be a second lieutenant in two months' time. Hans was still in high school, but there was already a place for him at the Naval Academy in Den Helder.

Père understood that I needed more time to mature for academic study, but did not suggest anything yet. He waited until the concept of military service was accepted in my mind, and until I myself came up with that possibility.

'But it'll have to be a sporty branch,' I quickly added. My father said there were many, very sportive branches in the military: those associated with horses, tanks, MTBs in the navy, flying, and sports like fencing …

'Flying, Père, are you serious?'

'Why not? You are more than qualified. Give it a try and if they don't take you, there are other possibilities,' he said.

What he did not say was that he had already made inquiries, and that he had talked to an old acquaintance, Professor Jongbloed (a physician and military pilot himself), and to Dr Brouwer, the medical examiner of the Air Force. Père knew all along that his sporty son had every chance in the world to be selected for training as a military pilot. He also knew that it would give me two more years to grow up, and very possibly open the door to a lifetime job in case my medical ambitions faded.

I applied. Papers arrived, there was a physical examination by Dr Brouwer, and then interviews, and before I realized what was happening, I received a letter to report for duty at Soesterberg Air Base to be trained for pilot in the Dutch Air Force. The two-year training would, if successfully completed, include a commission as second lieutenant/pilot. Again a tremendous change in my life, but I did not feel that I had entirely planned and executed this change. It happened suddenly, like exploding fireworks which would start off a whole series of other fireworks.

I bought a book about flying, I visited an aircraft factory, and I went to the airfields of Ypenburg, Schiphol, and Soesterberg to see airplanes take off and land. I visited the Meteorological Institute in De Bilt, near Utrecht, where my grandfather had been director only a few years ago. At home, I talked about airplanes and about the extensive medical examination I had to go through – the revolving chair, the low-pressure chamber, the measuring of my reaction time, the influence of G-forces, and various eye tests. The medical interest was still there, but at this time the only important thing was flying. The word *pilot* was magic.

The day to report came sooner than I could imagine, and before I had a chance to shout *Here,* when they called my name, I stood there in that horrible green uniform of the Dutch Infantry with thirty others – in boot camp.

'*Hee-aaaat ... oit!*' and Sergeant Hateboer had to explain what he meant. In his black uniform with the golden wings on the left upper chest, he instantly became our hero, in spite of his sincere efforts to teach us to stand in line without talking and turn left when he said, *left*. Dutch Infantry shoes, God forbid, had to be treated with whale oil, and sure as hell, we were infantry!

As in many countries in those days, there was no separate air force in Holland. The flying services were organized as a Flying Corps within the administrative jurisdiction of the army. The uniform was basically infantry, but there were the gold wings, and it had become tradition that the fly-boys would wear the black uniform with gold buttons and a red lining to the tunic. Very fancy indeed, especially with breeches and riding boots.

Our first meal was pea soup because it was Monday. On Tuesdays it was potatoes, carrots and a huge piece of meat, called *hutspot* in Dutch, and on Wednesdays pea soup again, of course, followed by *hutspot* on Thursdays and some sort of fish on Fridays. We never had the same thing two days in a row; we did every other day, of course. And then there was coffee, but how this was made remained a secret.

It is strange how some of these seemingly very unimportant memories can stay in one's mind, but they were my introduction to Soesterberg, the cradle of all Dutch pilots since 1913. I clearly remember that, one day, we had an extra large piece of meat in the pea soup which turned out to be a rag. No trouble. That evening we went to 't Zwaantje, a small restaurant just outside the base, where we ordered buns with roast beef and liver, which were flushed down with generous amounts of Amstel beer. Boot camp was not that bad after all.

On the third day, much to our surprise, we marched to another warehouse where we received a black leather coat, black leather leggings, a flying helmet, goggles, and gloves. The very next day we marched to the flying school to get our first real flying lesson. Again, my life had taken a new turn, and again I went through the experience of a first day in school. But this time there were no problems. Now, I fully accepted the new situation and there were no distractions. All I did was work and think airplanes and, consequently, I had no difficulties in officers' school and flight school.

I was well aware of the fact that my first dream was to become a doctor. But when I decided to go to the University of Leiden to start my medical training, things went differently. I had never seen myself as a pilot and now I found myself in the cockpit of a military airplane.

My class at Soesterberg became a group of friends very much like the fraternity brothers at the university. It was a matter of getting up in the morning at reveille, whether you liked it or not, and being ready at a certain time – no nonsense. In our most unbecoming, enlisted men's uniforms, we marched to classes and to the flying school. We saluted officers, and also sergeants if they had wings. At night we studied: aerodynamics, navigation, engines, tactics, strategy, military regulations and, again, mathematics. This time I did it with pleasure and did not feel that certain subjects were, perhaps, not directly related to flying. But we were trained to be officers as well, and that was a symbol of leadership and responsibility.

My instructor was Captain van Gemeren, and he had his own way of teaching. The S-IV trainers were biplanes, with pilot and pupil sitting in tandem – no breaks, no tail wheel. From his place in the front seat, he would turn around and shout,

'No. No. No. No. No, Vanderstok! Oh, what a rotten turn.' So I straightened out and tried again. 'No. No. No. No. No, Vanderstok! You must take the rudder back when you are in the turn.' And I tried again. 'No. No. No, Vanderstok! You must land exactly into the wind. The wheels have no brakes.'

I do not know how many times he said 'No. No. No. No!' But to my utter surprise, after about ten hours, he climbed out of the cockpit and said,

'Three takeoffs, three landings and then taxi back to the hangar.'

My face must have had an expression of despair and I couldn't say a word.

He grinned, and just pointed with a finger to the takeoff place on the field. Then he walked to the flying school hangar.

'Jesus Christ,' I said to myself. 'I am not at all sure that I can land this winged box.' But what else could I do? So I taxied to the wind sock at the edge of the field, looked around: 'OK … no other planes landing … turn into wind … and … Jesus Christ … here we go!'

The first solo flight is for every flyer a day of glory. When I came back, Captain van Gemeren stood there with a broad smile on his face, congratulating me. Three other cadet pilots also had made their first solos that same day. There was a big party at 't Zwaantje that evening.

The other soloists were Jan Bosch, Henk van Overvest and Herman Doppenberg, who were called 'Jan B.', 'Spanky', and 'Dop', by now. Other classmates soloed within a few days and, sadly, one was transferred to observers' school. He just tried to land the S-IV thirty feet above the ground every time – a nice guy but his flying was hopeless.

The training at Soesterberg was tough. But for me it was a pleasure, and often not without the old-fashioned Dutch humour, especially during classes in radio communications. We had to learn the Morse code, up to five words per minute. The very day we reached this incredible signalling speed we passed the test. Then we gradually sank to a level where we only could knock out a few dirty words, or even sing them – da-de-de-da-dit. Navigation I liked, and it came easily to me, but military air-combat tactics? Oh dear, were they really serious?

After the Fokker S-IV came the Koolhoven 51, and the Fokker C-V. Some of us were allowed to fly the Fokker C-X, the Air Force's newest reconnaissance plane. Spanky was by far the best overall flyer, and Jan B. the most accurate operator. I had a burning desire for stunt flying – upside down, performing stunts in formation, flying under bridges. One time I was caught when I flew under the double bridge at Moerdijk, and I found myself in an unpleasant situation in court. Someone must have saved me because nothing happened.

We first passed the so-called 'small wings', but after a year we walked around with the beautiful gold wings of the Dutch Air Force. Our shabby soldiers' uniforms were replaced with the black, officers' dress uniforms, with breeches and riding boots. The second year was a year of active service in one of the operational units of the Air Force.

Four of us were transferred to a fighter unit at Schiphol Airport, under the command of Captain van Weerden Poelman. The unit was called the *1st JaVA*, which means 1st Fighter Squadron. The four chosen for this honour were Spanky, Jan B., Dop, and myself. Flying was now in fighters only, first in D-16s and D-17s, and later in the Fokker D-21s and G-1s. We also had two Fokker D-VII fighters, the famous World War I fighters of von Richthofen. Every day Spanky, Jan B., and I flew and stunted in formation, or by ourselves, until we could handle those machines like a breeze.

At the completion of our second year, we became reservists and left the active service except for Saturdays, when we had to fly to keep up our flying skills. By now I could have stayed in the Air Force as an instructor, but two years of Soesterberg had done to me exactly what my father had hoped for. I went back to medical school, but this time at the University of Utrecht.

No more fraternity club life, no more ice hockey, no more rowing. This time it was just a matter of attending all lectures, attending all lab work, studying every evening, and nothing else. I even began to like the inorganic chemistry, the physics, and all those subjects I thought were not related to medicine. On my bicycle, I simply went to school every day. I began to know the professors and assistants, and after two semesters I passed my first exam.

I flew on Saturdays, but other than that it was medicine only. My next exam would include anatomy, pathology, physiology, and a lot of microscopy in various fields. Now that was medicine! Now I was a real medical student! That feeling of being a successful student also reflected on my life at home, and the atmosphere was once again one of happiness. It would not last for long.

Hitler and his new Germany had already broken the rules of the Treaty of Versailles. (Signed in 1919, the peace treaty officially ended World War I on 10 January 1920.) We could easily see the enormous buildup of the German military. We knew all about the Junkers, Heinkel, and Messerschmitt aircraft; Hitler made no secret of the huge militarization of our neighbours.

The construction of the *Autobahnen*, the super highways, already was viewed as a military preparation by almost everybody in Europe, except by some hopelessly naive government officials. We saw the *Putsch*, or insurrection, in Austria; we were not blind to what, very obviously, was being prepared. However, due to wishful thinking and the convincing lies of Herr Hitler – when he vowed never to violate any territory of

Queen Wilhelmina – the idea that, once again, the Netherlands could stay neutral in case of war remained the basis of Dutch military thinking.

Although there was 'absolutely no danger for our small kingdom', the Dutch mobilized in 1939. But that was only to ensure and maintain our neutrality. After all, Hitler had promised. Air Force personnel were among the first to be called up, and I also received the expected pink slip ordering me to report to Soesterberg for active duty. We were not at war; we flew some border patrols, but nothing of great importance.

My commanding officer allowed me to go to Utrecht to attend school as much as possible. But after two or three months, the Germans violated our neutrality almost daily. We increased our patrol activity, and on several occasions we met these German intruders, who quickly turned east toward their own country. Twice, I was in a position to open fire on the intruders. Twice I was ordered not to fire. This made me angry and I openly aired my disagreement with politics. But the Netherlands would remain neutral, as in World War I, and we should not provoke Hitler by shooting at German aircraft which probably were flying over Holland by mistake.

The squadron was transferred to Den Helder, the naval air station in the north of Holland. Our new commander was Captain Hein Schmidt Crantz, an outstanding pilot and instructor. We were now fully equipped with the new Fokker D-21 fighters – excellent fighters with, in our opinion, only one thing wrong. The planes had fixed landing gear.

There were other things about this fighter that could be discussed. For instance, we had only two machine guns mounted in the wings, which was very meagre armament. But the D-21 was an extremely manoeuvrable airplane. Any further disturbance of the airflow along the wings, plus the additional weight of two more machine guns and ammo, might take away much of the advantage of making small turns. With a maximum speed of about 200 miles per hour, we could not hope to beat the German Messerschmitts anyway, with or without extra guns in the wings.

On one of our 'neutrality patrols', we closed in on a German Heinkel bomber flying over the islands of northern Holland. We were supposed to warn the German planes, indicating by hand signals that they would have to leave. A gunner in the Heinkel opened fire and hit Spanky with one bullet, without doing any further harm. But Spanky did not like this and manoeuvred his D-21 behind and under the Heinkel. With a short burst he hit the *Mof* (the bad name we had for Germans), and a long stream of white smoke trailed from the intruder, who quickly disappeared in an easterly direction.

'He'll never make it,' I said over our newly installed radio, without identifying myself.

One time I intercepted a slow-flying Fieseler 'Storch' over the Zuider Zee. It was an easy target, but once again I was ordered not to shoot on the unarmed craft. When I came alongside to signal the plane that it was over Dutch territory and should leave, I saw the German pilot grin and wave at me. He quietly turned east, without the slightest visible efforts to evade me.

In spite of the numerous violations where we could have intervened, we also learned that bombers at high altitudes were impossible to catch. By the time we were close enough to intercept them, they would have crossed the entire width of the country. The aircraft warning system in those days was simply by observation from the ground. A very slow system.

The bullet that was shot at Spanky was lodged between the cooling ribs of a cylinder of the radial engine. Spanky kept it as a good luck charm after the incident.

The war in Europe began in September 1939, but not for us ... yet. Obviously there was some action, including English bombers over German territory, some of which were shot down. One of those unfortunate Allied pilots was Wing Commander Day, who was made a prisoner of war in the first week of September 1939, when his plane was shot down near Bremen, Germany.

'Wings' Day had already been a POW for more than two and a half years when I joined him as a *Kriegie*. The first months of the war were slow. Not much happened, it seemed. A few bombs were dropped and there was more German air activity, but we were not yet at war. The skirmish was seemingly just between Germany and England. For us in Fighter Squadron No. 1, it was damn clear that things would not stay this way. We felt that the policy of neutrality would become an impossibility.

It happened on 10 May 1940. We were in the air above our own base, Den Helder, in full squadron strength. It was about six in the morning, the sun just barely sending its first hesitant light from the east. The dawn patrol of nine D-21s was divided into three sections of three, and only the section commander had a radio. We could talk to the ground station and the other section leaders, but not to the other pilots in our formation.

Without warning we saw the Messerschmitts coming, one single *Geschwader* – a group of nine fighters with the very well-known black crosses on the wings and fuselage.

I tried to say something on the radio: 'We are being attacked by German Me.s!' But there was a lot of talk on the radio, all on the same frequency, and it would have made no difference if we had no radios at all.

The German fighters approached as if they expected little or no resistance. Two of them began strafing the buildings and some other planes on the ground, but then they realized that we were attacking them. A dogfight of at least eighteen fighters developed, right above our airfield.

Some of the Germans had used a lot of their ammunition on ground targets, and they had to fly a long way back to their own base in Germany. They had not counted on spending much time, or fuel, at their target. This unexpected situation probably caused a momentary hesitation, which put them at a disadvantage. I saw four Messerschmitts in their steepest turns with a D-21 on their tails. There was a lot of shooting as we saw the German tracer bullets streaking through the air. Wherever I looked I saw planes dogfighting; they were easily recognizable by their silhouettes. The Me.109s had sleek, liquid-cooled engines and retractable landing gear while our D-21s had stubby, radial-engined noses and fixed landing gear.

Our ability to make shorter turns taught the Germans an unexpected lesson in the very first minutes of their well-planned attack on the Netherlands. I closed in on an Me.109 and noticed immediately that I gained on him in our left turn. At close range, I opened fire with my two machine guns and a stream of white smoke came from the enemy plane.

'That's enough,' I thought. 'He'll never make it back over the Zuider Zee.'

Next to me was Dop, also on the tail of a *Mof* and shooting. Then I heard Spanky, who had a radio, say, 'I got him. He is making a forced landing on our field.' And I saw another Messerschmitt going down in a spin with black smoke coming from the engine.

Now I saw another attacker coming at me and I immediately threw my D-21 in a left turn, making it impossible for the German to adjust his aim at me as a moving target. He tried to close in, but in three turns I was on his tail. Half a turn further and I had the required angle to aim in front of him. I pumped him full. He went down and ended in a huge white splash in the sea. The rest of the German *Geschwader* disappeared in an easterly direction as we prepared for landing.

Over my radio I heard, 'German troops have invaded our Dutch territory, and the government considers itself in a state of war with Germany.' I think we knew that before the government did.

Once on the ground, there was excitement and a lot to talk about. My plane was entirely intact, but several of the others had bullet holes. One of our pilots had a wound in the calf of his leg. He had managed to land his severely shot-up fighter, but then collapsed and had to be taken to a hospital. None of the others were injured, but the damage to our planes was more than had initially been thought. And there was some minor damage elsewhere. Ground crews immediately refilled our fuel tanks and reloaded our guns, and Captain Hein called us together for briefing. We had shot down four Germans, one of them the commander of the German *Geschwader* (who had made the forced landing on our field).

In our briefing room the radio was on, and we heard the confusing news broadcast of the one-hour-old war. Further attacks were obviously expected, and Captain Hein quickly reorganized his remaining fighting units. Even planes with bullet holes and other minor damage were readied for flying.

'All our D-21s up in the air, you are probably safer up there than here,' Hein said. 'We expect Stuka bombing of the airfield, so as soon as your plane is ready you go and attack any German aircraft you see.'

We took off for the second time, and made a few primitive rules for the use of our radios. Seven D-21s were once again above the air base of Den Helder. The radio was quiet this time. The sun was up. It was 8:00 a.m. Suddenly I heard our ground station say, 'We are being attacked by dive-bombers and fighters.'

Simultaneously, I saw smoke coming from the hangars on our field and a number of German airplanes attacking. The air raid warning system was so slow that we never saw them coming, and identification and action all happened at the same time. The attack was short, but apparently extremely effective and, in spite of our presence, quite a surprise. The Stukas disappeared quickly, but the Messerschmitts were still over our field and we engaged in a fight again. This time it was short. I shot at one of them and I believe that I placed several hits. He turned east, and with his higher speed outran me immediately.

We were ordered to land. We also were warned about the condition of our airfield, because there were a number of bomb craters in and around our landing area. After I landed, I taxied to what had been one of the large hangars. When I reached the concrete in front of the destroyed building, an Me.109 came down in a dive and strafed the platform. My plane already had come to a halt and I jumped out. I started to run for shelter and heard the bullets hitting the concrete like a hail storm. Something hit me on my left shoulder, although there was no pain.

I had a camera, on a strap around my neck, tucked away in my leather jacket. In those days we had no camera in the wings and I was hoping that I could take a picture of a German plane going down in flames, perhaps as confirmation.

When I turned around to take a look at my plane, big, black smoke clouds billowed straight up in the air. I took a picture of my fighter, before the remaining bullets began exploding and the machine was reduced to twisted aluminium. I saw the immense damage to the buildings and equipment all over the place. I took more pictures of the shambles. Then I saw the Messerschmitt that had made the belly-landing on our field, and took a picture – our very first photographic proof of a shot-down German plane.

I found out that the pilot was the leader of the *Geschwader* which had made the initial attack on our airfield. The Germans had thought we would still be on the ground, and they could destroy our planes before we could take off. That may have been an expensive mistake, but with their second wave they achieved their objective anyway. As an air base, Den Helder was destroyed, except for seven D-21 fighters which could still fly.

The German commander was, officially, the first German prisoner of war. *Der Alte,* as his comrades called him, tried to bluff:

'Friends,' he said, 'why put up resistance? You have no chance against the German Luftwaffe.'

I was in no mood for that sort of talk and drew my pistol. But Hein quickly stopped the confrontation, and *der Alte* was taken away to spend the rest of the war in POW camps in England and Canada. I looked at my left shoulder, where the bullet had just grazed the leather jacket. I was not hit.

The Germans made rapid advances on all fronts at the Dutch–German border. The airfields Ypenburg, at The Hague, and Waalhaven, near Rotterdam, were taken by *Fallschirmjager,* as the German paratroopers were called. The bridges at Moerdijk were in German hands. Panzer tanks were moving along the rivers toward the south of Holland and Belgium. German Junkers Ju.52 transport planes landed on the beach on the west coast, creating havoc and establishing strongholds. German paratroopers in civilian clothing, one even disguised as a priest, landed everywhere.

Dutch radio announcers spread news which later turned out to be false information, supplied by Dutch-speaking Germans. There were rumours that all drinking water was poisoned. Dutch soldiers were not to accept drinks or candy from any patriotic citizens; it could be poisoned. The pro-German political party, the NSB, would take over the government. All of these rumours were not true. They were just products of the German propaganda machine. But they caused chaos throughout the country.

With our seven operational fighters, we were transferred to a small, so-called secret airfield near Amsterdam. From here we made several ground attacks on German units. The missions now were carried out by volunteers. On one of these raids, on Waalhaven airfield, which was already in German hands, we saw some thirty Junkers and Stukas neatly parked in two rows. Obviously, the Germans did not expect the crippled Dutch Air Force to be able to do any harm. We attacked and pumped all we had into the enemy planes, until all thirty of them were *kaput.*

The other Dutch squadrons had similar encounters, and also suffered heavy losses – both in planes and in personnel. Even the old Fokker C-5 and C-10 reconnaissance planes were used. But they were no match for the Germans. Our only bombers, the sluggish T-5s, flew a number of missions. But these pregnant ducks did little harm to the advancing German troops. All of the planes were shot down or crashed when returning from these futile efforts to stop the German *Blitzkrieg.*

My classmate Wim Rozenboom, in a Fokker C-10, was attacked by three Messerschmitts. With no other options, he fought back. Witnesses on the ground saw Wim and his gunner shoot down two of the attacking enemy planes. After that Wim himself went down in a spin, killing both Wim and his observer.

The war in Holland went on for five days, and there was not a single Dutch plane left that could fly any sort of a mission. The last few D-21s were now placed together at Schiphol, and set afire by our own personnel. It was the end of our flying in the short war of May 1940. Talk of capitulation was now heard, and we expected German troops at any moment. There would be no more resistance.

On the southern horizon, over the polders of Holland, we saw black smoke rising – an awful lot of black smoke. It could not be an ordinary fire. It had to be much bigger. Soon we knew what was going on. Rotterdam was being bombed, in spite of our General-in-Chief's declaration that Rotterdam was an open and undefended city. But the war was over. Why bomb a city when all resistance had ceased?

The attack was well-planned, and on a large scale. Stukas howled down, and with no mercy dropped their deadly cargoes on the city. It went on and on, until the centre of Rotterdam was a heap of rubble. There were fires everywhere, thousands were killed, and many more left homeless. The material damage was astronomical. Was it a mistake? The damage was done.

One of our pilots asked permission to go to Rotterdam, where his family lived. That evening he came back to our unit, which was still in Amsterdam. His father, his mother, and six brothers and sisters had been killed by one direct hit on their house. It was the only time that my eyes filled with tears – not only out of sympathy, but also out of anger and rage.

In five days the German Luftwaffe had lost more than six hundred of its planes, in its otherwise very successful advance through Holland. It was the Luftwaffe's biggest loss of the war. Many planes were lost in air combat – but mostly they were lost on the ground, and while trying to land on beaches, where they could not take off. It is believed that the Dutch anti-aircraft guns shot down some fifty of them.

On 15 May, we stood at Schiphol air base and saw the Germans come in. The Netherlands had capitulated to overwhelming forces. Further resistance would no longer make sense. For us the war was over. Or was it?

Persecution and Resistance

After the Dutch capitulation, the German High Command saw itself with the problem of what to do with 600,000 prisoners of war. It had more important things to deal with. On 16 May it announced that all Dutch forces were officially demobilized. We were told to go home.

Felix also had arrived home, that same day, and Hans came the next day. He had just missed the last navy ship that had left Den Helder for England. The cadets at the Naval Academy were caught by surprise; there were no plans for evacuation or deployment in case of war, and most of them, too, were just sent home by the Germans. Our Air Force commanders did not have the foresight to evacuate personnel and planes to England while it was still possible. Except for a very few, the Dutch were caught, beaten, and their country occupied – lock, stock, and barrel.

My mother and Père were in tears. The three boys were all but speechless. And then there was our little sister, Anky, who was in school in Switzerland. She might not be able to return to Holland at all until the war was over. The devastation not only disrupted our family life, but throughout the country there was chaos. Holland had not been in a war for more than a hundred years.

Inexperience and obsolete military leadership took its toll. The historical waterline, which typically formed a semicircle of flooded land around the heart of Holland, stayed dry. It would have stopped all German tanks and motorized equipment, but now they rolled in without much opposition. Later we were told that this was done to prevent unnecessary loss of lives, in a fight where the Dutch had no chance to begin with.

In our bitterness we did not believe this noble excuse for not being prepared in time, although it was true. The flooding of the waterline would not have stopped the German steamroller. And prolonged fighting would not have changed the course of events in May 1940.

My sister in Switzerland could not go anywhere. The country was surrounded by German-occupied territory and all travel had become impossible. The five-day war story told by my brother Hans was that he had stood watch at the academy, then stood watch again and again, until the Germans arrived. No shots were fired.

Felix had an even more demoralizing story. His field artillery unit had put up considerable resistance south of Utrecht, but a number of their ammunition crates were filled with bricks. Sabotage. Felix heard about the capitulation on a radio news broadcast, which also was controlled by Germans. His unit had lost all communication with their command, and just went home when they heard the news on the radio. He came home carrying his pistol and steel helmet, as if ready for his next orders.

The entire organization of the Dutch Army had collapsed, and the Germans had simply said, 'Children, go home.'

The next few days were confusing. It was difficult to realize that Holland, as a kingdom, did not exist anymore. From friends we heard similar stories about ammunition crates filled with bricks. Apparently, these were not rumours but first-hand reports. The German preparations for the invasion of the Netherlands were thorough, and the military plans obviously were not a last-minute decision.

We also received news of friends who were killed in these five days of war. A school friend from our days in Curaçao was killed when he led a counter-attack on German parachutists near The Hague. A school buddy with whom we played tennis was killed during a Stuka bomb attack. From my flight school class, four were killed. In total, the Dutch Air Force lost sixty-three pilots and observers.

The news about the damage was indescribable. A town in Zeeland, Middelburg, was bombed severely. The situation was disastrous, but not only in Holland. The Blitz went on in Belgium and in northern France. Roads were cluttered with fleeing civilians. Where they would flee *to* was an open question. So after a few days they turned around, with their belongings on carts and bicycles, and cluttered the roads once again. If anything, they held up the German troops, who were marching and singing their damned songs.

As if this was not enough, there were the pro-German followers of the Dutch Quisling, the infamous Mussert. They now walked the streets and terrorized the people as if they were part of the victorious German Army.

It took some time before the Dutch could catch their breath and adapt themselves to the new situation. So many families and businesses were torn apart, so much property was destroyed, and the general life-styles of the citizens had changed so abruptly, that no one could analyse where we stood or what the future would bring. There were rumours that Hitler could never keep up the tremendous effort of a *Blitzkrieg*, and it was actually predicted that the Third Reich would collapse within a few months.

For a short time we believed the rumours. However, already in the first few months of occupation, it became evident that the Germans would not have such an easy time ruling the Dutch in the German style. In spite of early attempts to pacify the Hollanders, the Germans realized that they were seen as enemy troops occupying another country, and that the Dutch considered Hitler a liar.

Many had lost their jobs and, understandably, after the succession of German military advances, began to consider the possibility of a German victory. Although not pro-German per se, many had to accept governmental jobs out of a need to make a living. They had to eat and look after their families.

Such jobs were held in accordance with the German occupation authorities, and often made it difficult to distinguish practical from pro-German attitudes. We did not know. Did the man take that job truly out of need, or was he one of those who could convert to German rule because a German victory looked very possible?

We had more than one enemy. The German soldiers were easily recognized, and the Dutch Quislings under Mussert also had uniforms which could not be mistaken. But there were civilians, German and Dutch, whose sympathies were not so obvious, and there were some who were patriots but who had now switched. Then there were the Dutch who did their work as civil servants in accordance with the rulers – but who at the same time had access to German files and information. Some had access to government printing facilities, where the new identification cards were made, and some had access to the warehouses of the Department of Economic Services, where food distributions took place.

There were extremes. Some men turned into traitors and informers, while others started the extremely dangerous game of organized resistance. The traitors were a much greater danger than the boys in quasi-Nazi uniforms. The traitors could not be recognized and were not known enemies. These people were Dutch and spoke the language without an accent. They became the country's most dreaded unseen danger. Soon we would not trust anybody anymore. A real cloak-and-dagger atmosphere developed – with codes, secret signs, and watchwords. The underground resistance also was organized.

I went back to school when the university opened again in September, but there I noticed similar situations. A pro-German assistant professor in the surgical department was promoted to full professor. There was a German in charge of administration. Conversations between students were cautious. As time went on, we discovered 'old friends' who had switched loyalties. Even in families it occurred. Initially, these people were not traitors. But many gradually became German sympathizers, and some became outright German agents.

At the university, we did not know who to trust. The interior enemy was the danger the patriots had to deal with, and this was something none of us was prepared for. The discovery of a treacherous person, who was thought to be a friend, was one of the hard realities of war.

In the beginning, our secret resistance efforts were primitive and amateurish. Once, I thought I could send radio messages to England with a small radio from a boat. But I soon learned it would not work. I had no organization to gather intelligence. I did not know to whom I could have sent my message. And, without a code, the Germans would have received my message as well.

Some underground workers, radio experts themselves, managed to build transmitters which were quite suitable for radio traffic between the

Netherlands and England. And they did, indeed, establish contact with radio operators in England. The Dutch government-in-exile, in London, had organized a regular broadcast, called 'Radio Orange', on one of the BBC channels. It was used as an encouraging and patriotic voice from a free country to the occupied people of Holland. The messages that came through were of little military value, and related to personal information.

Already, in the early days of the occupation, there were Dutchmen who tried to escape to England to join the forces fighting against the Germans. If they made it across the Channel, Radio Orange would then say something like, 'Kees has arrived.' The family in Holland would understand, and no sensitive information would be given away.

It was very necessary to establish some form of communication system between the underground resistance in occupied Holland and the government in England. We were unprepared for this kind of work, and the Germans had well-organized professionals in their counter-espionage. To make things worse, there was nobody in England with any experience in organizing things from that end. We wanted to have a way of telling the Royal Air Force to bomb this target, blow up that building or that bridge, but nothing happened.

Many people felt let down by the English, not knowing that our neighbour on the other side of the Channel was also totally unprepared for a war on this scale – or for the rapid collapse of its allies in Holland, Belgium, and France.

I was back in Utrecht, studying hard, but the social atmosphere of the place had changed. Students were cautious in their conversations with professors and others on the faculty. One never knew. Could that person be trusted, or would you be blacklisted as being unfriendly toward German occupation forces?

I started a cell system of students, a secret underground organization of friends we thought we could trust. Each member knew only the three members of his cell and the leader of the cell to which he belonged. By telephone or by word of mouth, about eight hundred students could be warned or informed within thirty minutes. We were not the only underground resistance group being organized. Everywhere in the country, the Dutch started underground activities.

These groups had to operate in utmost secrecy, because the Germans were no small boys in this sort of work. Their countermeasures were very effective – execution or concentration camp. It was important that we could warn each other, so that if something went wrong, a maximum of workers would know immediately and, if necessary, disappear. It was during these days that the term 'to dive under' was created. It meant that a person would simply disappear from daily life to stay hidden in the homes of friends or other underground workers.

Naturally, the Germans reacted with executions and concentration camps for those who were caught harbouring the 'divers'. It was equally dangerous for the fugitive and the helper who hid the resistance worker. Patriotism and hatred grew, and German measures became harsher. Felix was already doing nothing but underground work, and he had to dive under in the Biesbos, an almost inaccessible area of the Rhine delta, south of Rotterdam.

Hans tried to work his way through the maritime school in Amsterdam, but ran into an unbelievable incident with an 'old friend' who suddenly turned German informer. He left school and went home, ready to dive under at a second's notice. In Felix's group, they discovered one who gave information to the Gestapo. He needed the money. A girl in the group actually overheard him giving out the address of one of the leaders.

The entire group disappeared, but arranged a meeting at the girl's home. The informer was not aware of the fact that his treachery was known, and came to the meeting expecting business as usual. Once in the room, he was confronted with what had happened. With an air of, 'there is nothing you can do about it', he started to walk toward the door. The others stopped him and tried to explain. But of course, there was nothing to explain. With tears of emotion and trembling hands, they shot the traitor in the head. That same night his body was wrapped in jute sacks, weighted with stones, and dumped in a ditch. The group of underground workers dispersed and were not seen or heard from for several weeks. Then they slowly reorganized.

It was August 1941, and I sat in my room in Utrecht, trying to study, about 6:00 in the evening. My landlady knocked on the door and said there was a telephone call for me. I went downstairs and answered the phone. It was Felix, calling from my parents' home in The Hague.

'Bob,' he said, 'they came to pick you up.'

'Thanks. Bye,' I said, and hung up.

Without any delay I ran upstairs, packed a small suitcase, put my chequebook in my pocket, grabbed my fake glasses and walked out of the house. It was one of those moments when one does not ask questions, and one certainly does not tell anybody where one might go. On my way to the railway station, I saw another student and quickly stopped to look in a shop window. I was hoping that with my glasses and a hat on, he would not recognize me.

He came toward me and said, 'Hi, Bob. Hey, I didn't know you wore glasses.'

'Oh, well,' I said. 'Actually I sometimes do. Eh … I think my dinner is waiting. Bye.'

That was that for my disguise with glasses, and my friend knew I was a pilot. Ah, well. I walked on to the railway station and bought a ticket to Rotterdam.

Nobody could possibly know that I was on my way to Rotterdam, where I arrived about an hour later. There, I took a streetcar to a suburb and walked to the house of an old friend who I hadn't seen for several years. We knew the family so well that the chances of him being a traitor were slim.

I knocked on the door, and my friend Hans Maas said, 'Hello, Bob. What the hell are you doing here?'

'Hans,' I said, 'I am in trouble. I need to dive under for a few days. May I come in?'

'Of course,' he said, and quickly closed the door behind me. I told him the story, and with a smile he took me to his garage, where I saw a small boat in the final stages of construction. Hans Maas was preparing to escape to England.

The next morning we found out what the situation was. Two pilots of the former Dutch Air Force had stolen one of the repaired G-1 planes at Schiphol, and escaped to England. Both were employed by the Fokker factory, which was used by the Germans for repair work. Piet Vos and Hidde Leegstra were old friends from Soesterberg, and had just demonstrated that escape was possible, although they experienced great trouble when they arrived in England. The G-1 had German markings and the English opened fire, in spite of an effort to wave a small Dutch flag from the cockpit. They finally made a belly-landing in a field – and they were in England, unhurt.

The spectacular escape made the Germans angry. They ordered all Dutch Air Force officers to report for detention in a prisoner of war camp. Although many responded to this order, the Gestapo knew that not all of these officers would voluntarily report to become POWs. For that reason, they also started a general roundup operation – to arrest all Dutch pilots, obviously to prevent future escapes by planes.

They had me on a list, with my parents' home as my address, unaware that I had rented a room in Utrecht. When they rang the bell, my mother opened the door and, to her surprise, the Germans asked for me. She had fully expected that they had come to find Felix, who at the time was inside the house. My mother explained that I did not live there, and that I had rented a room in Utrecht. She gave an address, but with the wrong street number. This might give me a little extra time, and could be denied if the Germans should return and accuse her of giving false information.

When the Germans left, she called a quick family meeting and decided to telephone me, to give me a chance to decide what I would do. That was good thinking. Two hours after I left my room in Utrecht, the Gestapo came to arrest me, but found an empty room. Even my family did not know where I was. I had dived under, which meant a total disappearance from daily life.

The very next day, my classmate, Govert Steen, pulled a stunt which again made the Germans look stupid. Before their orders to guard their planes from possible theft were fully in effect, he stole a German flying boat in Amsterdam and made it to England. Govert had never flown a flying boat, but his plan was well prepared. He had studied the technique, and talked to an old navy pilot who had flown many hours on boats.

The escapes of the G-1 and the flying boat on the very next day boosted patriotic feelings, and everywhere one could hear the proud whispers, 'Here we have the real Soldiers of Orange.'

All soldiers in the Dutch forces wore the military uniform, which was, according to regulations, called 'Her Majesty's Tunic of Arms'. Those who wore it were called 'Soldiers of Orange', a phrase which indicated loyalty to the Royal House of Orange, and to Wilhelmina as our Queen.

As it turned out, Hans Maas was already involved in resistance work that would mean a concentration camp if he were discovered by the Germans. Therefore, he had decided that the best thing for him would be to escape to England. He was an expert carpenter and, as so many of us, an excellent sailor. With another resistance friend, he had constructed a seventeen-foot, unsinkable sailboat, with a well for an outboard engine. The boat could carry two persons, since much of the space was used for flotation compartments and storage. Although almost a ready-made escape plan, it was not suitable for three. I was, of course, not included.

Because I had nothing else to do, I worked on the boat. We painted it a blue-grey colour. Even the sail was painted the same colour, with a few wavy streaks of white as camouflage. I went to town, disguised with glasses and moustache, to buy a compass, some extra rope, and two waterproof cans as my contribution to the escape plan. After all, Hans and his wife kept me in their house at great risk.

In the meantime, I had to plan for my own escape and find another place to dive under. My next stay was with the family of a well-known judge in Rotterdam. I got his name from a person who had legitimate daily business contact with my uncle, who lived in Antwerp, Belgium. I did not know the intermediary, but when I went to the judge's house I was received with open arms.

My escape plan now was to just inch down through Belgium and France, to the Pyrenees, and try to get help there for the crossing to Spain. As a neutral country, Spain would be my first objective. I would travel by bicycle and whatever other means were possible. I had a plan to avoid the German sentries at the border. By now, I had a real moustache and a short beard. With workman's clothes, a bike, and Belgian and French money in my pocket, I was ready to go. The judge and his wife had filled my rucksack with various sorts of food and, after good luck wishes, I was on my way.

For the first part of my trip I pedalled eastward, to a bridge near the town of Schoonhoven. One reason for this was that it would seem that I came from Utrecht, not Rotterdam, where I had those two most reliable addresses. A little to my surprise, I reached the bridge across the Rhine with no interruptions at all. I carefully looked everywhere, but never saw Germans. So I just crossed the bridge and continued south to the next bridge, over the southern arm of the river. Again nothing happened, and I was on my way to the Belgian border.

By late afternoon I had covered fifty-five miles, and the Belgian border was only two miles further. I got off the bike, sat down beside the bushes at the side of the road, ate some of the delicious cheese the judge's wife had packed for me, and studied the map once again. When I had the geography well in mind, I continued my trip until I could see the border guard post, almost a mile ahead. Then I quickly disappeared into the shrubs which lined the road.

From my hiding place I could see the German post, and tried to figure out how many guards were on duty and what my plan would be. I had decided to try to cross the border under the cover of night, along the edge of a wooded area, some five hundred metres to the east of the post. It was now just a matter of waiting until dark, and I tried to relax, but with wide-open eyes and ears.

At 9:00 p.m. it was dark. The only light visible was the blue glimmer of a lantern at the border post. Walking and pushing the bicycle by my side, I proceeded in the field to a place well east of the road, seeking cover at the edge of the woods, which continued in a southerly direction. I could still see the blue light. A truck approached, it stopped and then continued on its way south. I also changed my course and turned south, trying to move with the least possible sound. When I had the post about 90 degrees to my right, I should have entered Belgium.

Suddenly I heard shots being fired, loud voices, and more shots. A man shouted in German, there were other voices, and – thinking I had been discovered – I froze. After a few minutes, nothing had happened and I began to wonder. Without the bike I crawled back where I had come from and heard no further alarm. I never knew exactly what the noise was all about, but I couldn't exclude the possibility that I had been detected. So I did not go back to the border.

Instead, I walked north along the road for several hours, and then stopped in the brush until dawn. When daylight permitted me to scout around, I saw a village about a mile further to the north and decided to go there. In the village I walked to the railway station and, seeing that there were no Germans around, I bought a ticket and arrived in Rotterdam two hours later. Another hour later I was back at the judge's house, explaining the whole story and wondering about the possibility that the commotion at the border had nothing to do with me, and whether I could have been in Belgium by now.

The judge had received a message from Hans Maas. His friend who was to have gone with him in the little boat had changed his mind. There was now an opportunity that I could fill his place. I liked the idea! The next day I went to Hans and we discussed the plan. The boat was ready and the judge, a yachtsman himself, gave us two large flags. One was the Dutch flag, the other, English. He advised me to display the flags as we approached the English coast, so the English wouldn't shoot at us. I found the boat plan very attractive, and put the bicycle trip out of my mind.

The little boat had a centreboard in the hull, and a well for a five-horsepower outboard engine at the stern. In the bow and aft there were three airtight compartments, which would make the craft unsinkable if kept intact. A partial deck provided plenty of room for stowage. There were two oars, a mainsail and a jib, ten gallons of mixed fuel, food for ten days, and water for fourteen days. Our masterpiece even had a large innertube from a car tyre and a hand pump to inflate it.

We called the little sailboat unsinkable, but that did not exclude the possibility of bullet holes in the airtight compartments. We could take any amount of water, but bullet holes, no. The next thing was where to put the boat in the water, and how to get it there.

An old school friend, who was married to a Jewish girl, lived in a house within walking distance from the beach at Scheveningen, the coastal suburb of The Hague. Behind their house, one could walk through the dunes to the beach, a distance of only four hundred metres. There was a German sentry post on the northern end of the boulevard, but then an empty stretch where we could see no Germans. This was a good place to launch our boat, paddle out about a mile, and then travel two hours on the outboard engine before hoisting sail.

Hans Maas' father, a contractor, provided a removal van. We did not ask how this was possible, but the huge van backed up to the garage, where our boat was, and lowered the ramp. With two other helpers and Hans' wife, we hauled the now very heavy thing into the removal van and closed all doors. The big truck started and moved toward our destination, The Hague, and the garage of Kees Kerdel, our most reliable school friend.

The transport arrived an hour and a half later and the driver rang the doorbell. We had told Kees we had to hide something in his garage, very temporarily, and, although curious, Kees had had no objections. When the enormous removal van arrived, he was no longer so sure of his decision. But when he realized what it was all about he laughed, and we slid the boat into the empty garage.

That night Kees went out to scout the way to the beach. Our original route had to be changed, because we would have come out on the beach much too close to the German guards. So we had to go further north. We needed more help, too, to carry the boat and its equipment – four hundred metres further. That night I slept at the Kerdel house, and the next morning we called some old friends, including two girls. So we had eight carriers to get the thing to the beach and the surf. The time of departure was set for 2:00 in the morning.

Hans and I stayed at the Kerdel house and checked our equipment and supplies. Kees and his wife had prepared a special dinner for us. There was laughter, and all were in high spirits, even when somebody said something like, 'the last supper'.

We thought it was funny and I said, 'Some more bread and wine please.'

That morning – at 2:00 sharp – with four on each side, we lifted the little, but heavy, boat and started walking through the dunes. Every hundred metres we put the load down to catch our breath, then on again toward the beach and the surf. There was more wind than we had thought, and it began to rain. We did not like the wind, but the rain made it unlikely that the Germans would notice us. We reached the sea, but the surf was much higher than we'd expected.

'We'll try anyway,' Hans said. 'It'll only be about a hundred metres. We'll make it.'

We walked into the water and the first wave slammed the boat and its eight carriers back, but nobody felt like giving up. We pushed and hauled further until we were waist-deep in the cold, salty water. The boat was floating, but in these waves, Hans and I could not get aboard.

Hans tried again, but had to jump out to prevent the boat from capsizing when the next wave thundered the whole party back. We tried several more times, but never made any further progress. Hans finally decided to go back and try again when the weather was better. The wind and rain were excellent camouflage, but the surf was simply too high to get started.

Eight wet, cold and exhausted bodies put the escape boat back in the garage, and all but collapsed in the house. Kees and his wife, Lieske, took care of us again. We tried to discuss what went wrong, and what we should do next time. It also meant we would have to use the garage longer, and again ask our friends to help us carry the same load to the sea.

The risk of helping would-be escapees was as great a danger as being caught in the act of escaping. It was difficult to ask such favours of your best friends. The day for the next attempt was not set; we had to wait for better weather. The best thing for now was to just go home, and be ready for action at all times. For the present, my home was the judge's residence in Rotterdam.

Hans and I discussed our plans. We decided to make four wooden bars, to make the carrying easier, but there was little else we could do but wait. The next day I went back to Kees in Scheveningen, to discuss further plans and to apologize for putting him in this spot.

When I arrived at his house, I could not believe my eyes. There was no garage and no boat. All the windows of the Kerdel house were shattered, and the entire lot was full of broken glass and other debris.

Kees came out of the house and said, 'Bob, you won't believe this. It was an English bomb. They tried to hit the railway station over there, but the garage got a direct hit. It was one hell of an explosion. Everything's gone. The house has very little damage, just glass all over the place. Lieske and I are OK. It was God's will.'

Perhaps it was. I looked around, and there was nothing that even resembled a part of a boat. The Germans did not bother to investigate, but they would not have found what was in that garage. All of it was gone. Kees' telephone was not working, so I called Hans from a public telephone. He was flabbergasted. I went back to Rotterdam to the judge's house and told him the bizarre story. It also meant that they would have to allow me to stay in their house, and take the deadly risk of being discovered or being betrayed.

But the judge and his wife did not hesitate a second. They said, 'Bob, you stay here.'

My uncle Charlie, in Antwerp, had provided me with Belgian and French money which I did not need anymore. It was a discouraging time. But then I suddenly got another contact. Via a complicated string of underground workers, the judge had heard of a group of young resistance workers who wanted to go to England. A meeting with their leader was arranged.

It was a group of five men. One of them was the skipper and owner of a self-propelled barge, which normally was used for transporting gravel or sand. The plan was to get the barge to Breskens, a small harbour in the south of Holland. It would be an ordinary delivery job. The load of gravel was to be left in the barge as ballast for crossing the North Sea. We would board the boat as sailors and bring the necessary supplies only at the last moment. So, if the Germans wanted to inspect, there would be nothing suspicious.

I bought another compass and we studied the charts of the waterways of the western Scheld. There were many shoals and sandbanks which would be dry at low tide. The tidal currents were considerable, and of course, all buoys and lights were eliminated. Furthermore, these waters were patrolled by the German Navy. The barge had a diesel engine, which would give us a speed of six knots. We tried to calculate the length of time we would need for the various legs, to navigate through the tricky channels of these waters.

The day was set. It was a slightly foggy day in October and we thought that conditions were ideal; very little wind and poor visibility – just right for us. I travelled to Breskens by train and dressed as a sailor, with a sailor's cap on my head, a small suitcase, and that little wooden box with the compass under my arm. All of us travelled alone, and one of us had trouble getting to the barge well before the 10:00 p.m. curfew. I placed the compass just in front of the large steering wheel, at the very stern of the vessel, and secured it.

At ten in the evening, in total dark, our skipper Cornelis started the engine and once again checked his fuel supply. One man had backed out, so we were five. This included the skipper, who was the only one I had met before.

To our surprise, we quietly steamed out of the harbour and soon saw little else but blackness. The shore was barely visible. There were no lights, and we did not carry any lights ourselves. We had to steer by compass immediately after leaving the harbour, because there were no landmarks to be seen anymore. We could see the shore for a while, but nothing could be recognized. The tide was coming in for the next hour, giving us high-tide depths. When the tide started receding, we should be well on our way out, and even have the advantage of the tidal current. For exactly fifty-five minutes, we happily steamed to England.

Suddenly we heard a loud scraping noise and Cor, our skipper, shouted, 'Jesus, fellows! We are aground!'

He stopped the engine, and with two long boat hooks we started pushing the barge back. Cor put the engine in reverse and we were afloat again. With no visible landmarks, it was difficult to choose another direction. We turned north, thinking we had made our turn to the west a little too early by making less speed into the incoming tide. We were on our way, but not for long.

Again we heard our bottom scraping on the sand. This time we were hard aground, and the tide would only lower the depth of the water. The waters of the western Scheld in Zeeland were difficult enough to navigate in bright daylight, with all the buoys and markers in place. We had got ourselves into a beautiful mess.

There was nothing we could do but wait for the next high tide. And that would be in bright daylight, not a pleasant thought. At about six in the morning, we saw the sun send its first glimmer of light over the eastern horizon. After an hour or so we could see the coast. There was a light fog, which burned away in the increasing rays of the sun, and after some time we recognized the harbour of Breskens, from whence we came. Shit!

The harbour was much closer than we thought. We had missed the channel to the west by some five hundred yards. Another nineteen minutes to the north would have placed us in a free run west to the North Sea, and on to England.

At 9:00 a.m. we saw the German patrol boat. Cor and I decided to stay on deck. The other three dug themselves into the gravel in the hold, so they could not be seen. They could barely breathe, through some airways they had made with large stones at the side of the heap. When the patrol boat was close enough to hear me, I waved my arms and started yelling in my worst mix of Dutch and German:

'Hey! You there! *Kommen Sie hier, bitte. Wir sind* on the ground. *Das ist* because you people have removed all the lights, and we could not see the *Kanal* to Breskens.'

The German coxswain shouted, '*Woher kommen Sie?* You are not supposed to be here at all. These are closed waters.'

I yelled back, 'I know! I know! I come from Rotterdam, with a load of gravel. I have a permit, but you made it impossible to navigate, goddamn it! You got me aground. You get me off.'

'*Wieviel Wasser haben Sie?*' asked the German.

I shouted back, 'About a metre and a half', indicating the depth.

'*Wir können es machen*,' said the German, and slowly came alongside our barge. Immediately, two soldiers jumped aboard and started searching.

I carried on in a very angry voice, saying, '*Das ist* all because of this goddamn war, and you people making the waterways dangerous. I have been here many times, never had trouble getting to Breskens. If we have damage, I'll send in a claim. Now you better pull me off.'

The German looked at me and said with an apologetic voice, 'The tide is coming in, we'll try. Secure the towline on that big cleat on your bow.'

The other two asked for our names and we both showed our ID cards, which were false, of course.

I went on, '*Donnerwetter!* How can these stupid people do this? I could have lost my barge. Nothing but *schweinerei!*'

'You better calm down, little skipper, or we'll arrest you for being in *verboten* waters,' the German said.

'*Ja, ja.* But that was not my fault. *Probieren Sie jetzt, bitte.* If you get me off, I'll shut up.'

Cor and I pushed on our boat hooks. The German patrol boat pulled and pulled. We heard the grinding noise of sand on the steel bottom. We were afloat.

The German patrol boat towed us toward the deeper water and Cor managed to start his engine again. I ran to the forward deck and shouted, 'Hey! *Wir sind* free now. *Danke schön. Ja, ja. Wir können* go on our own now. *Danke schön. Langsam, bitte.*'

The Germans slowed down, the towline slackened, and I freed the line from the big cleat. Then I threw the rope overboard. We set course for the harbour and the Germans followed us for some ten minutes. Apparently convinced that that was our proper destination, they left us and continued their patrol.

I waved and shouted once again, '*Danke schön. Auf wiedersehen!*'

Cor and I looked at each other, and with a sigh of relief he said, 'Jesus! Shit, that was close! Let's be careful. They may be looking at us with binoculars. Let's keep the others below.'

I agreed. I went down into the hold to tell our three friends what had happened, and that they could come out from under those stones and gravel, but not on deck yet. It took almost another hour to get back to the little harbour, time enough to enjoy a hearty breakfast with all the food we had with us. We had bread, butter, and cheese, and Cor had produced a kettle of coffee. Well, at least he called it coffee.

We realized now that we'd had a narrow escape, and that the danger might not be over yet. The skipper of the patrol boat might have radioed to shore. The Gestapo might well be waiting for us at the pier. We made a sort of plan. If there were Germans obviously waiting for us, the three in the hold would jump overboard and swim ashore. Cor and I would go in and try to bluff our way out. All but Cor would disperse as soon as possible, and travel on their own. Food and supplies were to be left aboard, a present for Cor.

Slowly we approached the harbour. There were a number of local people on the pier. They had seen us and the patrol boat. They knew, of course, that there was something fishy about the affair. But to our surprise, there were no Germans to be seen. I told Cor I would take the compass and my little suitcase and disappear in the crowd. The other three would do the same, leaving Cor, who was the only one on a legitimate mission. Cor agreed, and we moored our barge with help from the bystanders.

There were still no Germans around and I quietly stepped ashore to disappear, as planned. Walking across the village square, I asked somebody the way to the railway station, which was only one block further on. At the station, I found out that there was a train to Breda in about half an hour. I bought a ticket to Rotterdam. There would be a connection in Breda. At the station and on the train, there were German soldiers all over the place. But I mixed with the other passengers and there was no trouble.

With my wooden box containing the compass under my arm, the suitcase in my other hand, and my skipper's cap on my head, I stepped off the train in Rotterdam. The first person I saw on the platform was one of the other escapees from our unfortunate group.

The judge and his wife again received me with open arms, but I was depressed. Perhaps I took too much advantage of the patriotism and goodwill of these people. Hans Maas and his wife, the judge and his wife; they all took the dangerous risk of hiding me and what had I done in return? Already, three times now, I had tried to get out of the country without success and there was no plan for a next escape.

The underground resistance groups became bigger and more important. Some groups claimed they had established radio contact with the Dutch government in London, although I never saw real evidence of it. These operations were life-threatening and everything was, understandably, very, very secret. But we never knew if the claims were true.

One group claimed they had a regular exchange of agents to and from England. When I asked how this was done, the mysterious man told me he was actually not allowed to tell me – but, well, it was by submarine. At the time, I did not believe him. And I later found out there was no such thing as a submarine shuttle then. The poor man enjoyed his cloak-and-dagger play, and probably did not know that his spy stories were dangerous dreams.

Another group did much better. Originating in The Hague, these people organized a chain of addresses – from various places in Holland to Belgium. In Brussels, an associate group organized a similar chain to

Paris, and from there again an organized chain of addresses to southern France. Here the French resistance, the *maquis*, took over, and could guide the fugitives across the Pyrenees into Spain.

This was a serious group which indeed established a line from The Hague to Brussels. It was called the 'Dutch–Paris Line', and was mainly established to help Allied pilots get back to England when they were shot down over Holland. More and more Allied planes flew their night missions to German targets over the Netherlands, and the German flak was often all too accurate.

When the crews of disabled bombers bailed out in the dark, many of them received help from Dutch patriots. If they were wounded, medical help was given. If they were physically in good shape, the Dutch–Paris Line would try to help them to Brussels and Paris. The operation had initial success. But then we learned the hard lesson that the Germans had their own methods of countering.

The Dutch-Paris Line group had members from many different professions, and had access to essential government offices through underground workers who had kept their civil service jobs. For instance, the Line had its man in the office where the Dutch ID cards were made and registered. British pilots, when escorted via the various addresses down to Brussels, had real ID cards with real Dutch names, and were properly registered in The Hague.

The Germans had caught one of these escorted transports but kept it very quiet. The two Royal Air Force pilots were sent to prisoner of war camps. But when the Dutch underground worker was threatened with death or a concentration camp, he talked. He was forced to give the address in Breda, but the Gestapo kept it secret; the next four airmen quietly walked into German hands when they entered the house in Breda.

Almost immediately, the Dutch-Paris Line stopped operations and had to change all existing addresses. The workers who had offered their houses for sheltering the airmen had to dive under, because the Gestapo probably knew their names as well. The Germans managed to set up several traps in this manner, and it took some time before the resistance workers in Holland learned that the pilots they had helped never arrived in England. The trap in Breda worked so smoothly that some of the

Dutch-Paris Line workers could not believe it. So mistrust and arguments caused the operations to stop almost entirely.

Many groups split up and reorganized. Through my judge, I made contact with one of these groups. A very mysterious man told me that his group had regular radio contact with London, and I immediately thought, 'Oh, bullshit.'

However, he might help me to contact others. I had to start somewhere, after all. He told me the radio contact was extremely difficult because they had no code. In order to use a code, they needed agents who would act as couriers to take a code to England, which would have to be changed about every month. The mysterious man and his group were obviously interested in people who wanted to escape to England, and that was exactly my wish. He told me to see a man in The Hague; his name was 'Uncle Alexander', and at the door I had to say the word *Goudsbloem*, Dutch for 'marigold'.

The next day I went to The Hague, and rang the bell at the address that was given to me. A man of about sixty opened the door and I said, 'Good afternoon, sir. Would you be interested in buying plants for the garden? I have violets and very good marigolds.'

The man smiled and said, 'Come in.'

The house was one of the very large, patrician houses in a wealthy part of the city. I looked around, but did not yet say what I really came for. Neither did the man, Uncle Alexander. After some small talk back and forth, we both realized there was no need for secrecy, and Uncle Alex began with a long explanation about the need of contact with London. He belonged to the old Dutch nobility, and was mostly interested in a new Dutch government after the war. He was convinced that Germany would lose the war, now that the Americans had officially joined the Allied forces. Most of us were still very impressed with the capabilities of the German war machine. But this man, Uncle Alexander, had his own ideas. As a politician, he was already organizing a new government.

With a friendly voice he said, 'We are experiencing a great difficulty, and that is that the contact with the Queen and the Dutch government in London has been almost nil.'

I said, 'I was told that there were regular radio communications between us here, and London.'

'Unfortunately,' Alexander said, 'that is not so. The truth is that we have no contact at all. It has been tried many times but without success, and we think it is because the people in London are unable to respond to our efforts. Believe me, there has been no contact, and we do not have a regular exchange of agents by submarine. We are truly separated.'

'What do you expect from me?' I asked.

'Well, Vanderstok,' he continued, 'I believe that you want to go to England. Or should I say, must go? Knowing your background, we would like to propose a plan for just that. In short, we want you to take a code to the government in London, and organize the chain of communication between organized resistance here and our people in London.'

'All very well, sir. But my problem is to find a way to escape to England. I agree with you that there is a need for your plans, and I will certainly do my part in this. But, Uncle Alexander, and I do know your real name – how the hell do I get to the other side of the ditch?'

'First things first,' Uncle Alex said. 'I would like you to see somebody in Delft. This person is a professor in mathematics at the university, and he has designed a code which he will explain. It is, I was told, rather complicated. Once you know the code, we might have an opportunity that should not be overlooked.'

At least there was some light on the horizon. And if they could help me get to England, I certainly would be willing to act as a courier and take a code with me. I went back to Rotterdam and told the judge about my mysterious meeting. He was delighted, and we celebrated the new prospects with a bottle of wine, our spirits full of hope.

The professor in Delft was a tall man with a beard, and he expected me. No secret passwords, no nonsense or mystery. He started right away and to the point, as if I were one of his students:

'Sit down, please. A cup of coffee?' In those days coffee was already a luxury, and after months of drinking *ersatz* coffee, a real cup would be a special treat.

'Thank you,' I said. 'I hope you don't make the mathematics too difficult for me. I am only a medical student, not one of your engineering boys.'

The professor laughed, poured two steaming cups of coffee, and said, 'Oh, don't worry about that. The code I am going to teach you is easy to understand. But you must learn the key by heart, which requires a bit of memorizing. As a medical student, you won't have much trouble memorizing a list of details.' He was right there.

The system was based on the regular military code of a square with twenty-five fields. The row of five fields at the bottom had letters, and the left column had figures; so each field could be indicated by a letter and a number. The code was therefore a system with a double key, and each letter had a different key. According to the professor, it would take at least a month to decode a message. I would have to learn the key for the square by heart.

It was rather difficult, indeed. But after a week I had the square of figures and characters in my mind, and I could apply it to the regular military code system we had learned at Soesterberg during our officers' training. I also went back to Uncle Alexander several times. He gave me a number of instructions to be carried out in England.

He did not trust the Queen's secretary, nor did he like the man in charge of intelligence. He insisted that the code had to be handed over personally to Admiral Fürstner, the only man he really trusted. I said I would try to do all those things, although I did not feel any obligation to see myself as a servant under his orders. It was obvious that Uncle Alex had plans for himself in the political world after the war.

Alexander also talked about another Dutchman to whom he had given similar instructions. He openly admitted that if he could send two fellows, his chances of getting one through would be so much better. When I asked him about the actual arrangements for the escape, I found out there were no arrangements, and his underground organization had nothing. They tried, but their efforts, just like mine, did not get them anywhere.

At home, in the judge's big house on Rozenburg Lane in Rotterdam, I again waited with no plan. I visited an old friend of Uncle Charlie's who had a twenty-foot speedboat, and asked him if I could buy the boat. He was not very happy with my plan, since the boat was not designed for the open sea. And if I were caught with boat and all, it would be too easy to trace the boat back to him. Instead, he offered me some money, but I declined. So back to my hiding place – putting the judge and his wife in more danger again, although they didn't seem to mind.

Then a break came. The judge was a prominent person in Rotterdam and was, of course, a very well-known man. He also was an important member of the Yacht Club in Rotterdam, where he regularly met with old friends. It was here that he talked to my cousin, Jan Drost, a doctor who frequently examined the sailors and personnel for the merchant marine. He had just done the physicals for the crew of a Swiss freighter, which was to leave Rotterdam for the United States in about two weeks. He also knew where the ship was moored.

At home, the judge told me about his conversation with the doctor, and we laughed about the coincidence that Dr Jan Drost was my cousin. He lived only two blocks from the judge's house, on Kralingse Plas Lane, a place very familiar to me. The judge called him, and in the usual jargon that only a Dutchman would understand, arranged a meeting for me.

In most instances, Dr Drost did not know what kind of work these sailors did. Many of them had jobs on the Rhine barges. But the senior members at the Yacht Club had told the doctor they would be interested in any ship leaving Rotterdam harbour. These older gentlemen had their daily shot of Bols gin at the club, discussing news and world events. Not so well known to anyone was the fact that they not only secretly financed the underground movements, they also provided essential information they learned through business connections.

When I met with my cousin he told me about the freighter, *St Cergue*, which was ready to sail under Swiss flag and registration. The captain was a Lithuanian and most of the crew were foreigners, although he had examined a few young Dutchmen who had mustered as regular seamen. Jan asked me to come back that afternoon to meet a Dutch stoker by the name of 'Piet', whom we could trust, and who possibly could give more information about the ship.

When I spoke to Piet in the afternoon, he told me the ship was at Pier No. 4 in the Maas harbour. But the entrance was guarded by German soldiers and I would need a seaman's book and a special pass to get through the gate. He also told me the ship would leave at 4:00 a.m., four days from now, and that the destination was Halifax.

Both Jan and I listened with open ears, and we told Piet, the stoker, I had plans to get on that ship. He immediately offered help, and explained that the best place would be the poop – where the freighters have a vertical shaft with a ladder down to the engine room, a sort of escape tunnel. I told him I would be in the water at the stern of the ship at 1:00 a.m., and Piet said he would have a heavy rope hanging over the side.

That night I slept well. Suddenly there was light on the horizon. I had four days to prepare myself.

Escape to England

On 2 June 1941, I departed from the house on Rozenburg Lane in Rotterdam to the home of my cousin, Jan Drost, in the suburb of Kralingen, only a ten-minute walk. I had a white bandage on a finger, hoping I would look like a patient when I walked in the front door of his waiting room. There were two other patients, and Jan let me wait a short time to make everything seem like an ordinary doctor's visit. When the nurse called me in, Jan was behind his desk and another person was sitting with his back to me, but I soon recognized him. It was Piet, the stoker.

The three of us went over the plan in detail. Jan had a plan of the harbour and had sketched in the *St Cergue*, moored at Pier No. 4 in the northern basin. Piet would be on the poop deck at 1:00 a.m., with a rope that would be long enough to reach the water and at least one inch in diameter. I asked him to make knots in the rope, to make it easier to climb aboard. Then he explained where the escape shaft to the 'donkey tunnel' was. It was a square hole with a ladder on one side, running all the way down to the tunnel for the propeller shaft and its bearings, leading directly to the engine room.

When Piet got up to leave, I looked him straight in the eye and said, 'Piet, be sure to be there at exactly one o'clock. And, by the way, I have this 35-millimetre camera that I have to take along. Could you possibly get it aboard? You know that I shall have to go through the water. Not a good thing for a camera.'

'No trouble, meester. I can easily get it aboard.'

Piet left the room. I was sure I had given him not only a sense of importance, but also the awareness of having my camera, which made him a sort of accomplice.

Jan took me to the second floor of the huge house, where the living room was. His wife had prepared a meal of bacon and eggs, toast, and a bowl of soup. Jan gave me a small 6-mm pistol with some ammunition, wrapped in a surgical glove to keep it dry. I liked the idea of the rubber glove and asked for another one. I had a new film for the camera and some papers with me, which we stuffed into the glove and then sealed with a knot. Jan gave me a map of the city and a little small change. I had to take two streetcars to get to the vicinity of the harbour where the *St Cergue* was moored.

At five o'clock in the afternoon, I left the doctor's house, after a hug and many good wishes and encouragement. I was dressed in navy blue pants, a heavy black turtleneck sweater, black gym shoes and a skipper's cap. First, streetcar No. 11, then No. 5 to the very end. But I got off one stop earlier. Under the circumstances I thought it safer not to be recognized by anybody, not even Piet.

The long street along the large harbour had very few houses, this far outside the city. Between the road and the water was a stretch of muddy land, with a long row of knotty willows and thick with reeds. There was no traffic and I saw no people anywhere. I quickly stepped off the road into the reeds, where I was sure I could not be seen. Through pools of mud and clumps of soil, I made my way to the water's edge and found a reasonably dry, well-camouflaged place. From here I had a clear view of the harbour and Pier 4, where I saw a freighter with a Swiss flag at the stern – the *St Cergue*!

My waterproof watch read 6:15. It was still daylight, and I tried to judge the distance to the ship. It was about five hundred yards, most of which I would have to swim. Swimming – without splashing – would mean a speed of about half a mile per hour; let's make that twenty minutes, or let me take half an hour for that. Then a short walk through the shipyard, say about ten minutes, and then into the water again to swim to the stern of the ship. Let's call it one hour for the whole operation. I would leave at midnight. So, for the time being, there was nothing else to do but sit still and wait.

The waiting was long. I fingered the few possessions I had with me. There was the little pistol, loaded with a magazine of eight bullets, and one extra magazine. The small calibre was not too impressive, and the whole thing would be of little use if more than one German discovered me. On the other hand, a single person could perhaps be eliminated by the small weapon.

The rubber glove with the film also had the papers I wanted to take along. There were only a few sheets, and they could easily be destroyed if the need came. The information on these papers was my own little 'crib sheet', to make the code key somewhat easier to memorize. In spite of the professor's encouragement, I found the damn thing very difficult to memorize. Furthermore, I did not want to arrive in England with a forgotten key. That would be too stupid!

The thirty-six letters and figures I had to memorize were perhaps not too much, but I did not take the chance of forgetting. In my notes I had a list of groceries, with the cost of each item next to it. The third letter of each of the first five words formed the five letters of the first column of the key. The last digit of each cost figure fell in the order of the figures in the square of the key. Once I could reconstruct the square, I would know how to apply it to the key of the military code.

In the same glove I had a razor, six new blades, a box of matches, and a piece of soap. I noticed that Dr Jan had put a false moustache and a small tube of model glue in it, as well.

At 7:30 the sun went below the horizon, but it wasn't dark until about 8:30; I had not used the matches yet to look at my watch. I had to wait much longer. This was the fourth time that I was actually on my way to escape to England. It had to be right this time. My mind was not set for another failure – no, not again. I was pretty well determined to take advantage of the exceptional opportunity. The plan was well prepared. There was no point in repeating the sequence of actions again, so my thoughts went on.

I saw myself in England. What would I do there? I had some business with the government, of course, but my ambition was to join the Spitfire boys in the Royal Air Force. Contact between the government in London and the underground forces in Holland was important enough. I had a code with me, and I knew that the landing place on the beach at Scheveningen was a realistic possibility. Putting agents ashore by submarine would be much easier than getting them back; but there was the Dutch-Paris Line which would, no doubt, be activated again.

With the code, I had a time schedule for transmitting radio signals. This was easy enough for radio traffic from England to Holland, but in the other direction it was a different story. In those days, the radio frequencies which could be used could also easily be heard by the Germans and their direction-locators. They could plot the location of the transmitter in a short time, and the consequences would be disastrous.

The radio expert I had met during meetings with Uncle Alexander claimed this was no great problem. In the beginning, the transmitters would have to be relocated after each session. But once contact was made, the timing would be indicated by the code, which according to him was such a masterpiece the *Moffen* would never find out. I did not believe the story. But then, I was not a radio man and not a real spy either – I was a fighter pilot.

It was now 9:00 and dark, but I could still see the ship. Three more hours to the next step. The air was quiet. I heard no traffic on the road. An airplane passed over me but I never saw it. The night air became colder. I looked at my watch, but could not read it. It was too dark. About half an hour later I struck a match and saw that it was 11:45. I checked my equipment in the two surgical gloves, and considered myself ready to go. Slowly I moved to the water's edge and scouted the area once again. The ship was just visible – no lights anywhere, and only the sound of an occasional truck in the shipyard.

Time to go! Very gently, I slipped into the water and felt the cold water creep up my legs, my groin, my belly, and my chest. It was cold, but after a few seconds I was adjusted and began swimming without making a splash. I had kept my gym shoes on to protect my feet against broken bottles and stubble. My skipper's cap got lost somewhere but I didn't care. I didn't need a hat to swim across a harbour anyway.

I swam, but my progress was slower than I had planned, probably due to a little current. The harbour now looked much larger than it had at first, but that couldn't be. Suddenly my foot touched something and I discovered that this part of the harbour had shoals, and I could stand on the bottom. So, for the next two hundred yards or so, I walked through the water with just my head above the surface, like a periscope. I made much better time this way. But then the water became deeper again and I had to swim. I reached the shore at the shipyard but continued a little further in the direction of the ship; the shoreline, with all its junk and debris, offered excellent protection and gave me time to see if there were any German guards around.

There was a long extension of Pier 4, which I considered too far to swim around. So I climbed ashore to make the shortcut to the ship. A sort of road, covered with metal sheets, led to the pier. I saw that my wet shoes made a perfect trail of my steps. As an extra safety measure, I back-tracked on the footprints. Then I went on to the *St Cergue* walking backwards, leaving reverse prints as it were. If guards did find them, they might start with following the trail in the wrong direction.

It was only a short stretch to the pier and I could easily move between the stacks of steel plates, barrels, crates, and junk usually found in a shipyard. About fifty yards behind the ship's stern, I quietly slipped into the water again and began swimming toward the huge rudder of the *St Cergue*, fully expecting to see a rope hanging over the side.

There was a lot of dirt and debris floating around, and I even saw rats swimming between the hull of the ship and the shore. The tips of the enormous propeller were just above the water surface and, to my horror, I saw the propeller turning very slowly. Then I remembered that this was common practice with ships preparing for departure. It did not cause any wake to speak of, but near the propeller was not a place to be. First, I swam to the starboard side and looked up to the rail on the poop deck, but saw nothing. From my vantage point, the deck looked awfully high. I then swam to the port side, carefully avoiding the big blades of the propeller. No Piet, no rope.

What I muttered at that moment shall not be repeated. I was furious. But I immediately realized that anger would not help me at all; I just had to get aboard my own way. I swam along the port side of the ship to the bow, where I had noticed that in addition to the customary mooring lines, she had one anchor out – a common practice in areas where tidal currents are considerable. The anchor chain had links so large that I simply could climb up as if it were a ladder. However, at the top (thirty feet above the water level), I found that the hawser hole was not big enough for me *and* the anchor chain. Also, the board above the hole was too high to reach.

I had no choice. I had to descend into the water again, and I probably uttered a few more very angry words. Without making any noise, I swam to the starboard side of the *St Cergue*, between the ship and the pier. So far I had not seen any German guards, but now I saw them at the gangplank, talking and smoking. Between dirt, driftwood, other junk, and rats, I swam to the stern again.

Then I saw a hose from the shore to the ship. It was probably a water hose, for a last-minute fill of the fresh water supply, but I could not reach it from the water. The big rubber hose was pulsating slightly and I thought it would be strong enough to carry my weight. Silently, I climbed onto the shore again and quickly looked at the German guards. They had not noticed me, so I swung myself hand-over-hand to the railing on the poop deck. Then I found Piet, drunk as a skunk, sitting on a life preserver chest.

This was not a time for angry words, so I whispered, 'Hey, Piet. Where is the donkey tunnel?'

Startled, Piet got to his feet and said, 'Oh, yeah! Jesus, I thought you wouldn't come. How the hell did you …?'

'The donkey tunnel, Piet. Show me where the shaft to the tunnel is!' I said.

Piet took me to a nearby steel door and said, 'All the way down, and then follow the donkey tunnel to the engine room. Be careful that the engineer does not see you. Go on until you are in the boiler room. You can get under the steel deck through the space between the boiler and the floor itself.'

Well, Piet was drunk, and had not had the rope over the side, but at least he showed me how to get to a hiding place. I was on the ship and that was what counted at the moment. Wet and cold, I climbed down the shaft. At the bottom, I found myself standing next to a bearing of the propeller shaft. I could see all the way through the donkey tunnel into the engine room. The shaft was turning, very slowly.

I prayed that nobody would look in the tunnel, because there was no place to hide. In a matter of seconds, I stood in the entrance to the engine room and saw the engineer on duty sitting at a table, writing in a log or something, with his back to me. I slid to the side of the engine room, where there were enough pumps, generators, and other machinery to hide me so I could sneak into the boiler room. Just as Piet had said, the boilers were placed somewhat below the steel deck and there was an opening large enough to let me through.

The space in the bilge under the engine room was very large and dark, but only two and a half feet high. It was too low to sit, and I soon found out, littered with patches of oil and grease, three inches thick. My God, it was filthy and slippery. You couldn't see the dirt, just feel it. I crawled on hands and knees to a place at the side of the engine room, where I could see a light coming through openings in the floor. Again, there was enough space to let a person through, just behind a row of metal lockers.

Suddenly I heard voices – loud talk in German. It was obviously a detachment searching the ship for contraband and stowaways. One of them had a flashlight and looked behind the lockers, but I wasn't there anymore. Then I heard their heavy boots thud to the boiler room, and one of them beamed his flashlight into the bilge. But at that moment, I stood behind the lockers in the engine room. Standing in all that grease, I made no noise at all. They left.

Twenty minutes later I heard a sharp hissing sound, like that of escaping steam. There were more people in the area, there was more talk, and the humming sound of generators was like music to my ears. Another loud hiss blew steam into the bilge, but I was ready to accept almost any discomfort by now. The next thing I heard was the clang of the anchor chain being winched in, and then there was a vibration of the entire ship.

I tried to look at my watch but could not see the hands. So I crawled to the section of the lockers where there was some light, and from where I could look into the engine room. Slowly I peeked. There would be at least three or four men, and probably two or three in the boiler room. I could not see the boiler room, so I figured the people there could not see me. In the engine room, I saw one man at the entrance to the donkey tunnel, and three at the controls of the huge steam engine. It was 4:10, and the rods and crankshaft were moving. I now heard the rattle of the steering machine. Underway!

That was a good feeling, we really were underway. Now I could think about the things I would do in England. I had no food and nothing to drink, but I didn't care. If could only be a matter of perhaps two days before we would have to pass England, and surely the British would stop us to inspect a Swiss cargo ship on its way from Rotterdam to Halifax. Two days without water or food was not too bad; I could do that. I tried to twist my body into a position that I could relax in, and perhaps get some sleep, but wherever I put my hand for support all I got was a fistful of grease. Well, so what. I just stretched myself out in a nice bed of smear.

My body, full of the good stuff at the doctor's house, performed its natural duties and I began to realize there might be a problem. I had to urinate, and crawled a little to the side, where I simply pissed in the bilge. Every time I wanted to know what time it was, I had to crawl to the lockers to get enough light to see my watch, and I could roughly estimate where we would be, assuming that our speed would be fourteen knots.

After leaving the Hook of Holland, it would be a matter of possibly ten to twelve hours before we should be intercepted by the Royal Navy. That would be about three o'clock in the afternoon.

The hours went by. Three o'clock went by and nothing happened. I had to go to the head and there was no rest room in my uncomfortable quarters. I just had to go. It flashed through my mind that the bathroom problem might not be so simple. The smell of human waste could very well give away my hiding place. So when the act of nature finally happened, I buried the stuff in globs of grease.

That first day passed, with nothing eventful other than the little personal problems. I heard the machinery going at full speed, and I felt the ship's pitching in what must have been a moderately calm sea. At regular intervals, I made my trips to the lockers to see what time it was. This became increasingly disturbing, because my timing of a probable interception by the Royal Navy was obviously wrong. It was now 10:00 p.m., which meant we were eighteen hours underway and more than two hundred miles from the Hook of Holland. We should have been stopped. Something had gone sour.

After midnight, I made a mental note of the fact that it was now 3 June. My stomach began to send signals of hunger and thirst, but I still told myself that, even if this went on for two days, I could hold out. Surely it would not be more than two days.

Nothing happened on the second day, and I began to suspect that there had been a change of plans in the ship's voyage. This meant I would need food and water. My exuberance plummeted to a sense of being in danger again. I had no idea where we were going, and I could not just wait and see because I needed food and water – now!

I crawled to the big boiler. I could see a stoker cleaning a spray head and hear him talking to another man in the boiler room. They were speaking Dutch. After a few minutes, when I thought he was alone, I popped by head up between the floor and the boiler.

I said, 'Hey! Come here!'

The man was startled when he saw me, but he came. With my index finger on my mouth, I indicated he should be silent. Then I snapped, 'Tell Piet that I need some food and water! Don't tell anybody else! If I get caught, I'll say that you helped me! He can signal me with a flashlight at this spot.'

'OK. OK,' the man said. 'Piet is right here.'

But I had already disappeared. An hour later I saw a flashlight, held just below the deck, and I moved toward it. It was Piet.

'Here's a bottle of water and a tomato, we'll bring more later. We're going along the coast to Hamburg.'

He handed me the bottle of water and the tomato, then quickly disappeared. The little beer bottle with lukewarm water and the tomato were a more-than-welcome change for my stomach, but the change in the situation I didn't like at all. No one in Holland knew anything about my whereabouts. My friends in Rotterdam did not really know if I had made it to the ship, let alone got on it. I didn't know where we were going, and the prospect of being intercepted by the Royal Navy might have been a dream.

That same evening, I saw the flashlight again. When I crawled to it, a hand gave me a large piece of bread, a bottle of real beer, and another tomato.

A voice said, 'Hello, Bob. I'm Eric Hazelhoff Roelfzema. I'll get you some food every day. They changed the route. We're going to Kiel and supposedly to Norway.'

'Eric! How the hell –' I said.

But he got up, saying, 'I'll explain later.'

Eric was a school friend from The Hague and the University of Leiden. How did he get aboard, and how could he walk around freely? Later I learned that Eric had mustered as a regular crew member. He was the steward in the officers' mess. No wonder he could get a little food and beer for me.

On the third day, I felt the engines stop for some time and then go again. There was manoeuvring and commotion in the engine room. Eric kept me informed; we had gone through the canal and were now anchored in the harbour of Kiel. Piet also appeared occasionally, with something to eat or drink, and told me that the German battleship *Bismarck* was in the harbour, heavily camouflaged with nets and tarpaulins.

'Piet,' I said, 'you have my camera. Take a picture of the *Bismarck*. Then bring the camera back to me.'

'Oh Christ,' he answered. 'I lost the camera. It fell overboard. I'm sorry.'

I didn't believe the story but I couldn't do much about it. Later I found out he had to give the camera to somebody as payment for a debt.

The chance of taking a picture of the *Bismarck* was lost, which was a pity, but perhaps it was a blessing in disguise. A group of loud-speaking Germans entered the engine room and began looking everywhere. From my peephole by the lockers I could see them search, their flashlights shining into corners and under benches. When one of them approached the row of lockers, I slid under the floor and kept quiet. He looked behind the lockers and then went on to the next compartment, the boiler room. Like a snake, I worked my way up behind the lockers and saw the man go down on his knees, at the space between the boiler and the floor, and shine his flashlight into the bilge.

'*Alles in Ordnung,*' he yelled, and the inspectors left.

That same evening, I heard the encouraging sounds of the big steam engine running and the anchor chain being winched in. We were underway again. A little later, Eric came with some food. He told me we would go along the Norwegian coast to Bergen, and then head west to cross the Atlantic.

By this time, I had been under the floor of the engine room for eight days, and filth was building up on my clothes and everywhere on my body, but I didn't care. The initiative was still on my side. I was still on my way to England. I had to stay below because there were German soldiers on board, and we expected another search before the ship went west on her own. I got my food every day, but now someone else brought it. It was Peter Tazelaar, a classmate of my brother Hans' at the Naval Academy in Den Helder. He also had mustered as a regular sailor, and therefore walked around freely.

My daily food supply became better every day, and now included a piece of sausage. They must have had crates full of tomatoes, because they came two and three at a time. Eric told me Piet should be considered untrustworthy, but Peter Tazelaar had taken care of that problem. He simply told Piet that he would not arrive in Halifax if he said one word about the stowaway in the engine room, to anyone!

Eric and Peter were not the only Dutch escapees on board the *St Cergue*. There were two more who also had mustered as regular crew members, and several others knew about my being aboard. None of the officers, nor the captain, had any knowledge of what was going on deep in the bilge of the ship. Piet had understood Peter's threat very well, especially when Eric added that the Atlantic was crawling with sharks.

Four days after we left Kiel I felt the engines stop, but then resume again about half an hour later. When Eric appeared he had no food this time.

He said, 'Bob, the Germans have left the ship. We are at the mouth of the Hardanger Fjord and we are on our own. I heard that we will steam north as far as Bergen, and then west. Something about minefields.'

'That sounds awfully good, Eric,' I said. 'Are there any other *Engeland-vaarders* aboard? Other than Peter, you, and I?'

'Yes,' he said. 'There are two more, a fellow called Volckers and a real sailor, Toontje Buitendijk.' *Engelandvaarders* is the Dutch word for patriots who escaped from occupied Holland to England, to join the Allied forces.

'I believe that you can come up now,' Eric continued. 'There is no real danger anymore. I think you should breathe a little fresh air.'

76

I crawled out of my hole and we walked through the donkey tunnel to the escape shaft at the stern. The metal bars of the ladder were ice-cold, but I didn't feel them. I climbed to a blue sky and crisp, fresh air. On the poop deck, I found Peter and five other Hollanders who obviously knew about my presence down below. We were very close to the coast. I sucked in the pure air and was, for a moment, overwhelmed by the magnificent view of the Norwegian fjords.

One of the reception committee said, 'You need a bath. We'll put you in some clean clothes. I can wash those,' and he pointed to the oily mess that once had been my clothes.

'You think I am safe now?' I asked.

'Well, the captain and the officers don't know, so stay with us and don't go anywhere by yourself.'

He then led me to a bathroom, where I washed and scrubbed with real hot water and soap. The clean clothes didn't fit me too well, but they felt good and warm. On deck I noticed that we were steaming full speed in a northerly direction. Then I had my first regular meal in twelve days, *hutspot,* of course – carrots, potatoes, onions, a big piece of pork, and lots of gravy. It was fantastic – a feast!

That night I stayed on deck and enjoyed the view of the rugged Norwegian coast. The sun had just disappeared behind a cloud bank on the horizon, but it never got dark. I suffered from a form of time disorientation – twelve days in a dark hole, not seeing any difference between day and night. When I stood on deck, in the middle of the night but seemingly in full daylight, true time seemed unreal.

The next morning, I saw the sun shining on us directly from the rear. I knew we were on a westerly course now. The sea was calm and gulls followed the ship, waiting for waste to be thrown over board. I had a big breakfast of bread, cheese, and a variety of jams and jellies, with an unlimited supply of black ersatz coffee, which was ersatz indeed! The bosun had done a remarkable job of washing my clothes, so I sat on the poop deck in my own pants and sweater again. The day passed as if we had made a cruise to the Nordic fjords.

Another night without darkness passed. I was in the bathroom trying to shave off my beard of two weeks. Peter Tazelaar came in, all excited, and said, 'Bob, there is a ship on the horizon. We don't know what it is. Could be German. Could be English. I just came from the bridge and I believe that we were ordered to stop.'

With the soap still on my face, I ran to the deck and saw a warship signalling with a bright light. Everybody on the *St Cergue* came on deck. The officers on the bridge and all of us at the stern had our eyes glued on the ship on the horizon. With a slight vibration we felt our engines stop, slowing us down till we were just floating, dead in the water.

Peter, being a naval cadet, was our expert in naval affairs, so he should recognize things first. He did. When the ship came a little closer, he said it was an old ship the size of a cruiser. It was rather old because the bow was still sloping forward to the waterline. All newer cruisers had the so-called 'clipper bow'. Peter thought it very unlikely that the Germans would have a cruiser of this type, alone in these waters.

The impressive grey hull slowly approached us and started to proceed in a wide circle around us. We saw many signal flags, which I could not read, and on top – was it the British ensign? The cruiser narrowed its circle, coming closer all the time. Indeed the flag was the white ensign of the Royal Navy and we saw a name on the stern, 'HMS *Devonshire*'.

We started to cheer but the bosun calmed us down, saying, 'Cool it. You're not home free yet. You never know what they will do. Stay calm and don't pull any stupid tricks.'

The *Devonshire* circled us once more and then came to a stop. I could see her big cannon aimed at us all the time. They lowered a small boat with a boarding party over the side. The boarding crew consisted of one officer of junior rank, one midshipman, and four sailors. They were armed, but the detail obviously did not plan to engage in violence of any kind. They walked to the bridge, where they talked to the captain and some of the officers. Then they carried out a superficial inspection.

When the midshipman came to the deck where I was standing, I immediately identified myself, and explained the reason for my presence on the *St Cergue*. After Eric, Peter, and the other two did the same thing, the young Englishman called the officer, who quickly talked into a bulky, portable radio. Apparently, this was to inform his captain about the clandestine persons aboard. He ordered us to stay on deck and just wait for further instructions. At first, I don't think he believed my story at all. But after some time the conversation became friendlier, although we were not to move anywhere.

A second boat from the *Devonshire* was launched, this time with a detail of at least ten men. When they came aboard, the first group went back to the *Devonshire* and two of them took the second boat back. The cruiser started moving and we followed in her wake.

An English guard on our deck was a little more talkative. We found out the *St Cergue* was ordered to proceed to Thorshavn, on the Faroe Islands, where it would be inspected thoroughly by search parties. That might take several days. We asked what would happen to us, but he did not know.

Suddenly I saw the English officer come to our little group, accompanied by a snorting and cursing fat man who, according to Eric, was the captain of our ship.

In broken English, mixed with German and Lithuanian, he yelled at us, 'You God-*verdamter* idiots! You put de whole *Schiff* in danger! If de Shermans had found you, zey vould haf made me responseeble.'

Toontje Buitendijk responded with, 'Aw, shut up, you *Dumkopf.*'

The captain understood the word *Dumkopf* very well, and exploded, 'I vill report you *verdamter* Dutchmen …'

But the English officer took him by the arm and started to walk back to the bridge again. We could see the poor captain make all sorts of gestures, as he finally climbed the ladder to the bridge and his own quarters. Toontje Buitendijk was the only registered seaman and, under normal circumstances, he would have been in trouble with any maritime commission. But he did not care. He was going to jump ship in Halifax anyway to join the Dutch Navy.

At two o'clock the next morning, we arrived in Thorshavn, as if in daylight. There was an overcast sky, but it could just as well have been 2:00 p.m. We dropped anchor in the bay, where I saw several other British warships, a lot of barges, and fishing boats. The boarding crew of the *Devonshire* was picked up. When they got back on their ship, the cruiser began moving, soon to disappear over the horizon.

A heavy tugboat came alongside our ship and we were told to get ready to go ashore. They even had the gangplank ladder over the side to let us down to the tug. The captain, still furious, let four of us go but stopped Toontje. He was a regular sailor and he would not allow him to leave. From the tugboat we saw Toontje argue with the captain, who clenched his fists, ready to start a fight.

We joined the argument by shouting, 'Let him go. Let him go.'

But the English sergeant, pistol in hand, snarled, 'Be quiet and sit down.'

Eric tried to tell him we were friends – we were allies and on his side – but the sergeant wouldn't listen. Suddenly there was a tremendous splash in the water, right next to where we stood. Toontje had jumped overboard, and with loud cheers we hauled him onto the deck of the tugboat. The captain snorted something about international rules and waved his fists at us on the boat below, but the English officer patted him on the shoulder and began to laugh. This made the fat little captain even more furious. The Englishman calmly ordered the tug to leave.

'Jesus Christ, that water is cold,' Toontje said when we had him aboard. The poor fellow was shivering, but the stern sergeant had brought an army blanket so we could rub him dry.

Toontje looked up at the Lithuanian captain, shouting, 'Balls to you and Hitler! You *Dumkopf!*'

We were taken to Thorshavn, the capital of the Faroe Islands. These islands were Danish territory, but at the time they were occupied by the English. It must have been about 9:00 in the morning. But with the grey, overcast sky and no sun visible, it could just as well have been evening.

The sergeant took us to a small office, where a major with a huge handlebar moustache sat behind a desk. He told us our status was that of 'interned foreigners', but they had no camps in Thorshavn, so we could walk around town. We had to report to his office every morning at 10:00.

The sergeant then took us to an empty house and said, 'These two rooms are for you. The couple next door will bring you food. The major gave you this money, about ten shillings each, and you can have a beer or two in the pub at the harbour. Don't forget to report to his office tomorrow morning. Let me know if you need any clothing.'

This was our internment? Walk around town, buy a beer? Soon we learned there was not much need for a camp because we were the only prisoners, and there was no place to go to even if we wanted to escape. We already were in British-controlled territory, and that was good enough for us. The major had told us we probably would be transported to London within a week or so.

My watch had stopped. I had not seen a clock and had not paid attention to the time. We walked to the harbour and saw the *St Cergue* still there, still being searched under the eyes of a snorting captain. We entered the only pub we found and ordered beer. There was nobody else in the place, and the square in front was almost empty. After a while I discovered a clock in the taproom, which said 9:45. I thought that that was the reason I did not see any people; they would be at work. So we walked to the major's office to report, and discovered it was 10:00 in the evening!

We went back to our rooms, where we tried to get a little sleep, but that didn't work either – none of us could sleep. The food they brought us was fresh bread – still warm from the oven – real, unsalted butter, and goat's cheese. The coffee was steaming hot, but a bitter, almost undrinkable, brew.

We walked around in the little town and noticed sandbagged fortifications everywhere. Even at 6:00 in the morning, soldiers were marching or just standing near gun posts and artillery emplacements. We couldn't help but smile when we examined their uniforms more closely. It was a Scottish regiment. Most of them had very large moustaches, the kind of whiskers that were curled with wax into points. They all wore berets at a cock-eyed angle over one ear and many of them ambled around with very long walking canes.

The officers were armed with big six-shooters, those enormous revolvers quite in contrast with the elegant FN automatics we used to have. Some rode around on bicycles, others on motorbikes, and those small Hillman vans were all over the place. It was all so different from our uniforms and equipment. Their salute was different – very stiff with jerky, mechanical movements. After the salute followed a curling twist of the moustache, and they walked on again. Where to, we never discovered. Probably to the next hill or the next bunker and back again.

It made a comic impression on us but we knew better. These Scottish regiments were famous because of their history. They were units with combat experience, something most of our regiments had not had for more than a hundred years. A foreigner easily could have smiled at our Dutch uniforms with high collars, and at our pilots armed with three-foot sabres. We had seen the highly efficient and modern German troops in their streamlined uniforms; but what about the Hermann Goerings and their Johann Strauss operetta outfits?

The sergeant had given me new pants, underwear, and a new pair of shoes. We had nothing to do but hang around and wait to see what they wanted to do with us. And then it happened again. Eric and I walked to the pub for a beer but a corporal blocked our way.

'Out of bounds, gentlemen,' he said.

'But, Corporal, we were just here yesterday,' Eric said.

The Scotsman smiled and said, 'Not at four in the morning, buddy.'

When we walked on to the harbour, we came to a big stone pier. I tried to continue but a voice said, 'Out a'bounds, gents,' and we had to go elsewhere. So we walked up a small rocky hill, but halfway to the top we heard another 'out a'bounds' command, and realized we were being watched and our freedom was limited. The whole regiment probably had nothing to do but to watch us.

Every time we saw the major we asked what the plans were, but we got a standard, 'I don't know, boys' answer until he came to us almost jubilantly, saying, 'You're going to London!'

That was good news. The major told us we would be transferred to Leith, and from there probably to London. He was quite convinced we were escaped Dutch patriots. But he made it clear that, under the circumstances, we were prisoners and we'd better not try to run away from our guards. They had orders to deliver us at a certain destination and they would, no matter how.

It took another three days' wait at Thorshavn, but the prospect of moving on to England was so good that we didn't mind anymore. We just enjoyed the fresh bread, butter, and cheese. The guys in the pub began to greet us as old buddies when we came in for our daily beer, at 5:00 in the afternoon. It still looked the same as 5:00 in the morning.

A very old, black freighter of not more than eight thousand tons arrived in the harbour and started unloading its cargo on two big barges which had moored alongside. It took most of the day, but that evening the sergeant told us it was our transport to Leith. We were to report to the major's office at 8:00 the next morning. We were only too anxious to comply with these instructions, and at 6:00 a.m. five noisy young Dutchmen sat in front of the office.

The Scottish major, with moustache more fierce than ever, arrived at 7:45. He went into his office and came back with a large, yellow envelope, which he handed to the sergeant.

'Righto, Sergeant. Take them to the bark and give this envelope to the first mate,' he said. And then to us, he said, 'Cheerio, chaps. Good luck!'

A small launch ferried us to the black freighter, where the bosun took over, saying, 'This way gentlemen. We have two cabins for you, one for two and one for three. So split up into two groups.'

He took us down two decks and showed us to our quarters, which were very small. But both had a porthole, so we had plenty of ice-cold fresh air and we could see out. I shared my cabin with Peter Tazelaar and the other three were next door. The bosun smiled and said, 'Sorry', when he locked the cabin door with a big, brass key.

We left the harbour of Thorshavn almost immediately and passed several other islands, but with no sun visible and no compass, it was hard to tell which direction we were heading. The cabin was not uncomfortable, but there were just two bunks, a small washbasin in a corner, and no chairs. With the door locked, and a view through the porthole of nothing but grey ocean to the horizon, it was like being locked in a prison cell.

After a few hours, a sailor brought us each a big bowl of pea soup, some slices of bread, and a bottle of Coca-Cola. With a gentle roll, the ship steamed on until our next meal, at about six in the evening. That night we still saw the grey, overcast sky, just like during the day.

The trip took four days and three nights, but the last night was different; it became dark. When we looked through the porthole, we saw the vague contours of land, which gradually changed into hills with houses and factories. There was now much more traffic from other boats; no doubt we were entering a harbour. It was Leith, in Scotland.

After a breakfast of imitation scrambled eggs, sausage, and toast, we heard the cabin door being unlocked and two men in civilian dress appeared.

'Good morning, gentlemen. I am Inspector Jones, and this is Sergeant Hillery from Scotland Yard. You are under arrest. Please follow us.'

The bosun handed him the yellow envelope and said, 'All yours, Inspector. Five prisoners, alive and healthy.'

Hillery immediately pulled a pair of handcuffs from under his jacket and ordered Toontje to hold out his hands. At this moment, Eric burst out laughing.

While presenting his wrists to be handcuffed, he said, 'Mister Hillery, are you serious? We are not running away from you. We came *to* you!'

His laugh was contagious and we all began to chuckle. Then the bosun began laughing, and finally Inspector Jones joined the hilarity, and said, 'That's all right, Hillery. I don't think we'll need those things.'

Now I had my laugh. I took my little pistol, still in its rubber glove, out of my pocket and said, 'You know, Mister Jones, so far nobody has searched me. And, actually, I am armed – if you call this a weapon.'

Jones' mouth fell open and he said, 'You, you better give th-that to me.'

I gave him the pistol, which he put in the yellow envelope. After that we walked to an army van which was waiting on the pier.

We reached the huge railway station of Edinburgh in about half an hour. The two Scotland Yard men escorted us to a reserved compartment in a train and, after a while, one of them came with five box lunches under his arm.

It was a long ride. We nibbled on the food in the boxes Mr Hillery had given us and tried to sleep. The third-class compartment was uncomfortable and there was little to look at through the dirty windows. Nothing seemed to indicate that this country was at war except for the hundreds of soldiers who were also on the train. The train travelled fast without too many stops. At night the shades were rolled down and only very small, blue lights illuminated the corridors for navigating one's way. Our box lunches were quite adequate but no luxury; the two Scotland Yard men took turns eating in the diner.

Although it seemed that they viewed their job of bringing us to London as an easy one, I noticed that Sergeant Hillery had a revolver in his belt and that he always sat next to the door. I don't think the two Yard men would have been so easy going if we had tried anything. Early in the morning, Mr Jones disappeared for a while, only to return with a stack of sandwiches and coffee on a tray. This time it was coffee with sugar and cream … well, milk.

At last, with a lot of hissing and rattling, we rolled into Victoria Station. On the platform, right next to the train, there was a row of taxis. But they were not for us, at least not yet.

Hillery asked Jones, 'Irons?'

Jones shook his head and said, 'Nah, just catch them if they run.'

Hillery did not appreciate the humour and mumbled, 'Funny!'

Just outside the station, a big military bus with some uniformed personnel awaited us. There were many people in shabby clothing like us, escorted by properly dressed civilians. Some of them were handcuffed. The whole bunch, with plainclothes guards, was herded into the bus. Doors closed and we were off to our next destination.

The bus went through the centre of London, travelling on the left side of the road, passing red double-decker buses, square taxis, and policemen with cloth helmets on their heads. This was London all right. But then we also saw the ruins of houses and buildings, obviously hit by German bombs. We were in England, whose expeditionary forces also had to submit to the superior hordes of Hitler and Goering. England, the only country in Europe having the courage and will to fight the German invaders; it displayed a miraculous perseverance against the odds of an overwhelmingly superior power.

The ride through London took more than an hour, but finally we were delivered at 'Patriotic School', a large internment camp where, apparently, all escapees from the occupied countries were interrogated and screened. We shook hands with Jones and Hillery, who had given the yellow envelope to people in an office. A corporal gave us a card with a number and we had to fill in our names and other information.

'With this card,' the corporal said, 'you can get your meals in the mess hall.'

Then he assigned us to a ward, where each of us got a military-type bunk. There were hundreds of young men, speaking many languages. I even ran into an American. After two days, my name appeared on a bulletin board and I was escorted to an office.

'Come in,' a man behind a desk said in English. 'Sit down, please. What's your name?'

When I gave him my name, he continued in fluent Dutch, 'Do you want to continue in Dutch?'

Bandits Twelve O'Clock

The man behind the desk was a major in an English army uniform. He came to me to shake my hand and, with a smile, he said, 'Sit down please. That must have been quite an experience. Good heavens, almost two weeks in the bilge of that ship ...'

He offered me a Players cigarette and I tried to answer, 'Yes, yes indeed. My name is ...'

But the major interrupted, 'Never mind, I know who you are and let's continue in Dutch. After all, we're both Hollanders.'

I said, 'I have seldom heard a Dutchman speak English so well, I don't hear any accent at all, not even in your Dutch.'

'Well,' he said, 'I have been in the British Intelligence Service for many years. Whenever we have Dutch boys go through this camp, I test myself to see if they recognize an accent. In my profession the knowledge of languages is essential. By the way, my name is Major Pinto, British Intelligence.'

The major told me he had received our names and partial stories from Army Intelligence in Thorshavn. He had already checked with the Dutch Air Directorate in London, where several Dutch Air Force officers immediately identified me. It meant that I was considered to be on active duty. The Dutch government never officially demobilized me. So there I was, Second Lieutenant-Pilot Bram Vanderstok. It also meant I had some wages coming.

'How about that name?' Major Pinto asked.

'Bram is my real name. "Bob" is a nickname I've had since I was four years old. The last name is three words and a capital "S", but in

English-speaking countries they frequently write it as one word, "Vanderstok". It's OK with me, I can't very well explain every time somebody calls my name.'

I was given a temporary pass. Major Pinto had arranged a room for me in Brown's Hotel, within walking distance from Piccadilly Circus, where, according to him, I would find a number of my compatriots at almost any time.

'Oh, Lieutenant Vanderstok, before you go. I took the liberty of arranging something for you. Go to the Dutch Air Force Directorate as soon as you can to straighten out your salary and allowances, but here is a hundred pounds in advance for petty cash. You'd better buy some clothes, they may not allow you in Brown's Hotel with that outfit you're wearing.'

I looked at myself and couldn't help smiling. 'Right,' I said.

Eric Hazelhoff, Peter Tazelaar, Toontje Buitendijk, and Volckers received the same kind of treatment. That morning, five jubilant *Engelandvaarders* made their first acquaintance with the London 'tube', which took them straight to Piccadilly.

Tazelaar, Toontje and Volckers were taken care of by the Dutch Navy, Eric by the secretary of the Queen, and I already was considered to be personnel of the Air Directorate. The Directorate was a liaison unit between the Dutch government-in-exile and the Royal Air Force. We were considered to be on active duty, attached to the RAF.

When I arrived at Brown's Hotel, the man at the desk looked at me with an understanding smile and said, 'We've had quite a number of Dutch refugees here.' Looking at my clothes, he added, 'We understand.'

The man gave me a small map of the London subway (the 'tube') and explained where Austin Reed was, the big clothing store on Regent Street, where one could buy everything.

With a hundred pounds sterling in my pocket, I set out to get myself some clothes. The walk to the store took me to Piccadilly Circus, where a left turn and a block and a half put me in front of Austin Reed. Between the store and the square, a very obvious young lady tried to lure me to her apartment. But I was not about to spend my first pounds on that sort of thing in the middle of the day. A hundred pounds was a lot of money in those days.

I had better plans for my instant wealth and stepped into Austin Reed. The sales clerk over-suggested a little, but I finally walked out with new shoes, six pairs of socks, underwear, grey flannel slacks, four shirts, a plaid sport jacket, two ties, and a raincoat. A hat? The clerk showed me a bowler hat, but although I had seen several people on the street wearing such a hat, that was perhaps a little too British, too soon. He did, however, talk me into a black umbrella, which turned out to be a very handy piece of equipment almost all the time.

The London shops were full of merchandise. Nothing was rationed except petrol. And, having no car, that did not concern me. I also purchased a new suitcase at Austin Reed. And, like a new man with everything new, I walked back to Brown's Hotel.

The clerk behind the desk smiled and said, 'They all buy the same stuff. The only thing missing is a black bowler hat. Looks good on you, sir. By the way, there was a telephone call for you. Call this number.'

In my room on the third floor, I called the number and discovered it was Eric who had tried to reach me. He told me to meet him at a certain bar on Piccadilly Circus at 5:30 p.m. The name of the bar was 'Oddeninos'. Peter Tazelaar would also be there and we might meet some other Hollanders.

Dressed up in my 'everything new outfit', plus umbrella, I left the hotel at five. I met a young man in RAF uniform, with the word 'Belgium' on his shoulder. I told him about my adventure with the *St Cergue* and he told me his story. He was a Belgian pilot who had escaped via Spain, where he ran into great difficulties when he found out that Spain, although officially neutral, was quite pro-German. He had to escape from a detention camp and finally made it to Gibraltar. I told him I also wanted to join the flyers again. He knew where Oddeninos was and I entered the bar with my new friend.

Oddeninos was an Italian bar, but for some reason it had become the meeting place for the *Engelandvaarders,* the Dutch boys who had escaped from occupied Holland to England to join the forces fighting against Hitler. I never met Mr Oddenino and never saw anything Italian in the place. The drinks were more English than I had ever seen, gin and lime, Pimm's #1, shandy, and ale (at room temperature). Fortunately, there also were some ordinary drinks, like Bols Jenever and Amstel beer.

The first old-timers I met were Piet Vos and Hidde Leegstra, the two who had escaped by stealing the Fokker G-1 from Schiphol airfield. We celebrated the reunion with Amstel beer and decided to go to the 'Windmill', a not-so-terrific burlesque revue which became famous because the show went on even when the building was hit by a German bomb. Both Piet and Hidde were already in RAF uniform but not yet assigned to a squadron.

That night, in my room at Brown's Hotel, I started my diary. I had more things to do than just meet the buddies at Oddeninos and see what the Air Force Directorate had in mind for me. I had a secret code. I was to organize radio contact with the underground forces in Holland. I had to organize the routes and methods for agents from here to Holland and back.

I was convinced I could help the Dutch-Paris Line with constant new connections and addresses if it were done in a reverse direction – from here to Spain, France, Belgium and Holland, and back by the same agents, without escorts. Such agents could travel all the way on their own and take others with them on their way back. They would not need any other help than some money. My mind was racing with all the important duties I had established for myself.

A diary actually was against Air Force regulations. But I was more than a pilot. I had another mission, a secret mission, not related to the RAF, so I started the diary anyway.

The next morning, I reported to the headquarters of the Dutch Air Force Directorate at Hyde Park Corner, opposite the Cumberland Hotel. From the offices on the sixth floor one literally could look into the rooms of the hotel. That was exactly what my old buddies from Soesterberg, Lutz, and Aalpoel were doing, when I walked into the office.

Sneaking up behind them, I casually asked if I could borrow the binoculars for a moment. They jumped up and recognized me. There was laughter and camaraderie, as in the old times. Soon plans were made to eat that night at the Chinaman, in Soho, after meeting at Oddeninos, of course. Piet Vos inspected my civilian clothes from top to bottom and disapproved.

'You don't wear that kind of shoe here in London. And don't you have a hat?' he said, with an air of expertise. I didn't know what he was talking about, but he went on, 'We, I repeat, we here in London wear shoes that are hand-made by Pilkins, the famous shoemaker near St James' Court.'

In the office, I registered and received my first salary, plus an allowance for uniforms and overseas service, danger money for living in London, an extra flying allowance for pilots, and a salary, retroactive as of the day I left Rotterdam. With all this, I opened an account at Barclays Bank and tried to get used to the system of guineas, quids, pounds, shillings, sixpence, threepence, pence, and halfpence (pronounced 'hay-pennies'). For us, brought up with the metric system, it was a change to reckon with when paying any kind of a bill with pound notes when the price was quoted in guineas.

For the next few days I walked through Baker Street, with its fabulous stores, to the Directorate, as a morning exercise. There I met Govert Steen, my Soesterberg classmate who had escaped with the flying boat, and Captain Berdenis, who now was in charge of the Directorate.

One day Piet Vos walked in, complete with bowler hat, umbrella, thick-soled, light brown shoes and pigskin gloves. I wasn't too impressed with the slightly overdone Briticism. But the shoes were beautiful, except for the ghastly colour. So I went to Pilkins and ordered the custom-made shoes, but in regular brown.

The man looked at me as if insulted, and protested, 'But sir, this is the heavy country style. It is the natural colour of the leather. It shouldn't be –'

I quickly said, 'Well, OK.'

I didn't want to ruin his trademark. But on the other hand, I also found it unnecessary to display his advertising wherever I walked, and I could always polish them with a darker colour of shoe wax. Ten days later, I walked to Piccadilly in my genuine Pilkins, umbrella in hand, but no bowler hat.

Oddeninos had become a regular Dutch pub. All Dutch military personnel, especially Air Force, would meet and find friends at Oddeninos. Soon the Chinese restaurants in Soho also became familiar places where one could find the Dutch boys, many of whom had ties with the Dutch East Indies where they had learned to like oriental food.

The first few weeks in London seemed as if I were on leave. I had no assignment yet but I bought an RAF uniform with the rank of pilot officer, the equivalent of a second lieutenant. A patch on each shoulder of the uniform said 'Netherlands'. I then rented a small apartment, because I would have to pay to stay at Brown's Hotel after the first two weeks. Captain Berdenis, at the Directorate, had told me I would be attached to the RAF Fighter Command in about four weeks.

Meanwhile, I received a notice to report to Her Majesty Queen Wilhelmina, who had her residence in a beautiful villa just outside London. Her office and secretariat was in London, not far from my apartment. When I rang the bell the door was opened by Eric Hazelhoff, who already had a job there. The others who had escaped with me were also there when the Queen's secretary, Mr van't Sant, briefed us about the visit. All *Engelandvaarders* paid this official visit to Her Majesty. But since not all of them were officers, a quick reminder of protocol made good sense.

In two cars we drove to the Queen's villa for our royal tea and muffins. We were received in a large drawing room, where Queen Wilhelmina shook hands with each of us. This was an unusual procedure. Under normal circumstances, we would not touch Her Majesty except with a gloved hand, and then only after Her Majesty extended her hand first. But these were not normal circumstances, and the rules of protocol were eased.

After introductions the Queen said, 'You are very special to Us. You are the link between Us and Our country. Please tell Us all about the people in Holland.'

The rules of protocol may have been eased, but there remained the slight indication of majestic pride and unquestionable rank when the Queen said 'Us' and 'Our', instead of 'me' and 'my'.

We told our stories, trying to restrict ourselves to realities, but Toontje carried his story a little further than Mr van't Sant had planned.

With excitement he blurted, 'You know, Majesty, Bob was so god-damned dirty when he came out of the bilges that you wouldn't have recognized him!' The Queen smiled, and Mr van't Sant raised his eyebrows.

I explained the terrible situation of the lack of contact and communications between the government in London and the underground resistance in Holland. The Queen apparently knew about the failure of attempts to establish communications, and once again mentioned that we were the link between London and the Dutch resistance. She felt that both Tazelaar and I wanted to say more but for some reason didn't. Mr van't Sant was her aide, whom she trusted, but we had been warned by Uncle Alexander in The Hague not to trust him.

When our visit came to an end, Toontje had to go to the rest room and he was shown the way.

Soon he came back into the big room, saying, 'Jesus Christ, some toilet! Looks like a –'

Here van't Sant stopped him and we once again shook hands with the Queen. In compliance with the rule that one always faces the Queen, we tried to walk backwards, but stumbled against furniture and other persons.

Her Majesty laughed and said, 'Forget the protocol and save my borrowed furniture.'

On our way home Toontje had to describe the toilet. It was a ceramic bowl, painted with little flowers inside and out and set on a small platform, rather like sitting on a throne. And if this was probably only the servants' john, you can imagine what the real royal thing would be! We tried to tell him that this was not a royal palace, but he insisted that the 'pots' must have been specially installed.

Back in London, I arranged a meeting with Peter Tazelaar and Eric Hazelhoff at Oddeninos. That evening, with the blessings of Pimm's #1 and a Chinese dinner, we discussed our instructions from Uncle Alexander and the situation with Mr van't Sant. I knew him as the father of a girl we went to school with. He had been the chief of police in The Hague before he became special adviser to the Queen. The idea of van't Sant not being loyal to Queen Wilhelmina was simply unthinkable.

Peter and I decided we would go through Admiral Fürstner, as Uncle Alexander wanted us to, but since I had an appointment with our prime minister, Professor Gerbrandy, I would discuss the matter with him as well. Peter and Eric also had appointments with His Excellency and we decided we should bring up the controversy about van't Sant.

Although probably just a case of political animosity, the possibility of a traitor or foreign agent as the Queen's number one adviser was something that could not be ignored. We had come to England to fight for Holland's independence under Queen Wilhelmina of the House of Orange. We, as soldiers of Orange, were prepared to fight all enemies of our cause.

After our Chinese dinner we went to a nightclub. The joint was in the basement of a house opposite the Windmill theatre. When we knocked on the door, a tiny square window opened and a woman's voice asked who we were. When we said we were Dutch military she opened the door, but we could not enter because we were not members.

The girl said, 'Two shilling each, must have sponsor.'

'Here's two shilling, but I don't know anybody here,' I said.

The girl quickly answered, 'No problem, me sponsor for you.'

The club instantly had three new members. Armed with a little card, we entered the dimly lit club. We ordered a drink and enjoyed the floor show of a naked girl performing a sort of snake dance, and a very questionable pair of male dancers. A taxi took me back to my apartment.

During the next week we became members of about ten more night-clubs, so we could see that many floor shows for the price of a glass of beer. As a 'member' we could sponsor any of our friends, even if it meant being a member for just one evening. Sometimes we were admitted by showing the wrong card, but nobody seemed to take that very seriously.

Professor Gerbrandy, prime minister of the Dutch government-in-exile, received me with a handshake and congratulated me on my successful escape from occupied Holland. He elaborated on the complexities of government when there is no country to govern, and about his unpreparedness for the situation.

But then, as if he did not want to think about all those nasty problems, he smiled and said, 'But I have some pleasant duties as well. Her Majesty the Queen has ordered me to present you with the Bronze Cross for your outstanding performance as an *Engelandvaarder*.'

He pinned the cross on my lapel and gave me the citation. I thanked him appropriately but then changed the subject.

'Your Excellency, I am very grateful for the decoration, but I came here with something very difficult in mind.'

'Oh, what is it?' the prime minister asked, apparently totally unaware of the possibility that we had come with messages and plans.

I tried to explain that the resistance forces in Holland were screaming for support from their government in London, but that there were no realistic communications to speak of. The people of Holland expected more than prayers and kind remarks on radio programmes; they wanted help. They wanted leadership and action wherever possible, not a symbol of a government sitting and waiting for others to do the work.

Professor Gerbrandy was uncomfortable and didn't know what to say. It became painfully obvious that he had no knowledge at all of what was going on in the Netherlands. He knew of no radio contacts, and knew even less of any agents or assistance, financial or otherwise. The poor prime minister was hopelessly out of place, and thought more about his own forced separation from his family in Amsterdam than about his current obligations as head of a government.

'You must understand, Mr Vanderstok, that I am not a military man. I am a professor at the University of Amsterdam, and no expert in spy work or anything like that.'

When I asked him if he was aware of certain groups in Holland that were not only supporting the underground resistance, but also preparing a provisional government for the recovery after a German defeat, he was confused and had to admit that he knew nothing about that.

Disappointed and surprised, I did not even bring up the group of Uncle Alexander, the landing place for agents, the Dutch-Paris Line, or the code. I just left the office with a polite handshake, knowing that he was not the man for me.

On my way out he muttered, 'Perhaps Mr van't Sant, the Queen's secretary, knows more about these things. Why don't you talk to him?'

'Thank you, your Excellency. Goodbye.'

Of all people he recommended van't Sant, the man I was not supposed to talk to, the man who was under suspicion by the very people from whom I received my instructions. I did not feel an obligation toward Uncle Alex. After all, he had not arranged my escape to England, I did not owe him anything. It was actually the other way around; Peter and I did something for him.

Should I go to the English intelligence services? Or should I give it another try with the Dutch admiral, Fürstner, who had distinguished himself in the Dutch East Indies? Being a military man, he should have an open mind for my mission.

At the Directorate I made an appointment with the admiral, who I was to see the next day. In the meantime, I talked over my experiences with Peter Tazelaar and we both decided to try our luck with our admiral. Eric Hazelhoff, still working in the Queen's office, was in daily contact with Mr van't Sant and could not believe the information we were given by the Dutch group. Peter and I also began to have doubts.

My visit with Admiral Fürstner was of a different nature, and I immediately felt that I was talking to a man who knew and understood the situation extremely well. I told him the story about the feelings of Dutch resistance leaders toward Mr van't Sant, and related the instructions both Peter Tazelaar and I had been given. Admiral Fürstner quickly came to the point.

'Vanderstok, you may not like what I have to tell you. But it would be prudent to see the truth as it is and tackle our problems from a realistic point of view. One must define those problems and solve them with the tools that are available to us. These tools are not much of anything now.'

The admiral pushed a button and a girl in uniform entered the room. It was the first female in the Royal Dutch Navy I had ever seen. He asked her to type some names and addresses, and then to me, 'Coffee?' When I nodded, he continued, 'Give those addresses to Lieutenant Vanderstok when he leaves and please bring two cups of coffee.'

I told him the rest of my story – the code, the plans for the Dutch-Paris Line, the landing place on the beach, and the absolute need for communications with the resistance.

Admiral Fürstner went on, 'In the first place, may I call you Bob? I know that your younger brother is a midshipman at the Institute at Den Helder, and your uncle, Felix Snethlage, is a friend of mine. It is a small world. Next, put that idea of Mr van't Sant being a traitor or spy out of your mind. He is one of the most loyal and trustworthy men I know.

'His quarrel with Mr Schimmelpennink, alias "Uncle Alexander", is an old and well-known feud in political circles. It goes back to an alleged scandal involving Prince Hendrick, the now-deceased husband of Queen Wilhelmina. I guarantee you that Uncle Alexander's story is personal, and that you can trust van't Sant more than our friend Alexander.

'Now, I'll tell you what you may not like to hear. Contact with the Dutch resistance workers is all but non-existent. We have no reliable radio contacts at all. Some messages were received by the English intelligence, but most of them probably were of German origin and made no sense to us. Whatever messages we tried to transmit to them never produced any response. The only contact we have is through people like you, the men and women who got out of Holland and arrived in England to report for duty, the *Engelandvaarders.*

'What I would like you to do is go to Mr van't Sant in full confidence, and discuss your knowledge and plans with him. You know you'll be on the side of the Queen. One more point, Bob. Make a decision about what you can do best in our fight against the Germans. Are you a spy or a pilot?'

I was quite pleasantly impressed with the admiral's fatherly talk. I also took good note of his last remark. Was I a trained cloak-and-dagger spy, or were my background and capabilities more in line with a fighter pilot? That was easy to answer, but I wanted to see the other things done as well.

On my way out, the MARVA girl, as they were called, handed me a piece of paper with the addresses of Mr van't Sant and an English major in Army Intelligence. By this time I was convinced that van't Sant was OK and that politics were very dirty. I knew now that the thousands of Dutch resistance workers who thought they were doing their dangerous work under orders, or in compliance with their government in London and Allied commanders, were on their own. None of it was on orders received by radio or in any other way. Many sacrifices were apparently based on ... nothing at all.

Some of them, caught with their radio transmitters, never accomplished any contact, never received and never sent a true message. The stories of agents coming and going by submarine, the dropping of agents and equipment by plane at night at pre-arranged places, and transportation of shot-down airmen by the Dutch-Paris Line was all little more than wishful thinking. These stories were the way it should be. But it wasn't so ... not yet.

On my next visit to the Directorate, I received orders to report to the Medical Department of the RAF on Fleet Street. The physical examination was superficial, except for the eye exam, and I passed with an 'A' in the fighter category. Further instructions would come through the Directorate. I went back to the office at Marble Arch and contacted Peter, who now lived in the same apartment as Eric, just behind the office of the Queen where van't Sant had his headquarters. I also called the secretary, who invited me to see him that same afternoon.

Navigating in London became an easy thing, once I got to know the system of the 'tube'. Offices were largely located in the centre of the city, close to tube stations. It was a very inexpensive way to travel, although the little square taxis were also quite economical, especially if you could squeeze four or five people into the odd vehicles.

The office of the Queen was an ordinary, but large, house on Leicester Square. Peter opened the door and invited me to a large drawing room in the back, where Eric introduced me to Mr van't Sant. The four of us exchanged some small talk but we soon got down to business.

Again we heard the pitiful story of the incompetence of many of the members of the government, and were told that communications with Dutch underground workers had never been established. Just when I was ready to present my side of our concerns, Prince Bernhard walked in and greeted us with outstretched hands. With a big smile, he welcomed me and right away called us by first name. No formalities, no protocol, no hesitations. It was as if five old friends met.

Peter spoke about his instructions and what he suggested doing, since it was obvious that something had to be organized from scratch. After I told my story, Prince Bernhard shook his head and confirmed the sad situation. He and van't Sant were well aware of the negativism and fatalistic attitude on the part of most of the government officials who had escaped from Holland just before the capitulation. Then the Prince took charge.

'Listen,' he said. 'I have a suggestion. But first, I think we should celebrate your arrival in England with a drink.'

He left the room and came back with a servant carrying a tray with five glasses and a bottle of sherry. The glasses were filled and we proposed a toast to the health of our Queen. We talked about the adventure on the *St Cergue* and the hilarious farewell to the Lithuanian captain. But then the Prince shifted the conversation to the more serious purpose of our meeting.

Bernhard actually was German. Then he married the daughter of Queen Wilhelmina, Princess Juliana, who later became Queen of the Netherlands. Although German, he strongly opposed the actions of the Third Reich and openly denounced Hitler and his Nazi hordes. The fact that he mastered the Dutch language within a few years had made him popular, and his loyalty to the Dutch and the House of Orange was beyond any doubt.

'We are well aware of the incompetent group of people that make up this government-in-exile,' he said. 'But it is therefore so important that the younger people like you come here from occupied Holland. You know what the situation is, and you have a better idea of what can or cannot be done, with these Godforsaken Nazis in full command of everyday life. We need people like you, to organize and implement the support to the resistance at home.'

I didn't know yet what he had in mind, but it was obvious this was not just idle talk. He wanted action as much as we did. The people in Holland were screaming for help. We were not about to ignore that.

And he continued, 'Believe me, I have tried before but just ran into the wrong people every time. Too much confusion and no response. Let's start from the beginning, here and now, in this office, and see what will grow out of this. I feel confident that with a nucleus like this little group, we will expand and get the much-needed support.

'Eric and Peter, I have assigned you to assist Mr van't Sant, who will be in charge for the time being. Bob, I want you to work out those plans you brought along. Your headquarters will be here in this house, and you may use the office and equipment we have available. Your jobs must be considered classified. Just don't talk to anybody at all about this mission. I will expand our group as the need arises.

'And Bob, I want to talk to you privately. How about lunch at the Ritz Hotel, tomorrow about one o'clock?'

'I will be there, Your Highness,' I said.

The Ritz was an old but very distinguished hotel off Piccadilly. When I entered the lobby I told the clerk at the desk I had an appointment with His Royal Highness, Prince Bernhard. He ushered me to the dining room. I found the Prince at one of the tables with another person, who was dressed in a British army uniform. I was introduced to Major Higgins of Army Intelligence.

When we sat down, Prince Bernhard said, 'John is an old friend of mine, and as a staff officer in the British Intelligence Service, he might be just the man we are looking for.'

It was only common sense to understand that the kind of operations we had in mind would require the full knowledge and approval of the British. After all, who would have to provide submarines and planes for the exchange of agents, and where and how would we train our agents? It was clear that the British had to be involved somehow.

I explained my proposals once again, and stressed the basic objectives that had to be accomplished before any results could be expected. It was essential to send agents with radio capability from here to Holland. We had to establish reliable radio communications and we had to create one or more ways to get personnel from occupied territory back to England.

After the lunch at the Ritz, I went back to my apartment and started to work on my report and plan for the landings on the coast near Scheveningen. Every morning I reported to the Directorate to see what further developments there were with my attachment to the RAF. From there I went to the Queen's office to type my report, where I usually had lunch with Eric and Peter. We met with the Prince and Mr van't Sant almost every day. In the afternoon, I worked on the report and around 5:00, it was to Oddeninos to meet the boys.

On one of these days, during lunch, Prince Bernhard called me into his office and we talked about our plans. He said there were several *Engelandvaarders* who had volunteered to be sent back to Holland. They were about to start a training camp for Dutch agents to be dropped over Holland. Through Major Higgins, we knew that the Dutch persisted in trying to establish radio contact. But the messages were in plain language and did not indicate any use of codes. He also informed me that two Dutch officers, Captain Derksema and Lieutenant Commander Sobel, were now assigned to a newly formed Dutch Intelligence Unit in London. I was obviously pleasantly surprised to see such a promising response to the message we brought from Holland. But then Bernhard added:

'Bob, I know that you volunteered to go back to Holland as an agent. And you would do a good job, I am sure. However, you are a trained and experienced fighter pilot. I know that you will be attached to the RAF and deployed as a Spitfire pilot. Frankly, I see a better future for you as a pilot than this uncertain and extremely risky spy job. I believe that you would serve our country better as a pilot.'

I had to admit that this had been my first motivation all along, and the idea of being a secret agent was something I had accidentally run into. It was true, flying was far more in my line than spying. Nevertheless, I would complete my part in this facet of warfare but then concentrate my activities on the war in the air.

In the following weeks, I completed my report concerning the landing place on the beach at Scheveningen. The operations were described in detail. Agents would cross the hundred and fifty miles of North Sea by submarine, at night. Due to the gently sloping, sandy bottom, it would be possible to approach as close as three hundred yards to the coast at low tide.

The submarine would then surface very briefly and launch an inflatable boat with three men, who would row ashore. The inflatable would be pulled back to the sub by a long line, so there would be no evidence of any vessel on the beach. The place was to be the exact same spot where Hans Maas and I had tried our escape with the homemade boat. To return, the same procedure would be followed. The rubber boat would be rowed to the same spot, where returning agents would know when the next crossing would be attempted. The crew of the sub would give the agents twenty minutes to be on location, no more. By the same token, the agents would not wait longer than twenty minutes for the sub to appear.

Radio communications would be established by trained agents, using my code or a new code of their own. Radio frequencies should not be easy to vector, and antennas should be designed for directional beams rather than omni-directional. Agents could return by themselves, as a group, or could take someone along. If the inflatable was too small to carry the required number of persons, the extra passengers could be pulled through the water. Cold, but possible. The agents would not be allowed to reveal pick-up times to anyone, and no radio communications were to mention dates or times – ever!

A group of agents was to be trained to establish a series of addresses from Spain, through France and Belgium, to Holland. These people could well be women, and fluency in the French language was strongly recommended. Agents would be flown to Madrid as members of the Dutch Embassy. From there they would go to three places in the Pyrenees, with the aid of anti-fascist Spanish families, who were easy to find in those days.

Spain, under Franco, had just won a civil war with enormous German help. The victorious Spanish government, a fascist regime, was pro-German, a factor we had to reckon with. Our people had to cross the Pyrenees and make contacts with the French resistance, the *maquis,* and establish addresses where they could get shelter on their way back. They were to continue on their way through France and Belgium, to Holland, having a complete string of addresses for returning.

In Holland, they could contact our agents or members of the Dutch-Paris Line, but they were not allowed to reveal their routes. Each house would have a 'safe/danger' signal, so that agents would not knock on a door only to find themselves walking into a Gestapo trap. Such signals had to be simple but effective. They should not be recognizable by the uninformed, but yet should offer a clear indication for our agents.

Houses in the country, for example, could have laundry drying on a line, with one piece of green clothing as a signal that approach was safe. With no laundry on the line, agents should not come to the house. A similar warning should be displayed at houses in a town. A newspaper under the door, with a green mark on it, would mean 'ready to receive customers'. Nothing under the door, or a newspaper without a green mark, would mean 'stay away'. None of the owners of these shelters would know who or where the next links would be. Our agents were to create more than one string of addresses so unannounced changes could be implemented at any time.

Franco's government was strongly anti-communist, but those who opposed him often leaned toward communism. They were just the ones we needed for help. In France, the *maquis* were organized as armed resistance groups and openly members of the Communist Party. They operated in the foothills of the Pyrenees, where the Germans never caught up with them. Their organization needed funds, and they often demanded money or other valuables for their services.

Our organization of agents would need funds to make use of the incredible *maquis*. The link between our agents and the French underground could pinpoint sites for dropping supplies by parachute.

In less than a week, I presented the neatly typed package to Prince Bernhard. At lunch with Peter and Eric, I found out that British Intelligence was listening to our plans, and heard further confirmations of the incompetence of a large number of Dutch 'government officials'.

In the evenings, at Oddeninos, we met more Hollanders who had made it as *Engelandvaarders,* some of them old school friends or fraternity brothers from the university at Leiden. Almost all of them had offered their services as agents back in Holland. There was no shortage of enthusiastic workers, but an organization to use them was far from a reality.

The plan for the Holland–Spain Line was sent to the Dutch ambassador in Madrid, who instantly discussed the matter with Spanish officials. The pro-German officials declined any form of help, and probably went straight to the Germans to inform them. In spite of my protests against the involvement of the Spanish government, the Dutch ambassador had followed his official diplomatic 'bull' and almost ruined our plans.

I went to Commander Sobels to explain the mathematical wonder designed by the professor in Delft. It took me much longer than I had expected to show him the principle of the double key. Now, I sincerely believe that he never really understood the code.

Prince Bernhard and Mr van't Sant were enormously interested in the code, since this was the only form of possible communication between the Dutch underground and the government in London. The radio frequencies, the times, and the code were known in Holland; it certainly was worth a try. Messages would contain a safety signal with the letters a, b, or c, followed by a two digit number – b36 or a17. The signal for alarm was one of the letters x, y, or z, followed by a one-digit number – x5 or z9. Any message containing the alarm signal would mean, 'Do not believe this message, something is wrong!'

They gave me the name of a captain in the British Intelligence Service at an address on Fleet Street, where I should report and explain the entire radio plan. When I entered the building, there was considerable security checking. But after that, I was escorted to the office of the man who was to be the liaison between the Dutch government and secret operations in the Dutch sector. The captain was a very pleasant man who carefully listened to my story. I handed him an envelope with the written report, including an explanation of the code.

He glanced through the papers and then said, 'We will study your plan very carefully, and this may well be a fresh start for the operations of this nature. You see, so far all efforts to establish radio contact with the Dutch resistance have had no results whatsoever.'

When I discussed the exchange of agents by submarine, his tone was different.

'Now that is a different situation. What you talk about now is an operation where we control every movement of the plan. We do not have to rely on response or cooperation from people whom we do not know. I will submit this idea as well, but you should not discuss this with anybody else but Prince Bernhard.'

I gladly made that promise and left the office with a feeling of having accomplished something. Good heavens, who could have dreamt that I would be involved in a true spy adventure! The more I thought about it, the more I realized that sneaking around in a trench coat, dark glasses, and a felt hat with front and back brim pulled down, was not exactly my cup of tea. As a fighter pilot, I was in my own element.

During the daily contacts with Peter and Eric, I heard the discouraging news over and over that any form of contact with Holland had failed. Even more alarming was the feeling of many Hollanders in London that these efforts were carried out halfheartedly, and by totally incompetent people. The English had tried to transmit on given frequencies at given times without results. They had even tried to send a message in plain language, which promptly produced a response in the form of a joke, in German.

Finally, the long-expected letter arrived at the Directorate. I was accepted to be deployed as a fighter pilot in the Royal Air Force. Once again, I had to report to the Air Ministry on Fleet Street. On my way I stopped at Austin Reed, where a helpful salesman had the RAF wings sewn on my uniform.

He looked at me and said, 'Sir, you cannot report to headquarters like that', pointing a finger at the dull brass buttons on my jacket.

I learned that English uniform buttons had to be polished every day. So the man sold me a polishing kit and a shoe polishing kit, as well.

At the Air Ministry, I received my RAF ID card and a booklet especially designed for foreigners who joined the RAF. It was a most helpful little piece of literature, full of hints and rules about British services and traditions. It also contained a list of words that seemed innocent enough to a foreigner, but which would be considered bad taste in England. The word 'bloody' was to be avoided, British soldiers were not to be called 'Limeys', and 'Fanny' had another meaning besides a name.

In a few days I had to report for duty at Tangmere, a large RAF airfield where I was to receive training in an OTU (operational training unit) for Spitfires. The course not only included the conversion from whatever plane we had flown before to the Spitfire; it also dealt with a thorough review of the English language we would use in our radio communications.

The course was difficult at first, but soon we adapted to our new life as RAF officers. Our group was divided into classes of about twelve officers and sergeants, all military pilots with various levels of experience. When one class went flying with British instructors, the others went to school to study radio communications, parachuting (in classrooms), Rolls-Royce engines, aircraft recognition, armament, tactics, and the use of some techniques which were classified and very secret in those days.

One of them was the gunsight, which consisted of a little illuminated cross projected on the bullet-proof windshield. Around this marker was an adjustable circle, which could be set for a known wingspan. When the wing of the target plane fitted in the circle, the distance was then calibrated for the greatest concentration of fire from the machine guns. In other words, it was a simple distance meter. One still had to allow for the ballistic corrections to hit a moving target.

Another secret instrument was the 'cockerel'. If switched on, this ingenious little black box produced a small deviation of the blip on the radar screen, and so aided the radar operator in recognizing the plane. This radio signal was only used on request and not longer than for a few seconds.

The command was in the form of a question, 'Is your cockerel crowing?'

After recognition, the radar operator would say, 'Cockerel out.'

The gadget was the IFF unit, the method to Identify Friend or Foe. The little black box containing the IFF cockerel was very secret indeed. A red button, when pushed, would destroy the electronics inside. A hard impact also would set off a small explosive charge inside the box. The gunsight, with its optical distance meter, would also explode on impact.

Our code names were changed every day, which became rather confusing because there are not that many code names available so they had to be repeated frequently. Not only were code names given to squadrons, but the controlling ground station had to have a new name every day as well.

For instance, if a squadron name on a certain day was 'Jackknife', one could call any pilot in that squadron on that day simply by saying, 'Jackknife Red Four, this is Jackknife Leader. You have a bandit on your tail.'

The ground station was called, say, 'Olympic', and could warn us of approaching enemy planes. The station would come on the air with, 'Jackknife, this is Olympic. Bandits three o'clock above.'

We would look up and to the right, to see the German planes as reported by 'Olympic', but we would take no action. The actual air combat was directed by the squadron commander. With ink we wrote the code names for the day on our wrists. The ink could easily be washed off and, in case of emergency, one could lick it off as well.

It was all very secret and occasionally confusing, especially for those guys who had not taken baths and still had yesterday's code names on their hands.

One irritated voice blared into the radio, 'Well, what the hell is my name then for today?'

Newly commissioned Dutch Air Force officer, Bram Vanderstok, circa 1936

Pilot for Royal Dutch Air Force in the cockpit of a Fokker D-21 fighter plane, prior to Dutch capitulation in 1940

Squadron Leader Bram Vanderstok (centre-seated) with the entire RAF 322 Squadron

The Dutch Fokker D-21 fighter, May 1940. (Courtesy Royal Dutch Air Force)

Vanderstok's new Spitfire Mark XIVe, March 1945. Max speed 430 mph

Spitfire Mark XXII, the last operational model, in flight formation. Max speed 450 mph

The five *Engeland-vaarders* who escaped from Holland to England in 1941 aboard the freighter *St Cergue*. Left-right: standing: Buytendyk, Vanderstok, Tazelaar; sitting: Volckerz, Hazelhoff-Roelfzema

10 May 1940: Vanderstok landed his D-21, exited and ran as a German Me.109 strafed the field and set the plane on fire. One bullet grazed the author's jacket; he turned around and photographed his own plane in flames.

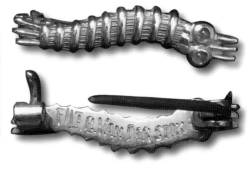

Caterpillar Club membership was awarded to authenticated individuals who successfully used a parachute to bail out of a disabled aircraft. Vanderstok received his membership certificate and distinctive lapel pin after bailing out of his shot-down Spitfire in 1942

Reconstruction of Stalag Luft III 'goon' security tower

Reconstruction of Stalag Luft III barracks interior

Stalag Luft III camp commandant, Oberst Friedrich Wilhelm von Lindeiner genannt von Wildau

Allied officers/POWs standing in front of Stalag Luft III barracks. Author third from left

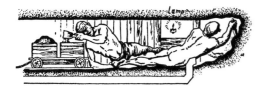

(above) Digging tunnels in confined space with oil lamps. Lighting was electrified later

(above, right) The jury-rigged air pump made of KLIM cans ('milk' spelt backwards)

(right) Stove hiding entry to tunnel 'Harry'

(below) Diagram of entire escape tunnel 'Harry'

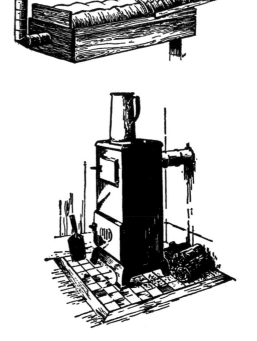

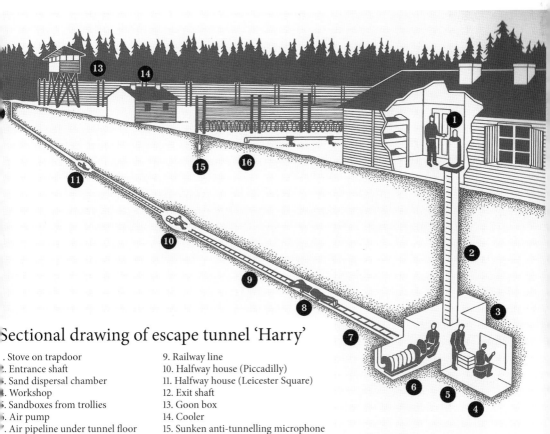

Sectional drawing of escape tunnel 'Harry'

1. Stove on trapdoor
2. Entrance shaft
3. Sand dispersal chamber
4. Workshop
5. Sandboxes from trollies
6. Air pump
7. Air pipeline under tunnel floor
8. Tunneller travelling on railway
9. Railway line
10. Halfway house (Piccadilly)
11. Halfway house (Leicester Square)
12. Exit shaft
13. Goon box
14. Cooler
15. Sunken anti-tunnelling microphone
16. Warning wire

Urlaubsschein

Der _Hendrik Beeldman_
(Vor- und Zuname)

aus _Alkmaar (Holland)_
(Heimatland, Heimatort)

geb. am _22. 12. 1917_ beschäftigt als _Installateur_

ist vom _24. März 1944_ bis _9. April 1944_ nach

Alkmaar (Holland) beurlaubt
(Urlaubsort)

Grund des Urlaubs : _Heimaturlaub_
(Familienheimfahrt, Krankheitsurlaub, Heimaturlaub, besondere Anlässe usw)

Der Urlauber hat Arbeiterrückfahrkarte bis _____
erhalten.

Der Urlauber ist über die für die Mitnahme von Geldmitteln in deutscher
bzw. der betreffenden ausländischen Währung geltenden Bestimmungen
unterrichtet worden.

Der Urlauber ist verpflichtet nach Beendigung des Urlaubs die Arbeit in
unserem Betrieb wieder aufzunehmen.

Breslau, den _23. März_ 1944
(Firmenstempel — Unterschrift)

Bescheinigung des Arbeitsamts
Breslau

Der Erteilung des Sichtvermerks zur einmaligen Aus- und Wieder-
einreise wird zugestimmt.

Breslau/Ohl, den _23. März 1944_ 194

I. A.:
[signature]
(Unterschrift)

(Stampel)

Vordr. Ausl. 5760 U
DIN A5

One of Vanderstok's false papers. This is a travel permit where Vanderstok travelled
under the pseudonym Hendrik Beeldman. All letters on this document are hand-
printed. It passed German inspection twice and took two months to make

Celebrating Queen Wilhelmina's birthday dinner at Stalag Luft III. Vanderstok is standing, second from left. Seated left–right: Casey, W/C Stanford Tuck, G/C Massey, Cdr. Hey Schaper, W/C "Wings" Day

Partial military medal collection of Bram Vanderstok

Victory Parade, London, 1945

Vanderstok receiving medal from Queen Wilhelmina, 1945

Vanderstok as a guest of the cast of American television comedy series *Hogan's Heroes*

Retiree Vanderstok was active in the US Coast Guard Auxiliary, a civilian support group to the United States Coast Guard.

Standing in front of his beloved World War II vintage Spitfire forty years later

Whereupon the ground controller calmly answered, 'I will forward your request to Hermann Goering.'

Another incredible advance for the time was the homing capability of ground-controlled assistance. By radar and with our cockerels, the radar controller could recognize the plane and its position. When necessary, we could seek cover in a cloud layer and simply ask for a homing. The GCA (ground-controlled approach) controller would literally talk us home.

Flying on instruments in cloud cover we would hear, 'Jackknife, this is Olympic. Steer two-seven-five.' And, after a few minutes, 'Jackknife, 2 degrees to the right to two-seven-seven', and more corrections, as needed.

At the right time one would hear, 'Jackknife, you can come down and pancake. Ceiling five hundred feet.' After that command, we would descend, make a left turn and find ourselves flying around our own airfield.

At OTU, my first solo flight in a 'Miles-Master' trainer ended in disaster. The Miles was a trainer for the Spitfire and had an identical cockpit. There was a second seat in tandem, for the instructor. I had no trouble flying the plane and he let me solo after an hour or so. When I rolled onto the concrete runway, everything seemed in order and I asked the tower for permission to scramble. The controller flashed his green light and I took off.

I opened the throttle and gained speed without any trouble. Suddenly, when I was not more than twenty feet in the air, at the end of the runway, I was sitting in a cloud of white smoke with a stalled engine.

I had just enough time to get the wheels up and shout, 'Mayday, Mayday! Just look for the guy in a lot of smoke!'

I quickly thanked the Lord for that small potato field just in front of me, and then made a model three-point landing in the mud. At the last moment my Miles dipped forward and came to a halt, standing 45 degrees on its nose. I jumped out of the cockpit and ran as fast as I could to a hedge, hoping to find some cover in case the darn thing might explode. Crash trucks and fire wagons rushed to the scene, sirens howling, and people were everywhere.

The flight engineer came to me, saying, 'Probably only a bent prop job because you made a nice belly-landing.'

That was my first solo in England.

The rest of the OTU was, much to my delight, a very thorough flying school. It was formation flying every day, not the fancy Vs and lines abreast we had done so often for demonstrations and parades, but battle formations. The basic pattern was three sections of four planes each. The Red Section, commanded by the squadron leader, was in the middle, with the Yellow Section on his right and the Blue Section on his left. The Yellow and Blue Sections flew in slightly staggered, line-astern formation, slightly below the Red Section.

After some training, the entire squadron could make 90 degree and even 180 degree turns almost as fast as a single plane. In a 90 degree turn, Yellow and Blue would change sides; so the section on the inside would go below and the one on the outside would go over. The buddy system of the numbers one/two and three/four of all sections provided a certain amount of safety, and an almost sphere-like vector for twelve pairs of eyes to see.

The three-dimensional directions were given by the clock system, above or below. So, 'twelve o'clock' was dead ahead, 'six o'clock' dead astern, and 'three o'clock' above was 90 degrees to the right, above us.

There were also words to learn. Enemy aircraft were 'Bandits', or 'Jerries', or 'Huns'. The Dutch called them *Moffen*. But then we had words for the foreigners on our side, too. We called the Belgians *Belzen* and they called us *Kaaskoppen* (cheese heads). Ah, and those words for the French, the English. The Belgians had a good one for the Italians, *Ysco manneke* (ice cream vendors).

We went through a parachuting course, much like we had done in Soesterberg, and extensive chart-reading sessions. For most of us, the flying was not the most difficult part of the OTU, as all of us were experienced pilots. Something new for those days was the Link trainer. In Soesterberg, we had flown 'blind flying' exercises with a black hood pulled over the cockpit, but always with another pilot to check on us. The Link simulator was a non-flying cockpit on the ground. It registered all flight movements on a table, where a very stern sergeant would approve or disapprove every detail of the flight.

There was a lot of training on the ground. Whatever we learned about parachuting was much the same as what we had learned in Soesterberg; have your straps tight, jump, count to ten, pull the rip cord, hope you won't forget the oxygen tube and headphone wires, and when you save your life with one of these 'Irvin' parachutes, you'll become a member of the 'Caterpillar Club'. I am ashamed to say that we did not take the parachuting instruction too seriously, because, well, who was thinking of being shot down anyway?

Other ground instruction was different, and for me, more than interesting. We studied the Rolls-Royce Merlin engines, the injection system for continuous power upside down, the hydraulic system of the landing gear, the flaps, the trim, the brakes, the steel plate behind the seat, the pyrotechnic signals and the marvellous layout of dashboard and handles. The cockerel, the radio and the gunsight, they were all different. Using the radio in the English language, understanding commands, and giving the proper replies, these were all new to us.

I quickly felt at home in the Spitfire cockpit. I enjoyed simply sitting in the machine to look around, absorbing all the little knobs, handles, and instruments that controlled this incredible flying machine.

The Link trainer plane impressed me most of all. We had very little experience in blind flying. Under a hood and with an instructor was about all we had ever done. But I realized the importance of instrument flying for the kind of missions we were to fly. I understood then that air-combat tactics had undergone enormous changes with the development of radar and ground control. They could send us places, flying all the way in a cloud layer; they could direct us back to base while we could not see the ground, or when we did not know exactly where we were. For this, absolute mastery of precise instrument flying became one of the most needed skills for a fighter pilot.

I spent hours in the Link trainer and became buddies with Sergeant Hopkins, our instructor. Although it was not a part of this particular training course, Hopkins let me go through the routine of what we then called GCA, ground-controlled approach. Over and over we went through the procedure, until he literally talked me down to complete landings. There were six Link trainers at the base, most of them with cockpits almost identical to the Spitfire.

For many foreigners joining the RAF, the English language could be a barrier. Not only did we have to speak in a foreign language, but we had to learn the slang and combat commands of the British. It took me a while to find out what 'Gremlins' were, and to learn that a 'U/S' plane did not come from the United States but was any plane temporarily 'UnServiceable'. We also discovered that everybody here was a 'chap', and if you didn't know his name you called him 'Charlie'.

Because of the technological advances of radar and GCA, flying had taken on new dimensions. Low clouds and fog had always posed a considerable drawback for navigation and landing. These weather conditions, much the same as in the Netherlands, were called 'flying in a thick soup', and made missions on such days almost impossible. Now we could be located and directed to targets, or rerouted to airfields with better visibility. On some bases one could make GCA landings and be 'talked in' all the way.

The gunsight was secret but I never understood why. It was nothing more than an optical cross, projected through the windshield, and an adjustable ring which could be set for a known measure of wingspan. For instance, when we set the ring for thirty-two feet, the wingspan of a Messerschmitt-109, and the enemy wing would just fill the ring, the distance was calibrated to two hundred yards, where the greatest concentration of fire would occur. We still had to aim at an angle well ahead of the target if it crossed our path. A target dead ahead was not subject to this correction.

The sight was a relatively simple distance meter and I did not consider it a tremendous technological advance. Much later, I learned that this gunsight was the forerunner of the new and fantastic instrument which later was installed in all fighters. The thing was so secret that there was a push button on the front panel which would ignite a small charge inside the instrument and totally destroy it. Also, an impact sensor would destroy the inside of the sight.

We learned about the daily code words. These were RAF slang for everyday business, such as 'scramble' for immediate takeoff, 'pancake' for landing, 'angels' for every thousand feet of altitude, and the various commands in the air.

The radio itself was much better than the radios we had in our Fokker D-21s a year ago in Holland. We learned about the IFF gadget (Identification Friend or Foe) and how to use it.

One of the most fascinating things we became acquainted with were the operation rooms of Fighter Command. These were the command centres where the respective positions of our planes and the German planes were plotted on large tables. Each table had a map of its operational area painted on it.

A number of WAFs, wearing headphones and using little rakes much like those used on gambling tables, moved models of airplanes on the tables. The WAFs received their information from the radar operators, who calmly figured out where each plane was and where it was going. Operations controllers could then direct us to the enemy planes. They could even manoeuvre us in such a manner as to let us approach the enemy from out of the sun.

The cockerel identification signal was not on all the time, only when the radar operator would ask for it and then for as short a time as possible. This brilliant system of directing our planes to the right place was no doubt one of the major factors for winning the Battle of Britain. The Germans were far behind in this detail of radio technology. Their radar did not have the IFF feature and could not detect planes flying under a thousand feet.

Another detail which I learned many years later was that the Luftwaffe radio operators had great difficulty in understanding our voice communications.

When we talked in our regular non-coded slang like, 'Blue Three, we go angels eight. Watch those bandits nine o'clock below. Think they are Me.s, span thirty-two feet', the German operators did not understand it at all.

I was told it took the Germans more than two years to train operators to where they could reasonably make sense out of our radio communications. Like most Europeans, the Germans were trained basically in the metric system and thirty-two feet did not mean anything to them.

The abbreviation 'Me.' for a Messerschmitt sounds like a girl's name to the German ear. 'Emmy', sure, must be a code word, they thought, but what the hell could it mean? And every time those English *Flieger* would land, they said, 'pancake'. Did they perhaps eat pancakes when they returned from a flight? The language barrier for the German radio operators was an unplanned advantage to us.

The controllers in our operation rooms had a difficult job. They were to coordinate our forces in the air against the German planes, almost like a game of chess. Surprisingly, only certain people were mentally suitable for this work. They often were called-up reservists who, in private life, were lawyers.

The English radar in the war year 1941 was superb in comparison with the German technology in this field, which could only be called rudimentary at best. There also may have been another factor. The German Luftwaffe was in every detail a reflection of Hermann Goering's thinking. His glory days in the air were World War I, and he predictably clashed with the ideas of younger, crack pilots like Adolf Galland.

The radar system also helped the fighter pilot, who is all alone in his plane, in navigating. In Holland we had to return to base by our own navigational ability after any mission, including combat. Holland is so small, and we knew the geography so well, it was never much of a problem to find our way home.

But England was not only that much bigger, it also was unfamiliar territory. Recognizing the terrain under us was quite difficult, especially in southern England, with its thousands of winding country roads through green hills which all look alike. But now we could call the radio controller at our own base and simply ask, 'Homing, please.'

After a quick identification we would hear, 'Steer two, one, five, angels four', and we would steer a course of 215 degrees at an altitude of four thousand feet.

This could be done in case we didn't recognize the geography on the ground or when flying in a cloud layer, without seeing or being seen by any friendly or not-so-friendly pilot.

The controller would follow us all the way to our base and then say, 'You can pancake now, ceiling angels one.'

On this command, we simply came down, saw the clouds break at one thousand feet and found ourselves smack above our own airfield. We made a left turn and pancaked (landed). All very easy if you knew how. But for a German radio man in a shack, it was a frustrating puzzle to figure out why we always talked about pancakes and angels.

The operation rooms conducted the war actions; the radar boys at the base controlled the traffic on the field and brought us home.

I began to realize the importance of these radar installations along the southern coast of England. I began to understand the incredible role the system played in the Battle of Britain, when the RAF held out against an overwhelming force of attacking Luftwaffe bombers and fighters.

Every time, the German *Staffeln* were intercepted – just at the right time in the right place. Every time our fighters were low on fuel, they were directed to the nearest field in a straight line. When German Heinkel bombers crossed the Channel in large formations, the Spits and Hurricanes were waiting for them, causing havoc and extreme losses to the attacking Luftwaffe.

Most of the fighting occurred over the Channel, close to the coast or over England itself. Damaged RAF planes often could reach England and the pilots could bail out over friendly territory. The Germans, on the other hand, were flying over enemy territory, much farther away from their bases. When they had to bail out they were lost for further Luftwaffe service.

Although the RAF losses were extremely high, the German losses in pilots and planes were considerably higher, so high that the German air offensive had to be stopped. The historic air victory of the Battle of Britain was not only an unbelievable show of the courage and skill of the RAF air crews, but it was won partly by the brilliant use of radar.

At the OTU, we first flew the Miles trainer with an instructor in the back seat. The cockpit was quite similar to the Spitfire, and like the Spits it also had a retractable landing gear. The performance was sluggish, but the classic stunts all could be done without problems. It soon became obvious that I was a much better stunt flyer than my instructor, but that was only play at the time.

We practised the RAF battle formations, turns, commands, and other radio lingo. We got used to the leather helmets with the built-in earphones, the oxygen masks, the throat microphones and the huge goggles with their light green lenses.

After ten hours of training, my instructor said, 'Van, you're OK.'

After the formidable refresher course at the OTU, the real fighter pilot mentality had awakened in me. Our dreams of 'dawn patrol' flying with

Errol Flynn and the seeking of the enemy now seemed a little naive, but they had not entirely disappeared. In spite of the beastly aspect of the war, I had to admit there was an element of adventure mixed with a not-so-Christian desire for revenge which, under the circumstances, was justified in my feelings. After all, we were attacked by Hitler's hordes without provocation. And, after all, they had bombed the defenceless city of Rotterdam and their plans for the future were not hard to anticipate.

After my delightful ten hours with my instructor and the Miles trainer, I was introduced to an enormous red-headed sergeant in overalls who said, 'This way, sir.'

I was dressed in the RAF uniform with that very thin blue stripe of pilot officer on my sleeve, and also the RAF wings on my chest. 'Thank you, Sergeant,' I said.

He quickly 'corrected' me saying, 'Jerry's the name, sir.'

'OK, Jerry, what's up?'

'Over there, sir.'

Together, we walked over to the enormous concrete platform, to a shiny Spitfire Mark V. During the course, I had sat in a Spitfire cockpit many times and I knew that cockpit from top to bottom. I even knew where the unfinished little screws were sticking out which could damage our watches. So my watch was already turned to the inside of my wrist. Jerry saw that I was beaming with pride when I took my first step on the wing of the Spit I would fly within a few minutes. There was nothing new to me; I knew the Spitfire very well, but this was the first time I would actually fly the famous machine.

I put the parachute in the seat and Jerry arranged the straps. I climbed into the cockpit, put the seat as high as possible and connected all my straps, tubes and wires. We had a short checklist, of which the first letters of each item formed a dirty word, easy to remember. Jerry and I went through the list together. Then he touched my shoulder, and with a, ''Ere we go, sir,' he jumped off the wing.

Jerry put two thumbs up in the air and I started the big Merlin engine, which was still connected to the big battery cart on the platform. With open cockpit, I taxied my Spit to the edge of the runway and called the control tower.

'Butterfly One, ready to scramble,' I said.

'Butterfly One, permission to scramble,' was the answer.

I rolled a little farther to the runway and gently opened the throttle. The engine roared, I felt the torque to the right and the pressure on my back caused by an acceleration I had never experienced before. Gently I lifted the tail, and at a speed of 120 mph, I pulled her up. Wheels in, pitch adjusted and I was in the air in my Spit! I climbed to angels seven and found a few small cumulus clouds, where I started to try out my Spit.

I had flown some fifteen different airplanes but never had I felt this sensation of power and sweet manoeuvrability. The feeling was indescribable. I simply had to try a loop, a slow roll, another roll, a flip, and finally a spin. The Spit responded to every subtle movement I wanted her to make, and finally I let her come down in a series of *Immelmans* and cartwheels.

On the top of one of the cumulus puffs I made my first 'landing' after a steep side-slip approach. My Spit obeyed every little movement of the stick and rudder. A few more times I climbed to ten thousand feet and throttled back to let her stall, just under 100 mph. The stall was gentle and gave plenty of warning, an incredible characteristic of a high-performance fighter.

After about twenty minutes of testing and playing I returned to the airfield and requested permission to pancake. After my left turn I made my approach with a little side-slip, because it felt so good, and put her down. When I taxied back to the hangars of the OTU flying school, the Spit seemed to wag her tail. Jerry motioned me to my parking place with a final 'two thumbs up' and I stopped the engine. Blocks were put in front and behind the wheels. The petrol wagon pulled up alongside and Jerry stood next to me on the wing with a broad smile on his face.

'How did you like that, Dutchie? I mean, sir?'

'Like a dream, Jerry. Like a dream,' was the only thing I could utter.

More training in lecture rooms followed. After about ten hours of flying on the Spit, I was transferred to a real operational squadron.

Not quite. My new squadron was No. 91 and was based at the same airfield – just across, on the other side. Originally a Hurricane squadron, it was now refitted with the new Spitfire Vb. The squadron's operations were almost like training flights and were restricted to patrolling the southern coast – and, specifically, to defending the radar installations. It was ideal for me; not too much action perhaps, but it would give me a lot of flight time on the Spit, which I had only flown some ten hours.

It was at this operational unit that I received my first operational equipment. It consisted of the coveted sheepskin-lined jacket, boots with a small pocketknife in the side, a newly designed leather helmet (with a microphone in front of the mouth), an even bigger pair of goggles (with light, amber-coloured, flat optical lenses), and an escape kit. The oxygen supply in the new machines was entirely automatic; it would go on at an altitude of five thousand feet and increase with the altitude. The special shoes and the escape kit were on the secret list. And, indeed, they were ingenious small details which proved their usefulness to many airmen.

These shoes were very special. Actually, they were sheepskin-lined, high boots. The lower part looked like an ordinary shoe with laces and the upper part had a zipper in front. On one side of the upper part, a small, stainless steel pocketknife fitted tightly in a sheath. The two parts of the boot could be separated by cutting along a groove designed especially for this purpose. When separated, the lower part of the shoe looked like an ordinary Oxford. The idea of such a boot was that it could be transformed into a civilian-looking shoe, in case the airman was shot down and had a chance to escape before being caught.

Another part of the uniform was a small item, but with the same idea in mind. A button of the pants could be placed on another button to make a compass. The top button had a small fluorescent dot which always pointed north. The secrecy of these small details was perhaps not too important, but under certain circumstances they were extremely handy and should not be discovered by hostile people.

The escape kit was a plastic box which fitted snugly in a breast pocket. It contained two maps, one of Western Europe and the other a large-scale reproduction of a localized area. The maps were printed on silk. This was not only much stronger than paper, but meant they could be used for other things. Torn in strips, the silk maps would serve as bandages, tourniquets, slings, and perform many other functions, such as keeping splints in place.

The kit had a small compass, a bar of soap, a razor, fishhooks and line, a morphine injection, sulfanilamide tablets, and some food tablets in the form of chocolate-malted candies.

My squadron was made up of English pilots, except for one Belgian and myself. The squadron officially was operational, but during the transition to the new Spitfires we were a defensive unit. No sweeps over enemy territory. But since it was still 'Battle of Britain' time, we were constantly on daylight readiness. Scramble alarms were a daily routine and Squadron Leader Vic Moser was proud to be able to have his squadron airborne, in full battle strength, within three minutes. This was a good performance, as our field had a runway which permitted only two Spits to start together. On grass fields, we could take off in fours.

Once in the air we received orders, 'Course zero-six-five, angels seven', and in due time a correction. Or, 'Single bandit, three o'clock.'

The squadron was identified by a name which changed every day and the ground station at our base also had a name of the day. To remember these names, we wrote them with ink on the palms of our hands. With a little spit they could be erased.

If the target was only one enemy plane, our squadron leader would order one section of four to attack. More than one plane would be attacked by two sections and the third section would stay in reserve, some five hundred feet higher and 'up sun' if possible, to make it more difficult for the enemy pilots to see us.

The massive attacks by German bombers had resulted in such enormous losses that the Germans had changed their tactics, to more attacks by single aircraft, using the element of surprise. In military teachings, a surprise action is almost always successful, at least in the initial stages of the move.

These attacks, if carried out by fast-flying fighters approaching at low altitudes, were indeed often a surprise. But the damage they could do to ground targets was limited. The bombers, on the other hand, could do much more harm but did not like to make low-level approaches. Their relatively slow speed could only be increased by diving, and for that they needed altitude.

At night, they still bombed in groups of at least forty to sixty Heinkels, or used the slightly faster Junkers. But during daylight they came alone, seeking cover in cloud layers. The German Command had not fully realized that our radar systems had practically eliminated its element of surprise.

Single bombers were detected long before they crossed the English coastline, which gave our squadrons time to scramble or be directed to a location where they simply waited for the intruders to arrive. A single bomber had little chance against a few fighters, so sometimes the bombers were escorted by their own fighters. But to us, that would be no surprise. Our Ops room would have warned us well in advance. The advantage was on our side, but when it came to air combat, it was still a matter of slugging it out, man to man.

It was during these days that I had my first operational experiences with modern warfare, as an RAF pilot. I had made many scrambles with the squadron, or in sections. On one of these flights we were directed to two Heinkels, approaching apparently without fighter escort. The weather was awful, so bad we had trouble staying together. Ops told us the bandits were within a mile to our right but we saw nothing. My section leader climbed a little, just above a stratus cloud layer, and there were the two Heinkels, three o'clock at the same height.

Without a second's hesitation I heard the command, 'Attack!'

The four of us instantly swayed to starboard and placed ourselves behind the Heinkels. Only the number one and number three planes initiated the attack; two and four followed after our first run. I was number two to the section leader, and pumped my machine gun bullets and my 20-mm cannon slugs into the fuselage of the Heinkel and then quickly formed up with my number one.

The other Heinkel also was hit, making a smoky left turn which put us in a very good position again. We made another run on the *Mof* before they disappeared in the cloud layer.

We resumed our battle formation and, not knowing where we were, I heard, 'Moonshine, this is Marco. Homing please.'

Moonshine immediately answered with, 'Marco, this is Moonshine. Steer two-seven-eight.'

Without being able to see the ground, and after the action, we did not know where we were. But that didn't matter. We just closed into a tight formation and our section leader steered the given course.

After about fifteen minutes the same voice said, 'Marco, this is Moonshine. You may pancake.'

In tight formation, we went down through the cloud layer and suddenly saw our base right in front of us.

Our section leader said, 'Line astern. Pancake one by one,' and right away started his left turn around the field.

Victory rolls over the airfield were not allowed anymore. Besides, this section leader was one who had seen action many times. He had lost one of his best friends when two Hurricanes collided and plunged into the ground after making victory rolls.

Another time, I scrambled with my Squadron Leader Vic Moser, just the two of us. One or possibly two bombers were reported approaching the coast, at an altitude of ten thousand feet. We were vectored to intercept and soon saw the German plane, which must have seen us as well. Vic did not go straight for his target because the German did not make any attempt to take cover in the cloud layer. First we saw only the Heinkel, but soon we discovered two Messerschmitts, halfway hiding in the misty cloud layer just above the bomber.

Vic knew the pilot of the bomber could not release his bombs without seeing the target, unless he wanted to drop them just somewhere over London, which meant at least another half-hour of flying. Furthermore, the Messerschmitts would not be able to escort the bomber all the way to London; it simply was too far. So he waited and let the Me.s use a little more of their fuel.

If the Heinkel dived through the cloud layer, we would be told by Ops in which direction to follow. The escorting German fighters would have no way to know where to go. The only thing they would be able to do would be to fly east, to France. Vic flew parallel to the invader, in the opposite direction, then suddenly made a sharp turn to the left, saying, 'Attack.'

I swung with him and we both made a run at the bomber, which returned fire. We probably scored some hits but she continued her flight without changing course. Immediately the Me.s were at us and a dogfight developed. But in my first pull up, I found myself in the thick soup of the cloud layer above us and lost my orientation. I made a half-roll to gain a little time, and when I dived down I saw one Messerschmitt spiralling down with a black plume of smoke coming from the cowling. To his right, I saw the other Messerschmitt, followed by Vic, both coming in my direction. I had to evade the path of the Me. and pulled hard to the right. The German pulled to the left, putting me in a very good position to follow his turn.

Over the radio, I heard Vic's calm voice, 'Attack, Dutchie!'

The Spit made a better turn to the left than the Messerschmitt, and after two turns I had my angle. I opened fire with the machine guns and the cannons and hit him. Something flew off the German plane but I never knew what. The Me. pulled up in the layer of stratus and we didn't see her again.

I formed up with Vic, who called our base to report, 'One Messer-schmitt-109 destroyed. One Messerschmitt and the Heinkel bomber damaged. Check with Ops, please.'

Ops came in and confirmed the Me. The bomber and the other Me. were reported to fly southeast for a while, then disappeared from their radar screens. This could mean they went down in the English Channel or that they had reached an altitude and distance which no longer could be detected.

I had hoped to get credit for the bomber and one Me. but I did not. Vic got another deserved victory to his name, which was witnessed by me, but the other two enemy planes were classified as 'probables'. Well, better than nothing.

Our squadron engineer came to me in the readiness room and said, 'Van, do you know you have holes in your tail?'

'What – bullet holes?' I asked. 'Jesus, I never felt or heard anything.'

We walked to my Spit, and there I saw four holes in the elevator of the tail. So, I took two hits. Must have been from the Heinkel. He had found no other damage and the elevator was replaced that same afternoon.

The next morning, Vic scrambled again. This time, with a section of four and I did not take part in it. Like the day before, he intercepted a group of two Junkers-88 bombers, escorted by three Messerschmitt fighters. Again they were flying between two layers of stratus, which was a good tactic for their approach. At almost any moment they could pull up or dive down into a cloud layer and fly home on instruments, depending on what kind of opposition they encountered.

A messy dogfight developed, with our Spits and the Me.s going in and out of the clouds. In our readiness room I heard the radio communications. After a while, I heard Vic reporting that the German planes had turned around, seeking cover in the clouds, and that he had lost contact. Ops ordered him to return to base.

When the four Spits appeared over our airfield, number three reported that he could not lower his wheels and might have to belly-land. Base instructed him to try the hand-operated gear that lowered the landing gear. But it was impossible; the wheels would not come down. They told him to circle the field until Vic and the two others had pancaked. The crash team was already in its special truck, and the young English pilot was ordered to belly-land.

In most cases the procedure could be carried out with relatively little damage to the plane, sometimes just a bent prop. On a grass field the chances of going over the top were greater. He was to land on the runway. He made a good approach, a perfect landing, but the Spit burst into flames.

The fire truck was there within seconds, spraying foam on the violently burning Spit. The crash team was there and they got the pilot out of the cockpit, alive. By this time, Vic had arrived on the scene and an ambulance sped over the grass and runways with its siren howling. Steve Cummins, the young pilot with a brilliant Battle of Britain record to his name, was alive. But his face and hands, the only uncovered parts of his body, were very badly burned.

We infrequently scrambled at night for ground-controlled interceptions, but the Spit was not specifically suitable as a night fighter. I much preferred the flights at dusk or early in the morning, with at least some light to see by. Trying to find an enemy plane in the dark – only by directions from our Ops – was indeed extremely difficult.

Our gunsight also was not ideal. The little optical cross, projected on the windshield, was still far too bright, even when fully dimmed. It was almost impossible to identify another plane of about the same size. A Messerschmitt at night looks very much like a Spitfire. But, fortunately, the Germans did not send fighter escorts with their bombers over the areas they had designated as targets. So we considered bombers to be enemies and fighters to be friends.

On four occasions I made contact with Luftwaffe invaders during such night missions, all at dusk, with some visibility. Without radar gunsights, we depended entirely on our ground control.

As soon as they manoeuvred us to within about a mile of the enemy plane, they directed, 'Is your cockerel crowing? Five degrees to your right, look eleven o'clock above. You should see the bandit now.'

They were our miracle boys because frequently they placed us correctly.

The first time I experienced this kind of mission, the radio insisted, 'Straight ahead, right in front of you!'

I looked my eyes out and saw nothing, until I noticed an air turbulence I knew only too well. First, I saw the red-hot exhausts. Then the dim silhouette of a twin-engine bomber. I throttled back and tried to adjust my distance, then let all four machine guns rattle their steel into the German plane. My first burst did nothing but the second hit an engine, which immediately caught fire. I pulled to the right, having little desire to get debris in my face. I never saw the bomber again but Ops had been able to follow me because I had left my cockerel on. I did get the credit.

The second time, I saw the German bomber before Ops told me where to look. He saw me, too. It was not quite dark and I could position myself. The German opened fire with tracer bullets, which were frequently used by the Germans because at very short distances one could aim them almost like a water hose. But beyond three hundred yards the tracers were more deceiving than of any help. Ballistic curves and moving targets play hell with guesswork, and the tracers went wild.

On the third night-scramble, I fired at things I thought were flaming exhaust pipes, but nothing happened. The last night mission was another 'probable' for me, although I tried to convince our intelligence officer with all my might that it should be counted as a victory. The IO was not convinced. That night fifteen German bombers were shot down. But in the pitch-dark night it would, of course, not be possible to determine who shot down what. More than twenty-five RAF pilots reported air victories.

I heard one of our boys call for a homing. I, too, had lost track of my whereabouts. I also asked for a homing and our GCA superbly brought us back to base. I was told to orbit at angels two until my buddy landed, then I had permission to pancake.

Our night landings were tricky. When we were actually over the field, they lit the small lights along the runway. And – during the last phase of the approach only – two searchlights would illuminate the landing path. The moment we touched the ground the lights would go out, and all one could do was look for two tiny blue lights, in the hands of a member of the ground crew who directed us to our parking place. On the grass fields, they only used the searchlights. I didn't like night combat.

Then came the bad news that two of our pilots had not returned to base. Had they bailed out, made a forced landing? We heard the next morning. Both were hit by the Germans; one bailed out, the other crashed. The one who bailed out died of a bullet wound in the head later that night.

The pilots of Squadron No. 91 were mentally exhausted. They had fought the Battle of Britain in a magnificent manner, but they were depressed and exhausted. The strength of the German Luftwaffe was broken but the RAF was exhausted. A depressed morale is the worst thing that can happen to any fighting unit, and for me, it was not the best place to be. But the experience of being part of this crack squadron was unforgettable.

'Battle fatigue' was never mentioned and our squadron leader, Vic Moser, flew all missions during the last three days before the squadron was transferred to Liverpool for a well-deserved rest. Vic, with fourteen victories and a double DFC (Distinguished Flying Cross) on his chest, was up for wing commander.

I did not go to Liverpool; they had other plans for me. I was transferred to Squadron No. 41 at Westhampnett, one of the grass satellites of Tangmere. This squadron, of World War I fame, had a South African commander by the name of Peter Hugo. The motto of the squadron was 'seek and destroy'. The young Afrikaaner already had an impressive record of eight air victories to his name, and he was the kind of pilot who could turn the motto into deadly reality.

Just as we had heard of the Luftwaffe's famed Adolf Galland, the German pilots knew the name Peter Hugo. The alarming radio command *Achtung, Schpitfeuer* was known throughout Hitler's Air Force. Most German pilots said a little prayer when they heard the feared *Achtung Schpitfeuer,* and hoped the damned *Schpitfeuer* would not be piloted by Bob Tuck, Douglas Bader, or Peter Hugo.

Transfers always were preceded by a few days of leave, and that meant London and Piccadilly Circus. It was only a few hours by train and the Cumberland Hotel at Marble Arch always seemed to have room for operational RAF pilots. How did the girls at the registration desks recognize us? There were, after all, far more people in RAF uniform who were not operational. Well, there was a very unofficial sign. All pilots wore wings, of course, but operational fighter pilots were 'allowed' to leave the top button of their tunic open. This unofficial honour was respected by all pilots.

The Dutch Air Force Directorate was on the corner just opposite the hotel, and I visited the office every day. I also kept up my contact with Mr van't Sant and Prince Berhard, who literally had become the patron of Dutch pilots. My code and the plans for communications with the Dutch underground workers had been watered down to almost non-existence, and other efforts at radio contact also had failed entirely. The spirit of the Dutch government-in-exile had become an attitude of fatalistic inactivity.

Indeed, there was a war on and Holland was occupied by the enemy, like the other Western European countries. Even England was exhausted. There were nothing but black clouds in store for the future of the occupied countries. The only silver lining was the incredible success of the RAF in its defence against Hitler's bombers. The success of the Battle of Britain was a turning point of immense importance, because after their huge losses the Germans decided to cancel, or at least postpone, their invasion with ground troops.

We were well paid, compared to our English colleagues, so we had parties every night. After a few drinks, we would go to the Chinaman for dinner and then to the nightclubs. We drank too much Pimm's, ale, and Bols, which Oddeninos had for its Dutch customers. We ate too much and went to too many nightclubs, where we drank some more Pimm's and shandy (a mix of ale and Seven-Up at room temperature).

I met more *Engelandvaarders* and old friends from The Hague, who were all very quickly introduced to the universal meeting places of Oddeninos, Soho, and nightclubs in the cellars of the houses around Piccadilly Circus. Girls? Everywhere, and with enthusiasm on their side. The general evaluation of the English girls had been that they were slightly cool, a little snooty, and a little Victorian. But … at night, they're all right!

We criticized our government, and we had arguments, little fights, and big fights. We had nice parties and raw parties, and occasionally very distinguished meetings over dinner at Claridge's or luncheon at the Ritz with Prince Bernhard.

The Dutch government in London was sometimes seen as a most useless group of nothings. But at other times its officials were seen as sturdy fighters and compared to the historical *Geuzen* who, as pro-Orange Hollanders, kicked the Spanish out of their country. With all of the criticism, arguments, and disagreements, our Royal House was never included. Not because it was our Royal Family and we were in Her Majesty's service, but because we genuinely loved Queen Wilhelmina, Princess Juliana, and Prince Bernhard. Like the *Geuzen,* we were the loyal Hollanders who would fight for Holland's independence under the House of Orange.

Some of our fellows developed outstanding talents for their few days of leave in London. A young sergeant-pilot, very good looking I must say, mastered the pick-up technique better than any of us. In the great hall of the Cumberland Hotel, with hundreds of people around, he would simply scan the crowd until his eye caught a pretty girl. A few seconds of staring (and the sweetest smile I've ever seen) was enough to take the pretty thing straight to his hotel room. We loved the Cumberland Hotel and its understanding staff.

When I reported at Westhampnet, I became friends almost instantly with Squadron Leader Peter Hugo, who, as a South African, spoke *Zuid-Afrikaans*. This is nothing less than an old form of the Dutch language. We could converse in Dutch, and since his nickname was 'Dutch Hugo', my nickname of 'Dutchie' had to go. From now on I was 'Van'.

Squadron No. 41 not only had a defensive task like Squadron No. 91; it also carried out offensive sweeps over France. Westhampnet was only some ten miles from the coast, and the Channel there was only forty miles wide. We also flew escort missions for the light, twin-engine bombers on their attacks on coastal targets in France. The sweeps were meant to get the German fighters scrambled, like a challenge, but mostly to help our radar operators estimate the strength of the Luftwaffe in case of massive attacks.

The Germans were aware of the superior efficiency of our radar and consequently we were kept at readiness for intruders who had our radar installations as their targets. The Germans tried to attack these structures with fighters but they didn't cause enough damage. Then they tried Stukas, but these were too slow and none of them came back. Their best plane for this target was their relatively fast Messerschmitt-110, a twin-engine fighter-bomber. The German attacks were carried out mostly with single planes, and we often scrambled with two – or at the most four – Spits.

It was on one of those scrambles that I flew with Dutch Hugo as his number two. After some vectoring by Ops, we suddenly saw the Me.110 on our starboard side, not more than three hundred yards away. Immediately, Dutch Hugo said, 'Attack!'

Under these circumstances, we didn't bother to call or identify first. There was no time to lose and the order was too obvious to be misunderstood. He made a sharp turn to the right and placed himself behind and well below the Me. I followed, increasing my distance behind him, and placed myself straight behind Hugo and the German intruder. Small puffs of smoke from the Spit in front of me indicated he was firing and the Me.110 pulled up into the cloud layer.

Peter and I followed and for a few moments we saw nothing but grey fog. But then we shot through above it and had the German in clear sight again. I was in a much better position and Peter immediately said, 'Attack, Van!' So I did, and with my machine guns and 20-millimetres rattling and thundering, I saw the tail unit of the Me.110 tear off. The Me. flipped into a spin, down into the cloud layer.

'Good shot, Van!' I heard in my earphones, and immediately after that, 'Lime Tree, this is Bengal One. Homing, please.'

Lime Tree answered with, 'Is your cockerel crowing?'

Peter said, 'My cockerel is crowing.'

And then, 'Bengal One, this is Lime Tree. Steer two-four-four.'

During the radio communication, I closed in to about one span from his wing and together we descended through the cloud layer until we could see ground again. Within ten minutes we were over our base and heard the familiar, 'You may pancake now.'

Dutch Hugo and I walked from our machines back to the readiness room with big smiles on our faces. Inside the Nissen hut, our intelligence officer was on the phone and confirmed the kill. The Me. had come down twenty miles northeast of us. Both crew members were injured but had managed to come down by parachute.

I wasn't too sure about who had done what and said, 'Dutch, you probably had him with your first run.'

Hugo smiled and said, 'Possible, of course. But you shot his tail off, I know that for sure.'

The credit was finally given to both of us, one-half each.

These scrambles for single intruders happened quite often but in many cases the Germans would turn back, not chancing a dogfight. They only continued if they saw no RAF planes when they approached at very low altitudes. Flying only ten or twenty feet above sea level was relatively safe for the Germans, but as soon as they crossed the coast line they would be detected immediately. At very low altitudes, navigation becomes difficult, especially if the terrain is not well known.

There were other occasions that I scrambled to protect our radar installations from marauding enemy planes, flying on two of them with my flight commander. First a Heinkel He-111, escorted by two Me.109s, was the target. I got the Heinkel, which exploded in front of my eyes, but we did not get the escorting Me.s. My flight commander fired at one of the German fighters, but had to make an evading turn when the other one tried to close in. They disappeared and Ops ordered us to return to base.

The other time I scrambled for intruders was again with my flight commander, and we engaged one of the new Junkers-88 bombers. The Ju-88 was designed as a horizontal- and dive-bomber and, for a bomber, was extremely fast.

We were over the Channel when we heard, 'You should see your bandit now, nine o'clock above.'

We indeed saw the speedy bomber at about seven thousand feet. Although we didn't know what his target would be, it was obvious that the German would try to outrun us at his advantageous altitude, dive-bomb his load, then fly back as low as possible. We had to climb another thousand feet, which slowed us down to about the same speed as the bomber, but the weather permitted us to see her all the time.

When the Ju-88 crossed the coast, she made a turn to the north and we could close in by cutting the turn short. The Ju-88 had a turret in the belly of the fuselage and began firing at my leader, who was not quite in position yet. I placed myself behind him but saw him pull up, probably to avoid the fire from the belly, and immediately make a dive with all his guns wide open. He overshot the Junkers, which put me in an ideal situation to attack.

I had set the gunsight on the measure of the Ju-88 wingspan and the moment the wing filled the circle of my sight, all machine guns and cannons rattled their steel into the Luftwaffe plane. In a spiral of black smoke the thing went down. I saw no chutes. In bright sunshine, with only an occasional cumulus cloud, we didn't need any assistance to fly back to our base. Back in the readiness hut we discovered my flight commander's Spit had two bullet holes in the tip of its wing, which meant he had been hit by one bullet that went in and then out. By his report he witnessed the air victory to my credit.

These scrambles were numerous but always done with a minimum of planes because Ops knew the size of the attacking force. The Germans usually launched raids by one, two, or three planes. The much bigger operations were the sweeps over France, which were carried out in squadron strength, together with ten or more other squadrons. We also escorted larger groups of bombers, which would plaster the coastal defences, but never strayed far into France because of the limited range of the fighters. The sweeps did not cause much damage to the Germans but they were very impressive. Some three hundred Spitfires and Hurricanes in one huge formation were quite a sight.

It was on these sweeps that I learned something about anti-aircraft guns. When escorting, we were not concerned if we saw the black smoke puffs of the German flak because we would fly well above our friends; and the Germans were shooting at them, not us. But on sweeps, there were no bombers and the shooting definitely was directed at us. It was quite common to feel a small air disturbance when the black puffs were at our altitude.

Once, after feeling such an air pocket-like turbulence, we found a scratch and a small dent on the leading edge of my wing, probably caused by a piece of shrapnel. That was too close; we knew the German flak would shoot at us as well.

Dutch Hugo was a born leader, especially when we went out in greater formations. He seemed to see things before we did. His orientation in the air was at all times superb. On the return flight of one of these sweeps, near Calais, we were jumped by a *Staffel* (squadron) of the new Focke-Wulf Fw.190s. This new German fighter had a radial engine and was therefore easy to recognize. The Fw.190 was faster than our Spits and we didn't like it.

Just when we crossed the coast of France, they came from nowhere and speared right through our formation. Again, Hugo had seen them first.

He calmly said, 'We're being jumped by bandits. Tally-ho, but do not follow them.'

Several Fw.190s overshot their targets, hanging like lame ducks in front of us. As Yellow Three, I had one of them in my sight without much correcting. I opened fire with all weapons and saw a long streak of white smoke coming from the cowling of the Fw.190. I immediately returned to my place in the enormous formation of more than two hundred Spits and Typhoons (the newest version of the Hurricane).

'Good shot, Van!'

I recognized Peter Hugo's voice and was glad to see the protective mass of my own buddies around me, because that Fw.190 obviously had made a run at me.

We learned that the Focke-Wulf Fw.190, in spite of being a little faster than the Spit, was difficult to fly. It had a nasty tendency to stall without much warning, and its manoeuvrability was even worse than the Messerschmitt's. We still did not like that extra speed, but it wouldn't be long till we were better equipped.

In the next few weeks, we were re-equipped with the Spitfire Mark IX. The wings were clipped and we had a bigger engine, a four-blade propeller, and a 16-mm movie camera in the wing. By flying the new machine, one could not feel much difference; it was still the sweet, responding Spit. But in the takeoff, she had much more torque and was almost 50 mph faster than the Mark Vb.

I had had a lucky shot at that Focke-Wulf over Calais. But now, less than two weeks later, we had Spits that were slightly faster than any Luftwaffe fighter and could make shorter turns.

A week later, we were scrambled in squadron strength to seek and destroy a German PT boat. Ops led Hugo in a straight line to the place where the boat was reported, so he had no trouble finding it. Ops had not reported any bandits around and we attacked in sections of four. After the first run of Dutch Hugo's section, I saw no action of the guns on the deck of the PT boat.

It was now Blue Section's turn and we attacked from abeam. I could see the bullets hit the water and then 'walk into' the boat, which began to smoke. After Blue Section, Yellow Section squirted steel into the now-completely lame vessel. Red and Blue made second runs, but then came the warning from Ops that bandits were approaching from the east.

Hugo said, 'Battle formation, follow me.'

And after one more look at the sinking boat, we flew back to base without ever seeing any German aircraft. At home we eagerly took our film cassettes out of the cameras to have them developed by Intelligence. We should have prize movies.

Our work became daily routine. We had snow and there was no flying for several days. One Australian pilot had never seen real snow, and he had to make a snowman and throw snowballs. He looked at his Spit and saw a layer of three inches of snow covering his machine and wrote on it, 'Balls to Adolf'.

The winter weather and the incredible German losses had slowed the German attacks and we had more time off. I was given the opportunity to make a three-day trip on an English destroyer in the Channel. It was cold, and the constant 'ping' of the sonar made me more nervous than did a briefing for an operational mission. The quarters for the crew on a destroyer must be the worst on any ship.

A small group of Dutch pilots was invited to have tea with Anthony Eden at his estate in the country. The foreigners who filled the ranks of the RAF were well taken care of. We became well-known characters in the local pubs and made friends with the girls who lived or worked around Westhampnet airfield. There were parties, and we learned the traditions of the officers' mess – how to pass the port wine and how to serve oneself when there was an enormous chunk of roast in the dining room. The food was anything from a superb roast to Brussels sprouts, three times a day. A 'batman' or 'batwoman' was not available for us at Westhampnet, so we had to polish our own buttons and shoes.

The attack on Pearl Harbor was already several months old and we saw more Americans in London than before. At Oddeninos we analysed world politics, in the Chinese restaurants we discussed the fate of China, and at the Air Force Directorate we collected our salaries. I met with my old Soesterberg buddies and saw that Govert Steen, Hidde Leegstra, and Piet Vos were wearing the ribbons of the Dutch Bronze Cross. They had received it as *Engelandvaarders*.

Most of us had no ribbons of any kind at that time. The race for decorations became questionable, with ribbons everywhere. And certainly, some of the most avid contestants were the Americans, who already wore a row of ribbons before they had seen any action. Air victories were reported by the hundreds; there were so many reported victories that we would have shot down the entire German Air Force – three times over – if they all were true.

All our fighters now were equipped with the 16-mm movie cameras and air victories had to be confirmed by photographic evidence. The cameras were activated by the machine gun and cannon triggers, and stopped when the triggers were released. Frequently, the most dramatic evidence, like an explosion, would not be on film. After all, one does not shoot at an explosion. We could not follow a burning plane down with the camera without shooting at the same time, so the combat films were extremely short. Later, the cameras were adjusted so they would continue rolling for four seconds after the triggers were released.

One day, the squadron was scrambled in full strength to engage a large group of enemy airplanes, about halfway across the English Channel. Another Spitfire squadron was to accompany us, in case Squadron Leader Hugo wanted assistance. Ops vectored us to the correct location and Hugo ordered us to fly in regular battle formation. The other squadron was well above us and separated from us by a thin layer of clouds. We could not see them, but Ops kept them about four miles behind us and we knew they were there.

It was again Dutch Hugo who saw the German formation first. It was a *Staffel* of twelve Messerschmitt 109s, flying in the typical German V-formation. They obviously saw us much later, and tried to spread out. But Hugo had already given his familiar command, 'Attack, attack!' and his Red Section initiated the dogfight.

At first, he tried to offer us some direction, but the fight soon developed into a whirl of twenty-four fighters circling and looping around each other. I saw the first Me. go down. Immediately after that, another one, trailing a black plume of smoke, went spinning down. I gained little by little on the bandit in front of me. After two turns, I opened fire and caught him with the first burst. When I looked down, I saw at least five large, white 'mushrooms' in the water, obviously caused by downed planes, but I had no idea if they were theirs or ours.

Another Messerschmitt veered across my starboard side and I noticed some smoke coming from the exhaust. With a right turn I was on his tail, and pumped a burst of machine gun bullets into the *Mof*. His canopy flew off, black smoke came out of the engine and that was the end of another Me.109. In the sea I saw many more of the big, round, white 'mushrooms'.

Then I heard Hugo's voice, 'Form up, angels four.'

The leader of the other Spitfire squadron, who had witnessed the whole scene from above, came on the radio saying, 'Damn good show, Dutchie!'

When I looked around, I saw Hugo's Red Section of four, all there, and Yellow Section to his left was also intact. My own Blue Section was the only one that could have suffered any losses. But when I heard our Yellow Section commander report, 'Red and Blue Sections all present', I realized we had suffered no losses and had shot down twelve Luftwaffe Messerschmitts.

Back home at Westhampnett, we were welcomed by Wing Commander Larry Jackson and the whole gang. The news had spread like fire and a party was organized for that evening. From intelligence, we heard that all twelve kills would be confirmed and written reports were requested. We had lunch in the officers' mess, where spirits couldn't be any better, in spite of the Brussels sprouts.

That afternoon we were sitting in our readiness room in the Nissen hut at the airfield, in a business-as-usual fashion, when our sour intelligence officer came in.

'Well, I thought all the time that it was a little too incredible,' he said. 'Twelve Messerschmitts down and not a scratch on any of our Spits. Intelligence thinks that it was a practice flight of German student pilots who had no ammunition in their guns.'

As if on command, we jumped up and booed the poor IO, who suddenly felt very unpopular. It was possible, of course, and we never learned the true story from the German side. But in spite of the damper on our glorious victory, we had our party in the officers' mess.

That evening the story was on the BBC news and the next morning it was in the papers. Credit for one air victory was given to a Dutch pilot in Squadron No. 41. No names were given of those who might have relatives in occupied countries. The second Me. I shot at was already damaged to the point where it could not have reached the French coast, so the credit went to my flight commander. It was his last flight in our squadron. He had been promoted to squadron leader and had received orders to outfit another Spitfire squadron for duty in North Africa.

The position of flight commander was vacant in our squadron, but not for long. Two days after the former flight commander had left, Peter Hugo called me into his office and said, 'Good morning, Flight Lieutenant Vanderstok.'

When he looked at the surprised expression on my face, he added, 'And you are in command of A-Flight.'

That was a big reason to have another party in the officers' mess that evening. The rank of 'flight lieutenant' was two up from my current rank – so I had skipped 'flying officer' and become 'captain', straight from 'second lieutenant'.

The next two months we flew our regular sweeps, escorts, and intercepts as daily routines. During that time I added two more air victories to my name. But I also had a few very close calls after encounters with the new Focke-Wulf 190s. Since they could not out-turn us, they tried to make high speed, hit-and-run attacks on single planes in the big sweep formations. They came from out of the sun in steep dives, and I had all machine guns and cannons firing at them, but the films showed only planes crossing my path, nothing else.

We made a big sweep with three hundred Spits and Hurricanes on a beautiful day. It was also the day that the Focke-Wulf shot me down.

Organization Big X

The reality was that I was a prisoner of war in Dulag Luft, the passing-through camp for all Allied air personnel, and waiting for transportation to a permanent camp. My search along the barbed wire for escape holes was discouraging. The guards, the dogs, the towers, the searchlights and the machine guns made escape from this camp seemingly impossible.

In spite of this, I heard of tunnels that had been started by prisoners in this camp and which were continued by newcomers when the originators were moved to another camp. One of these tunnels was discovered by the German guards only one week before it would have been finished. Nobody ever escaped from this camp. It was relatively small and POWs only stayed there for a couple of weeks. There was never enough time to really get organized. My stay at Dulag Luft was only ten days.

With a group of about a hundred Allied pilots and other air personnel, we marched to a small railway station nearby. Many guards, with orders to shoot, escorted us from the camp to the waiting train cars – ordinary third-class passenger cars. The compartments, normally for eight passengers, now were filled with at least fifteen of us. This made it even more crowded than on our first train trip as *Kriegsgefangenen* (POWs), which had been from France to Dulag Luft.

The guards were all Luftwaffe soldiers, and not unpleasant. One could speak to them without being bullied. But, as before, we had to take off our shoes. These were thrown into a freight car, together with all sorts of other stuff, including a load of Red Cross food parcels. It was hard to believe, but I still had my plastic escape kit in the breast pocket of my battledress uniform.

The two-day trip was not as repulsive as the first train trip, except for the overcrowded compartments. We could use the train toilets, but a guard would stand close to the door, which had to be left open. The train made many stops, and travelled at a very slow pace through hilly terrain and forests. It all seemed so friendly and easy that I played with the idea of jumping off the train from the rest room. With three years of junior college in Switzerland, my knowledge of German was more than adequate to address the guards in their own language.

I went to the toilet and tried to talk the guard into letting me close the door. He said 'no'. When I tried to fraternize, with my hand on his shoulder, he hit my shin with the butt of his rifle, grabbed my neck, and thrust me back into my compartment.

'*Aufpassen, mein Lieber!*' he said, and I understood that the guards' apparent friendliness was not to be taken for softness.

These guards had already made many trips transporting prisoners of war, and my idea of simply jumping off the train probably was a little naive. They were no small boys, and after their tremendous successes in the last two years, I should know better.

After two days we arrived in a small town, Sagan, not far from what used to be the Polish border. The train halted outside the actual railway station and we were ordered out. Again came the routine of officers handing over big, yellow envelopes while shouting '*Heil Hitler!*' and raising their right hands like Roman emperors. I took a good look at the railway station, considering the possibility that I might use it sometime. It was a typical, old-fashioned brick building with natural stone corners and a blue, slate roof.

The German officers spoke fluent English and were actually friendly. Not exactly a welcoming committee, with all those heavily armed guards around us, but there was no hostile attitude and no roughness of any sort. Of course, we didn't try anything, either.

At Dulag Luft they had given each of us an RAF overcoat and a Red Cross blanket. With that luggage on our shoulders, we were told to take one pair of shoes from the freight car, no matter what size (they could be sorted later). Our group of about a hundred *Kreigies* then marched for about one kilometre to the main camp, Stalag Luft III.

The road cut through a thick forest of pine, and a New Zealander, who had been very quiet until then, suddenly dashed off to the woods in an apparent escape attempt. A shot was fired in the air and a guard let his German shepherd go with a short command. Within seconds, the dog stopped our would-be escapist and the trembling New Zealander was brought back to the marching column. The other guards laughed. The attempt obviously was not considered of much importance. True, the attempt was rather silly.

Stalag Luft III was an enormous camp – rows of wooden barracks surrounded by a double, barbed wire fence, and rolls of barbed wire between the two fences. At distances of three hundred feet there were watchtowers, each equipped with a machine gun on a tripod, a search light, a guard with binoculars, and a telephone. Each tower was manned by a Luftwaffe soldier. Between the outer fence and the forest, a hundred-foot-wide strip of land had been cleared.

I saw a small group of Russian prisoners, with big, yellow triangles painted on the backs of their great-coats and shovels in their hands.

When one of the officers drew next to me, I asked him in German, 'Are those fellows also prisoners?'

'Ah, you speak German,' *Hauptmann* Pieber said. 'Yes, they are Russian *Kriegsgefangenen*. But they can walk around freely, they don't want to go back to Russia. Some of them are Polish, others are from the Ukraine. They hate the Russians. Some are even serving in the German Army.'

'Are these prisoners Slavic, and not really "Russian" themselves? Or are they actually "Russian" deserters from their own race?' I asked, but Pieber did not answer.

Inside the double fence, there was a ten-metre-wide strip marked with a single barbed wire not higher than two feet. This was the so-called warning fence. No prisoner was allowed to be in this warning area without specific permission from one of the tower guards. The guards had instructions to shoot without warning. Special permission was granted, for instance, when a ball rolled into this warning zone, so it could be retrieved without trouble. The clear area on the outside of the compound was often, but not regularly, patrolled by guards with dogs.

Before we could enter the actual camp we had to go through the so-called *Vorlager*. It also was a fenced-in area, but was much smaller. It contained a sick bay, a delousing unit, and a shed for Red Cross parcels and materials – like clothing, blankets, shoes, some YMCA equipment, musical instruments, books, and various balls for sports.

Next to the compound, but with a space in between, there was an administration complex for the German officers and troops. It was a large set-up and was designed for possible extension. When I entered Stalag Luft III, there were three thousand officers in the East Compound and about twelve hundred non-commissioned officers in an adjacent compound.

The barracks were simple wooden buildings which would house a hundred prisoners, in rooms for six. Each barrack had one simple kitchen and one general washroom. Each room had three double bunks, six lockers, a table with two benches and a coal stove. The rooms had electric lights and two windows each, which had to be covered with shutters from the outside. The floor was about two feet above ground, so the accommodations could be inspected from all sides. Except in one place. The coal stove was placed on a platform of red bricks, forming a sand-filled square to support the stove.

Each compound had a general kitchen, run by German personnel with the help of a few *Kriegies*. Although officers are not required to perform any labour, according to the rules of the Geneva Convention, we were expected to keep our own rooms clean. And little jobs – such as helping in the kitchen, the hospital, and the administrative building where food parcels and clothing were kept – were gladly accepted. Most of us not only preferred to do some work, but it gave us access to places and materials which could be useful.

There were many kinds of specialists among the guards. The commanding officer, Colonel von Lindeiner, was a highly educated man and a member of the old German nobility. He spoke several languages fluently, including Dutch. His wife was Dutch and they had visited the Netherlands frequently to see her family. Among the other officers were language teachers, security specialists, a doctor, and several administrative professionals. They all spoke fluent English.

The guards were divided into groups: for manning the towers, performing duties inside the camp, working in the kitchen, and handling maintenance and sanitation. But there was one specialized group of ten guards who we called the 'ferrets'. These were the ones who were trained for dealing with prisoners. They walked around with flashlights, pliers, and screwdrivers; constantly searching for hidden objects, tunnel entrances, radios, and all the forbidden things *Kriegies* would make to obstruct the German cause. They even crawled under rooms and tried to listen to our conversations. This seldom occurred without our knowledge.

I was put in a room with three other Dutchmen, one Canadian, and an Englishman. Heye Schaper, a naval commander, was one of those Dutchmen. He was shot down over the North Sea and picked up by a German air-sea rescue plane, after sinking a German freighter with a bull's-eye, five hundred-pounder. Later, Heye became general of the post-war Royal Dutch Air Force.

I wanted to escape immediately and discovered there was a committee for escape activities. There had been a number of escape attempts but none were successful. I also found out I was not the only one with plans and that the Germans were well aware of our activities. The ferrets were highly trained sleuths, and had, so far, discovered every tunnel or escape attempt. No one had escaped since the opening of this camp three years ago.

They had already dug more than thirty tunnels but none of them had succeeded. The tunnels had collapsed or been discovered before the would-be escapees reached the fence. One of the tunnels had reached the warning wire; the diggers needed more air to complete the remaining twenty feet, so they made an air hole straight up. The gush of fresh air was such a relief that a digger relaxed for a moment to smoke a cigarette. A guard saw a thin spiral of smoke coming out of the ground and sounded the alarm. The tunnel, with its beautiful entrance in the general kitchen, was discovered.

Another tunnel showed the inventive imagination of *Kriegies* and almost made it. As stated earlier, the Geneva Convention said officers had to keep their own quarters clean but, other than that, did not have to perform labour unless on a voluntary basis. Some of us joined such working parties, pretending we liked the exercise and promising we would not try to escape while outside the fence.

Such gentleman's agreements were honoured on both sides; no escapes were ever tried on such occasions. However, our boys kept their eyes open and produced valuable reconnaissance information about the terrain around the camp. It turned out there was an ideal spot in the woods for a tunnel to have its exit. Unfortunately, the place was just across from the sports field and the tunnel would have to be very long.

The escape committee in those days was just three men, and Wing Commander ('Wings') Day decided that a tunnel would be constructed and that the entrance would be on the sports field, about forty feet from the fence. An entrance in the middle of an open field?

It was the first time that an effort to escape was organized on a large scale. We would need many workers. Since we didn't have to work, much time was spent on the sports field. This was nothing but a level area of sand, and was used constantly for cricket, baseball, fencing, athletics, and gymnastics. For our gymnasts, a 'horse' was built, with a padded top and a 'spring board' to boost their jumps and tumbles.

Every day our gymnasts performed their exercises, and even the guards became interested in the performances of some. They were happy that we kept ourselves busy with harmless activities on the sports field. What they didn't know was that the 'horse' was put on the exact same spot every day, and that two *Kriegies* were sitting inside the horse with their digging equipment. For four months they opened and closed the tunnel every time we brought out the horse. And every time, we carried the contraption, with the diggers and their sand, back to the storeroom in the kitchen. Here, the two workers and their heavy load of sand quickly disappeared, only to repeat the whole process the next day.

The Germans did not notice that we needed eight people every time we carried the horse, a heavy load that included two diggers and the sand. The progress was obviously slow, since we could only stow so much sand inside the horse. The entrance was a masterpiece of camouflage. It was a box-like trapdoor, fitted on a frame above a vertical shaft of about fifteen feet. From there, the horizontal part of the tunnel was forty feet from the fence.

The extremely well-planned project, code named 'The Wooden Horse', went unnoticed for four months. Now the end of the tunnel was just outside the fence. The committee had decided that three *Kriegies* would give it a try at night, in the hope that they could reach the edge of the forest unseen. This meant they would have to spend the time from the end of the gymnastic exercises until dark inside the tunnel. Light flurries of snow had already made the tumbling operations difficult, so there was no time to lose. The plan had to be carried out now.

It was during Project Wooden Horse that I became acquainted with other escape activities which had nothing to do with the actual tunnel construction, but which were just as important. Escapees needed German money, civilian clothes, papers allowing them to travel, maps, compasses, and information about their proposed travel routes.

Everything they had should look German-made, so we changed labels in underpants and jackets. We provided packages of German cigarettes and German matches, and even razors and combs were made unrecognizable. A small amount of food, at least enough for the first two days or so, was provided from escape kits such as my own. I discovered myself to be a rather promising false-paper artist, and my knowledge of the German language also came in very handy.

Not all items could be manufactured by *Kriegies;* many simply had to be real to pass any possible inspection. For instance, money, German cigarettes, photos on ID cards, and such items as pocketbooks had to be real. Bribing of guards became a most necessary and highly efficient *Kriegie* occupation.

The three would-be escapees were caught just outside the fence. They had almost run out of air after the long wait and had to make an air hole. By making the air hole, they had discovered they were only one foot from the surface. Part of the exit shaft collapsed, just outside the barbed wire fence, and this was seen by a guard who happened to pass by. Searchlights went on and, with a lot of shouting, the three unhappy escapees were marched off to the 'cooler'.

It took the Germans several days to discover where the tunnel originated. None of them had much desire to crawl into the hole, which could collapse at any moment. The snow and drizzle had softened the soil around the entrance until the box of the trapdoor became visible and a ferret almost fell into the entrance.

The 'cooler' was a separate building, in the *Vorlager*, and was a simple prison block with twelve cells and a watch room. The cells could hold up to four bunks and contained no other furniture. For washing or using the toilet, one had to call one of the guards. They provided food twice daily, but it was always the same – a soup of carrots, potatoes and bits of meat, and a piece of sourdough bread.

The Germans were half-flabbergasted, half-amused by the wooden horse. They couldn't believe their eyes when they dismantled the contraption and found two seats and twelve hooks in the innards of the horse. But now they understood why those two carrying-bars had to be so big and strong. The horse was used for firewood and we were no longer allowed to use the kitchen storeroom.

Another escape was psychologically well prepared and carried out with skill and courage. One of our Czechs, Arnost 'Wally' Valenta, was prepared to cut through the barbed wire fence in broad daylight. I began to realize what kind of a workforce we had. Of three thousand officers, less than 10 per cent were regular, professional soldiers. All the others were civilians in temporary service, draftees, mobilized reserve officers or volunteer specialists.

Almost all of them had a profession or job and possessed some skill other than their military occupation. There were tailors, artists, engineers, radio experts, chemists, mathematicians, and almost any profession one could think of represented. We could speak forty-three languages between us. We had professional distillers who could make booze out of almost anything – especially the tons of Sunmaid raisins which came in the Red Cross food parcels.

Valenta was well equipped with civilian clothes, papers, some German money, and a homemade wire-cutter. The site for the escape was chosen carefully; it was just where the guards in the watchtowers had almost no view of the base of the fence. The escape attempt went as follows:

On the sports field, a group of fencers started their regular exercises. A little to the right, gymnasts were making human pyramids and practised their gymnastics. On the left, just past another watchtower, a *Kriegie* sat on a tree stump practising beginner's scales on his saxophone. The guard in the tower looked at our musician in obvious disgust, but tried to ignore the annoying screeching sound. After a short while he leaned over and suggested that our boy practise somewhere else – '*Gehen Sie etwas weiter bitte*' – but our musician was insulted. He started an argument about his right to exercise his musical talents in a flow of words which temporarily kept the guard busy.

Meanwhile, one of the fencers got hurt. He fell on the ground, holding a hand to his shoulder and screaming in pain. I ran to the rescue with a first-aid kit under my arm, and soon a little group surrounded our wounded fencer. Then I ran to the guard in the tower on the right and asked him to call the doctor – an accident had occurred. The guard immediately picked up his telephone and started calling.

At this moment, Wally Valenta walked to the first fence, stepped over the wire into the warning strip and threw himself flat on the ground against the second fence. In bright daylight, we watched him cut his way through the barbed wire fence. At that angle, the Germans could not see him as he quietly walked into the woods and disappeared. The fabulous stunt had worked all the way, from the distracting scenario to the actual act of cutting a hole through the wire in broad daylight!

Valenta was caught a few hours later when he tried to buy a train ticket at the railway station in Sagan. After ten days in the cooler he was brought back to the general compound, where he received a hero's welcome, of course. A well-prepared plan, brilliantly executed, and we learned a little more about the art of escaping. It was difficult enough to get outside the barbed wire, but what the hell do you do once you are outside that blasted fence?

When the doctor came to the scene of the fencing 'accident', two ferrets accompanied him and immediately saw the hole in the fence. Within half an hour they had held *appel* (roll call), and discovered exactly who was missing. An MP at the station recognized Valenta, in spite of a professionally made civilian suit and a very non-military suitcase in his hand. He had failed to escape, but came back with precise information about the terrain around the camp and the railway station itself.

I began to realize that escaping from this camp required more than courage and good luck. Plans would have to be worked out to the smallest detail – not only how to get outside the barbed wire, but how to get all the way out of Germany. To travel through Germany one needed permits, travel orders, ID cards, passes, and money to buy train tickets and food. I reported to Tim Walenn, an Englishman and a master forger, and started to practise drawing printed papers, first typed characters and later regular printed script. It was the beginning of an elaborate false-paper department.

Every day I practised, drawing letters of various types and sizes, using watercolours or an ink I had made myself. I obtained a YMCA watercolour set and trimmed one of the brushes to five short hairs. A pair of reading glasses, swiped from one of the older guards, served as magnifying lenses.

As a medical student, I was allowed to work in the small hospital which was located in the *Vorlager*. I gladly promised I would not make any escape attempt from the hospital. Gentleman's agreements such as these were honest and never broken. Not only should a word of honour not be broken; but, if caught, punishment probably would be execution.

In the hospital I cleaned and redressed wounds, visited our colleagues who were treated for injuries or illnesses, and fraternized with the German doctor. I also swiped alcohol, glycerine, needles, syringes, tape, and many other things that might be useful for our secret activities.

With the help of a Polish chemist we made a usable black ink out of soot, glycerine, ether, and a pinch of mineral oil. This could be applied by brush and would be waterproof when dry. Watercolours would run with the slightest application of water, which instantly distinguished it from printed matter, which never runs at all. In the hospital, I noticed a large kit for eye testing. It was the standard set of forty-eight spherical and cylindrical lenses for optometric measuring. I instantly obtained the strongest positive spherical lens and vastly improved on my magnifying glass.

Almost every week a new contingent of *Kriegies* walked through the main gate. On one of these occasions I saw a man with a big cigar in his mouth, in the middle of the new group entering the camp.

The man was Squadron Leader Roger Bushell, a South African serving with the Royal Air Force. Roger was a well-known fighter pilot of Battle of Britain fame. And because of his reputation as an 'ace', he was, at first, put in a special POW camp. After several unsuccessful escape attempts, the Germans thought he had given up these 'foolish' escape ideas and transferred him to Stalag Luft III.

In the camp he was welcomed by a number of fighter pilots who knew him well, including Bob Stanford Tuck, considered England's top ace at the time. Booze suddenly appeared on the table, and it became clear that Roger had not given up anything, especially when he produced an incredibly civilian-looking raincoat and an ordinary felt hat. How he managed to smuggle these most valuable items through the gates will remain an eternal secret.

Within two days we knew that a new escape committee had been formed, called 'Organization Big X', and that Roger Bushell was 'Big X'. Our senior officer, Group Captain Massey, issued a secret order that, from now on, orders from Big X would take precedence over anything.

Bob Tuck shared a room with Roger Bushell and became his chief of staff. A Polish officer by the name of Tobolski was appointed head of the clothing department. He and his staff of professional tailors provided civilian clothes for prospective escapees and manufactured other items if cutting and sewing were involved.

Tim Walenn was made the head of the false-paper department. He gathered a group of twelve artists and photographic experts to create passes, ID cards, permits, and the ways and means to obtain the all-important German money.

The technical branch was headed by Wally Floody, a Canadian engineer with more tunnelling experience than anyone else. He was in charge of designing tunnels and their entrances, as well as all other sorts of engineering, like the manufacturing of tools and equipment.

Another department created by Bushell was security. At least a hundred *Kriegies* helped in this most essential part of our operations. In the barrack closest to the gate, we had a man who registered all Germans who entered and left the camp. There was only one gate, so our security knew at all times which guards were inside the compound. This was important information for other workers, as we will see.

The security department also had a group of members who simply would sit at strategic places around an area where secret work was being done. Whenever a tunnel entrance had to be opened, the diggers would need time to do this and our security boys would warn or clear the area of approaching Germans. A security member sitting with a towel around his neck meant 'all clear;' putting the towel on his knees meant 'German in sight'. If he sat on the towel it meant 'ferret near', or 'German approaching the barracks'.

The same warning system was used for the room where we drew false papers. If a German (and certainly a ferret) came too close we stopped our work, hid our papers, and instantly listened to a well-prepared lecture on bird watching. It actually happened that the ferret called 'Rubberneck' entered the room and was invited to participate. When the 'teacher' explained that the area around Sagan was exactly the place where the 'three-toed-speckled-woodfinch' made a migrating stop in the fall, he asked Rubberneck if he had ever seen one. The ferret shook his head, said he did not come from the area and left the room. When our security men gave the 'all clear' sign, we continued with the drawing of false papers.

Roger also created a large department of 'stooges'. They were non-specialist helpers and could be assigned to a variety of jobs as courier assignments, distraction tactics, and the tricky job of sand dispersal from tunnels. There were more than two hundred men available in this department.

Another department was made up of *Kriegies* who spoke German. Several Czechs, some Poles, and a number of other men in the camp were bilingual. I also volunteered for work in this department.

In our bribing and wheeler-dealing work we had many valuable items at our disposal. Germany had been without coffee for several years now, while we received real coffee in our Red Cross food parcels every week. It was a mighty bargaining weapon. We had unlimited amounts of very good cigarettes, real butter, chocolate, and Sunmaid raisins – all desirable items which the Germans could not buy themselves. The raisins, though, were not used for bribing Germans because they were important for our distillers; they could transfer the 'Sunmaids' into 100-proof booze.

Other non-military groups developed parallel to Bushell's operational forces. There were study groups, language groups, musical ensembles, and theatre troupes. They blended into the other organizations and served as an intellectual means of keeping the prisoners busy in legitimate workshops, and as a disguise for not-so-legit activities.

The false-paper factory worked every day. For security reasons, we didn't even know too much about the other departments. For instance, we had a radio department and the BBC news from London was read to us every day. After a year and a half in Stalag Luft III, I never saw one of these receivers, nor did I know who operated them.

Although I fully realized the necessity of Big X's methods, I became restless and asked Roger Bushell's permission to pull a so-called 'quickie'. With my Canadian roommate, Jim McCague, we would run to the fence at night and 'mole' underneath it to the outside, then try to catch a train before we were discovered. With my knowledge of German and Dutch, we could go to Holland and get help there. I knew Roger had done this himself in another camp and, indeed, had 'moled' himself out, although he was caught later.

Roger said, 'Well, Van, I must admit that it is possible. But chances are poor. I'll OK your plan but do it from hut No. 16, which is much closer to the fence, and promise me you'll run back to the barracks when you hear my whistle.'

With Jim, I prepared what I thought was needed for our escape, and we waited for the 'go' signal from Big X. On the chosen night we exchanged places with two prisoners from hut 16. We checked our equipment over and over again to shorten the long wait until 11:00 p.m., just after the rounds of the German guards who checked the shutters on the outside of the windows. There were no lights and our security boys had no trouble reporting where the guards were. After they passed our window, we waited quietly until we got the signal that they had left through the main gate.

Jim and I opened the window and slid out of the room. It was only about a hundred feet. Armed with a small homemade shovel, we crawled to the warning wire and crossed it at a place just between two towers. All was well, we thought. At the base of the fence I started to dig. It seemed so easy.

Suddenly there was commotion. We heard voices in German and somebody fired a rifle shot. Searchlights flashed on but the action seemed to be somewhere else. The lights were not trained on us, and there were no guards or dogs near us.

'Van, what the hell's going on?' Jim asked me.

At the same time, we heard Roger Bushell's two-tone whistle and I said, 'Back to the hut, Jim. Run!'

We ran to the open window in hut 16 and jumped into the empty beds in the room. The shutters were closed silently and we all pretended to sleep. The noise in the next barracks continued and then all was quiet.

The next morning Roger told me what had happened. An Irish hothead had stolen a field cap from one of the guards, and to hide it he threw it on the roof of the building. That night he tried to retrieve it by climbing on the roof but a tower guard heard something, trained his search light on him and fired a warning shot. Within minutes our Irishman was escorted to the cooler.

The entire incident had nothing to do with us and may even have been an unplanned diversion to distract the guards. But security had reported to Roger that the guards who came for the Irishman had a dog with them so he ordered us back, knowing that the police dog would not fail to detect us.

We returned our civilian clothes to Tobolski, who now operated a full-scale factory – included the shaving and dyeing of RAF uniform material to change the rough, blue-grey cloth into a smooth, brownish fabric that looked and felt very civilian.

The departments of Big X became more and more professional, with more experts coming in on a weekly basis. An Australian goldsmith joined our false-paper plant and became a master at making stamps from rubber heels which, for the purpose of shoe repairs, were sent to us in Red Cross parcels. On the flat side of a heel he would have one of us draw an official German stamp, in mirror image, with white watercolours. With a broken razor blade mounted on a small handle, he carved the stamp into the rubber so accurately that it could not be distinguished from a real stamp – except for a blank space where the name of a city would be painted in. This way, the stamp could be used for different cities and would coincide with other papers which were prepared for 'civilians from various cities'.

The chemical experts who dyed the fabrics for Tobolski also were master brewers. From our Sunmaid raisins they made a kind of vodka. Before long, one simply could exchange so many cartons of raisins for a pint of 'vodka'. The brewers kept a small amount of each order as profit, a fully accepted form of trading. After all, they made the stuff. It was officially *verboten* by camp rules, but I never saw a German guard discover the homemade stills, even when the room stank of fermenting Sunmaids. Occasionally, on very cold days, the wheeler-dealing department even offered a steaming cup of freshly brewed coffee with 'something extra' to promising guards who were still in the stage of softening up. This 'something extra' was, of course, our famous vodka.

For some of us, the Polish vodka was a little raw. I thought I should improve the liquor to drinks of my own taste. The first product was so successful I even made a very Italian-looking label, 'CINZANO', to honour the first bottle in our bar. I made syrup by boiling down sugar and water, added a touch of cinnamon from the Red Cross parcels, and with the proper proportion of our vodka, we had vermouth. Later I produced 'Crème de Menthe' from peppermint tablets and a pinch of green watercolour paint. Whisky was made by mellowing the raw booze with dark Karo syrup and sticking a burning piece of wood into the liquid. After putting a suggestive label on the bottle it went for Scotch.

We took turns cooking, which resulted in five days of horrible meals and one day of proper meals. I volunteered to be the cook every day in exchange for cleaning duties. Our Red Cross parcels often contained essential little goodies for cooking: pepper, salt, spices, sugar, butter, coffee, chocolate, egg powder, milk powder, mustard, vanilla, and often a package of flour. The parcels also provided us with cigarettes, pipe tobacco, rubber shoe soles, and other little things to make our lives bearable. With all of these ingredients, cooking really was possible. Special banquets with guests were no exception at all.

Even more important for Big X were the materials in which these things were packed. Powdered milk ('KLIM') came in cans which fitted on top of one another when the bottoms were removed by a clean cut.

Every parcel had such a can and every *Kriegie* received a parcel weekly. We received three thousand cans per week. Put together, they could form a tube more than four hundred yards long. Coffee and soap were the most valuable products for trade with the Germans. We made them expensive!

There were many items we could not possibly make, no matter what expertise was available. Paper money is simply too difficult to draw by hand, and metal items such as buckles or buttons for German uniforms could not be made. Tobolski wanted insignia for a German uniform, a leather belt, and a real field cap.

Big X did not concentrate only on tunnels; he evaluated and supported every serious plan. Several *Kriegies* escaped by making use of 'quickies', and did get out, but all of them were caught sooner or later. They organized another escape attempt for me, this time with Commander Heye Schaper. We would get out during a delousing day and become 'Russians' inside the delousing building, which was in the *Vorlager*.

Through Big X, Heye and I were well equipped. We packed civilian clothing under our uniforms and had papers, maps, and money. When it was announced that our barrack had to be deloused, Heye Schaper and I were ready. Our civilian clothes were carefully hidden under our uniforms. The Russian overcoats were carried by two other *Kriegies*, folded in such a manner that they looked like the blankets we all carried with us. Two Russian-speaking Big X workers had arranged that there would be two shovels against the wall of the delousing building. The Russian POWs gladly obliged, for a pack of cigarettes.

At the gate we were counted, then marched on to the brick building with four guards and one ferret escorting us. Inside we had to undress, hang all our clothes and blankets in a steam room, then proceed to a large shower room where soap and towels were provided. We were given twenty minutes to wash, while at the same time our clothes were treated with hot air and steam. After our shower, Heye and I dressed in our civilian outfits. But instead of our uniforms we put on the Russian great-coats and khaki stocking caps, and on our way grabbed the shovels and walked around the corner of the building. Two other *Kriegies* put on our uniforms over their own and the group, minus two, marched back to the gates of our compound. Heye and I shovelled a little sand and tried to look Russian.

We knew that there would be a count again, and that detail had been organized as well. When the incomplete group stopped at the gate, the next group to be deloused was standing ready. The moment the gate opened, they started to walk out.

The guards shouted, 'Vait, vait, one group at the time *bitte*, ve still haf to count.'

The boys apologized and stepped back, except two who had smoothly mixed with the incoming group so that its number would be the same again.

Schaper and I were outside the compound but still in the *Vorlager*. However, that was not too much of a problem because the towers around the *Vorlager* were not manned. Only a patrol, circling the entire complex, occasionally passed by and we did not consider it a big problem to cut through the fence. Obviously, we had to wait until dark and the best place seemed to be the attic of a latrine. Without any trouble we walked to the wooden structure and hoisted ourselves into the space under the roof, to wait it out until dark.

Back in the camp Big X and Bob Tuck were smiling. The counting foul-up at the gate had worked perfectly, but there was another obstacle to be cleared. At 5:00 p.m. there would be the regular *appel* (roll call), and there would be two unaccounted for. A clever artist had made two life-size mannequins, dressed them in RAF uniforms and at *appel* the two phoneys were standing between two real *Kriegies*, ready to be counted.

Hauptmann Pieber and his staff carried out the counting – '*drei, vier, fünf, sechs* – well, everything in order …' until the ferret Rubberneck shouted,

'*Halt! Herr Hauptmann, kommen Sie mahl hier!*'

And when Captain Pieber came and saw the two mannequins, he could hardly suppress a smile. Naturally, they called a big alarm and within minutes the compound was swarming with ferrets and other guards. All *Kriegies* were ordered to their rooms, where a quick count immediately revealed that the two *Hollander* were missing. Several dogs were brought to our room, where they sniffed our clothing and beds, and the manhunt was on.

Heye Schaper and I were not aware of the commotion. We just waited in our hiding place, looking at our watches with a so-far-so-good attitude, until we heard the growl of a dog. Then the short bark of another dog. Within seconds we saw two huge German shepherds showing their teeth and growling, just a few feet below us.

'*Raus!*' ordered the dog trainer, pointing his pistol at us.

I looked at the dogs and said, '*Ja, ja, wir kommen.* But what about those goddamn dogs?'

By that time they had put the dogs on their leashes and we had no choice but to climb down and be very polite for a while. They marched us to the cooler, where we were put in the big cell.

Before a guard slammed the door shut he said, '*Ach, kinder,* don't you know zat you cannot escape from zis *lager*?'

Another guard came in with two sets of regulation, battledress uniforms and made us change in his presence. Our coats and civilian dress underneath were carefully examined by a ferret who, while shaking his head, asked, 'How did you get these clothes?' Heye said we had found them but nobody believed him. We were not about to tell them that they were made by the professional tailors of Stalag Luft III.

The two weeks they kept us in the cooler were boring, and not easy, with only two, soupy meals per day. The guards were not unpleasant but they were very strict. We had to call them for bathroom necessities and they would place themselves in front of the open door. The cell doors had small square windows in them, with lights burning day and night. There were more *Kriegies* in other cells and we tried to establish secret communications with them by knocking codes on the wall.

After a few days we had to admit that knocking out Morse code on a wall was not a very effective way of communicating, especially when we discovered we could talk to the others anyway during the morning wash time. We could even talk right through the square holes in the doors and the guards didn't object at all. The Germans were right; our knocking on the walls belonged in Hollywood but here in the cooler it would not very likely change the course of the war.

When we were taken back to camp, we were received with cheers, special vodka and my own vermouth. I became sick and when Heye saw me, he also vomited the poisonous brew, while bystanders roared with laughter.

The speciality departments of Big X became better, more specialized, and more incredible. I went back to the false-paper factory to produce more, improved documents. Tobolski was in the process of making a German uniform that supposedly was not distinguishable from a real one. The Czech mechanics had made a handle of a Luger pistol which looked identical to the real thing, when kept in its holster.

Our compound was now filled with more than three thousand *Kriegies*. A steady stream of new prisoners arrived week after week, and we knew the Germans were building a new compound next to the one we now used. In October 1943, we received the order to move to the new 'North Compound', which was at least twice the size of the one we then were living in. Entrances of two new tunnels were sealed off for the next occupants to reopen, secret hiding places were emptied, and in four huge moving operations we managed to get everything – including Tobolski's tailor department – to our new quarters.

In the new compound, the sports field was much larger and new camps were already being built to our south and west. This made tunnelling in those directions totally impossible. There were two small rooms at both ends of each barrack, no doubt made to house senior officers or act as supply rooms. When two more Dutch pilots came in, they were placed in our room and Schaper and I were given one of the end rooms, just for the two of us.

The Germans had left many more trees between the buildings, which made the camp nicer, and they had converted one entire hut into a theatre and library, with several classrooms. Over the years, the YMCA had sent musical instruments and the International Red Cross had given us a piano, which was brought in by a team of Swiss Red Cross inspectors. Among the professionals in our camp, a number of them were first-class musicians. Small wonder that we had an eighteen-man band of Glenn Miller-calibre and a symphony orchestra of forty 'Beethovens'.

Security was better than ever for us in the false-paper department, so we had more time for our work than our eyes could stand. I concentrated on bribing. I had received word that my friend Tobolski needed German uniform buttons, a leather belt with buckle, a field cap, and an embroidered corporal's insignia. These items were simply too difficult to falsify. Money was always welcome, of course.

My victim was a guard of about fifty, by the name of Heinz. He was an Austrian from Vienna, spoke no English and made no secret of the fact that he was not German. After several cups of coffee, I gave him some tobacco because, I told him, I didn't smoke a pipe and would throw it away. We became more friendly and I invited him into the room where Heye Schaper 'accidentally' had brewed fresh coffee and left four packages of cigarettes and three bars of chocolate on the table. When Heinz came and saw this Horn of Plenty on the table his eyes popped.

'*Himmel!*' he said. '*Ach, Sie haben es besser als wir!*' ('You have it better than we do!')

Heinz enjoyed his cup of coffee and was genuinely thankful that we shared our limited luxuries with him, an ordinary citizen, who didn't like the war any better than we did. On his way out I slid a chocolate bar in his pocket and invited him back – 'Anytime, Heinz.'

This fraternizing went on for several weeks, until we thought Heinz was ready. We filled his pockets with a little more than the usual store of goodies and I escorted him on his way to the gate.

About halfway there, I said, 'Heinz, you know that some *Kriegies* want to escape. And for these idiots, I need six of your buttons, your field cap, and those embroidered patches on your collar. You are wearing a helmet and a great-coat; nobody will notice anything and you can easily replace those things.'

'But Herr Captain,' Heinz exclaimed, 'that goes a little too far. Don't forget, I am the guard and you are the prisoner!'

'I know, Heinz, but those guys want them and if you don't give us the things I asked for, I'll call the guards at the gate and tell them you stole the things in your pockets.'

'Captain, that is mean!' Heinz grumbled, but then gave us the items we wanted.

'Heinz, I know it is mean. But I knew that all the time. Come and have your coffee anyway. Next time we make a deal we'll do it in my room, so you'll have a chance to say "no" if you think it's too risky. Don't worry, Heinz, I won't tell anybody.'

He walked off, confused, not knowing exactly what to think or what to do about the situation. The next day he was back for his coffee and we had a regular source of supplies.

One of the Czechs convinced a guard there was a serious epidemic of tuberculosis in Vienna, the city the guard was from, and that there was a shortage of medicine. Fortunately, we the *Kriegies* were protected from this dreaded disease by a drug we received in our Red Cross parcels. He showed him a can of Ovaltine. After a few days, the guard himself asked for the 'drug' in exchange for German money. He wanted to send Ovaltine to his family in Vienna. This one, also, became a regular supplier.

The methods of our wheeler-dealing department were not the most ethical one could think of. However, we considered our cause much more important than the relatively harmless small business we did with the guards. We never reported any of these simple-minded guards, and none of the guards ever reported each other, because a certain amount of trading was done by most of them.

When I walked into Tobolski's room, I said, *'Djen Dobri* (Polish for "good morning"), how about this?' and sprinkled a buckle, buttons, and insignia on the table.

Tobolski could hardly believe his eyes: 'How the hell did you –?'

'Well,' I said, 'I just saved a guard from being sent to the Russian front.'

That afternoon, Roger Bushell came to our room and congratulated me on the deal with Heinz. We got some vodka and vermouth out of the bar and made 'martinis' – with snow instead of ice, which was still present under a few trees.

Roger was pleased and said, 'I don't know how you did it, but that was quite a haul. It'll come in handy, very soon. By the way, Van, meeting in my room, tonight after roll call.'

'What about cooking?' I joked.

To which Roger answered in Dutch, *'Schaper moet die kok speel.'* ('Schaper must play cook.')

Hauptmann Pieber performed his daily roll call, which now was called *appel* by everybody, and I walked back with him to our barracks. We talked about the Russian front and about the 'flexible corrections' the German High Command made on an almost daily basis. These flexible corrections always were made in a Westerly direction and we all knew that the Russian campaign did not go according to Hitler's plans. After Stalingrad, it was one disaster after the other. Pieber was aware of the fact that I was well informed about the military situation on the Russian front, which puzzled him.

'Herr Vanderstok,' he said, 'you seem to know about these events on the Eastern Front, sometimes before we get the information ourselves. How do you do that?'

'Well, *Herr Hauptmann*,' I replied, 'As you know, we have a large map in the library and all you have to do is look at the woollen thread to see where the Eastern Front is. The red thread and pins are updated every day.'

'*Ja, ja*. I know that, of course, but how do you know where to apply the changes? They always seem to be correct.'

'Military predictions,' I said, knowing that Pieber was trying to get some information about our radios. It was too obvious that the map in the library represented facts we could not have obtained from the German newspapers, which always were three or four days old. The truth was that we received the BBC news from London, Stockholm, or Moscow every day and our 'military predictions' were more than mere guesses. Most German guards and officers found some reason to inspect our library to take a quick look at the map, which spelled out the bad news day by day.

When security gave the 'all clear' sign I went to Roger's room, where I was told where the meeting would be. We never had meetings in his room, always somewhere else, and never twice in the same room. In the meeting room I found Roger, Bob Tuck, 'Wings' Day, Hornblower (Chief of Security), Tim Walenn (Chief of False Papers), Tobolski (Chief of Clothing), and Wally Floody (Chief of Tunnel Operations). That was just about the entire Big X leadership, and a feeling of pride went through my veins when I knew that I was considered one of them. I learned that Big X was now an organization of more than a thousand workers, each with a specific task.

In a quiet but business-like voice, Roger explained about the big projects he wanted carried out. Floody was in charge of the digging of three tunnels – 'Tom', 'Dick', and 'Harry'. They were to be built at the same time so that if one had to be discontinued for any reason, there would be two others underway. There would be a party of twenty senior officers who would walk out in bright daylight, escorted by a German *Feldwebel* (sergeant).

'By the way, Van, you'll be our German *Feldwebel*.' Roger said, and continued explaining his plans.

We needed samples of passes to walk through the gate. There would be an evening of entertainment by the band, with German officers and sergeants invited. The Germans would be seated in the front row, together with some of our senior officers. A team of pickpockets would sit in the second row and collect wallets. Wally Floody needed boards to strut the tunnels. Heye Schaper was put in charge of getting bed-boards. All of our bunks had about twenty loose boards, which were just the right size and strength for this purpose. If we could get three boards we would have enough for a start. Transportation of bed-boards to the various tunnel sites was the duty of security and stooges. We heard a knock on the door.

One of Hornblower's men came in and said, 'Rubberneck entered the compound. He's at the gate.'

'Thank you,' Roger said. 'Everybody out of here!' and we strolled back to our rooms, minding our own business.

There were single-escape attempts. An American tried to hide in a garbage truck but got hurt when the 'goons' at the gate poked their bayonets into the rubbish. It was almost comical when our boy came out screaming, 'Stop, stop!' with curls of rotting potato peelings on his head and shoulders. Another attempt was made by a prisoner in a Russian uniform when a smelly tank wagon came in to pump out the latrine pits. Our 'Russian' simply sat next to the driver, who did not suspect anything at all, but he was caught at the gate.

Another fantastic plan was considered, but turned out to be too ambitious. Four Americans had designed a hot air balloon, including the airtight material for the balloon itself, and a gasoline burner to provide the heat. The only impossible task was hiding the enormous amounts of material for the balloon, which they tried to make of rubberized bed sheets. They had made a black rubber paint from shoe soles dissolved in gasoline, which was stolen from trucks that entered the camp for kitchen supplies and garbage.

The burner had a pump which had to be operated all the time but it worked well. The 'gondola' was nothing more than a system of straps and a multitude of wires, connected to a wooden ring at the base of the balloon. It was impossible to hide the enormous balloon and the plan was given up before completion. The gasoline torch, however, was used for manufacturing tools.

During the building of the North Compound, many POW sergeants from the Centre Compound had worked there. They had their own escape committee and their spirit was nothing less than in the officers' compounds, but escaping was even more difficult because their camp was surrounded by other compounds on three sides. The fourth side was their sports field, where tunnelling was almost impossible. One of them, while working in the North Compound, swiped two new spools of electric wire and threw them in the attic of one of the new barrack buildings. He speculated that they might be useful later, no matter who would occupy the hut. Big X already knew about this very large supply of electric wire before we moved to the North Compound, but he did not know exactly where to look for it. He ordered all hut commanders to search their attics and the spools of wire were promptly found.

The ferret 'Rubberneck' never was included in bribes or any other favours, such as coffee, because we simply could not trust him. Apparently the ferrets received bonuses for finding escape materials and Rubberneck was, no doubt, their best man. He had found a few minor items – a screwdriver, a half-finished wire-cutter, and a stolen flashlight. He became arrogant and tried to make life as unpleasant as possible by searching rooms just when a meal was served, or kicking over a basin with fermenting raisins.

We could make life unpleasant for him, as well, and some of the *Kriegies*, perhaps psychologists by trade, were real masters at that when they said, 'Hey, Rubberneck, would you please take a bath before you enter our room? Here is a piece of soap, we can't stand your "BO"!'

He couldn't accept the soap because he knew we would accuse him of theft if he took it. He had, on several occasions, hit prisoners with the butt of his Luger if they didn't move out of the room fast enough, and made others strip in the cold corridor for no good reason. He became one of the few real enemies, while many other guards were just strict but not truly hateful.

One of the good guards was *Feldwebel* Glemnitz. The man had lived in New York and spoke excellent English, even with a Brooklyn accent. He was strict, never accepted anything but an occasional cup of coffee, and could not be talked into bribery of any kind. Like the commandant of Stalag Luft III and several officers, Glemnitz was regarded as a gentleman and a very good soldier, but one who was just on the wrong side.

The day of the band concert arrived. There were posters and there was excitement, because everybody knew the band was outstanding and it would be a special evening. We dressed for the occasion and, precisely on time, twelve German officers and our senior officers were ushered to the front row of seats. All others present rose and stood at attention until they were seated. The light dimmed, talking stopped, we heard the roll of drums, the curtain opened … and the show was on.

It was hard to believe that a bunch of prisoners of war were able to present such a production of jazz and contemporary music. But then, more than half of the musicians had played in big bands at home. A famous song of the time was 'Lili Marlene', originally a German hit but later adopted by the Allies in North Africa as their 'pin up' song. 'Waltzing Matilda', the 'Lambeth Walk', 'Roll Me Over', and the classic big band songs were a huge success and honoured by thundering applause.

At the end of the performance, the enthusiasm became even greater and the entire audience stood up, giving the band a standing ovation. Many of the Germans had made themselves comfortable in their chairs by loosening their leather belts and pistol holsters, and even stood up, leaving these items in their chairs. Four wallets and one pistol plus holster were missing and the *Kriegies* in the second row had disappeared.

None of the officers sounded any alarm; the situation was too embarrassing and they all thought they had a better chance to solve their problems by negotiation. This proved to be true when *Hauptmann*

Wiegel came to me the next day. When he told me his pistol had been stolen during the concert, I expressed concern and said I would try to get it back for him. I told Wiegel to be back in half an hour. To make it impossible for anybody to follow me, I asked Jim McCague to see Roger and ask for instructions. Jim came back with the pistol, but also with a demand.

Wiegel anxiously walked to meet me at the pre-arranged place and I put him at ease by saying, '*Hauptmann* Wiegel, you have nothing to worry about. You will get your pistol back. Some over-zealous *Kriegie* stole your gun but we have no use for a pistol. Just imagine, one pistol against ten machine guns.'

'Oh wonderful!' Wiegel said. 'Can I get it now?'

'Well, as I said, *Herr Hauptmann,* you'll get it back but you must do something for us in return. I want your pass for the main gate for about an hour. You'll get your pistol and your pass back, I promise – gentleman's agreement – OK?'

Wiegel didn't like the deal at all. But considering the consequences, and the relative assurance that it would stay a secret, he gave me the pass. And in exactly one hour I returned the pistol and the pass to him.

Roger did not consider the pistol of great value. If any of us was caught with a real gun, shooting would be justified and not much advantage could be expected. But to use it as a trading item was very desirable. The pass was taken to Casey, one of our most talented false-paper artists, who studied it and made a rough copy of this most essential document.

Pieber came to us with the same embarrassing request as the other two pickpocket victims. They all were treated the same way.

Much later, I found out that the story about the pistol was not quite complete. Roger had sent it to the engineers and carpenters to have the handle copied before giving it back to *Hauptmann* Wiegel. What they didn't tell me at the time was that the engineers also filed the firing pin short so it would never shoot. The money was taken out of the wallets, but other than that they were returned intact, after a thorough inspection by Tim Walenn and his forgers. In one of the wallets we found complete travel permits and a sheet of food stamps.

An increasing number of German officers were ill at ease about the bad news from the Russian front. They knew the possibility of being transferred to the front was not at all imaginary. Quite differently from their arrogant attitudes in 1940, they now began to see that a German victory was not so certain at all. More and more, we heard them say that they were not Nazi but simply were doing their duty. In the meantime, Big X took advantage of every opportunity.

Flowers in Stalag Luft III?

After passing two security posts, which gave me the 'all clear' sign, I reported to Tobolski's room, where I found Roger and Tim Walenn. Immediately after me, twenty-one other officers arrived, most of them of the rank of major or higher. Wings Day started to try on a civilian suit, followed by the others, but for me they had the uniform of a German *Feldwebel*.

The uniform looked as if it had been taken from one of the guards – the material, the colour, the texture – it was unbelievable. On the collars there were the real, embroidered insignias, and in the front was a row of metal buttons. I recognized the field cap, the leather belt with buckle, and a large holster with the handle of a Luger protruding. The entire outfit was a breathtaking copy of the real thing. With a few pins in his mouth, Tobolski fitted the length of the sleeves and added a small red, white, and black ribbon on the left chest. I was, at least to the eye, indistinguishable from a German *Feldwebel*.

Tim Walenn showed me the pass he had produced and gave me another paper to serve as a travel permit from Sagan to Amsterdam. Tim also gave me sixty German marks in paper, money which I had to hide.

The other officers took their civilian clothes to their own quarters so that if found, the Germans would not catch the whole arsenal of escape clothing but, hopefully, just one outfit. During the next three days there were rehearsals of the choreographed operation until everybody knew exactly what to do.

Group Captain Massey had requested a meeting of our senior officers with the camp commandant, to discuss the regular flow of Red Cross parcels and their distribution through his own officers. There had been irregularities, such as opened or damaged parcels, all of which could be corrected by organization. The commandant OK'd the meeting, which was set for a certain time in his own headquarters. The group would be escorted by a German *Feldwebel* of the Censor Department, who would meet the prisoners at the gate at exactly 1400 hours (2:00 p.m.).

At exactly 1300 hours (1:00 p.m.), I appeared as *Feldwebel* Schwartz-mann, near the gate, and collected my senior officers in a column of three abreast. They were neatly dressed in their uniforms, which bulged a little on some of them, but *Kriegies* were not expected to wear well-fitting gear anyway. We were exactly one hour too early, speculating that the real guard would arrive perhaps ten minutes ahead of time.

When we came close, the guard on duty opened the big gate to let us through. I shouted, '*Einundzwanzig*,' and waved my pink pass at the guard, who said something like, '*Jawohl*,' but hardly looked at the pass. We simply walked through.

With a commanding voice I ordered, '*Also, weiter bitte!*' and we marched out of the camp on the road along the edge of the forest of small pine trees.

I felt certain that I had not talked too much because of the easy way we walked through the gate. After three years of speaking the language in school in Switzerland, my German was reasonably good. No accent could be detected if I said only a few words. But, when telling a longer story, the Dutch accent would be noticeable to any German.

We were ready to quietly disappear into the woods but Wings Days said, 'Would you believe it, Van, we just walked out! We'll disperse into the woods, but let's just wait until that goon has passed.'

A single *Feldwebel* walked on the dirt road in the opposite direction and did not seem to pay much attention to us.

But when he passed, he said, '*Was ist los? Woher gehen sie?*'

'*Zum Kommandantur,*' I said, but then he started shouting.

'*Wieso? Wieso? Das ist doch mein –*' and suddenly he understood the situation. He grabbed his pistol and yelled, '*Halt!*' and fired two shots in the air.

One of my group tried to run into the woods, but another '*Halt*' and two more shots from his Luger stopped all attempts to run. By this time we heard sirens, more shots, and barking dogs; and we saw Germans running toward us from every direction. In no time we were all in the guardhouse at the gate. The real guard, who was supposed to escort the group, had come half an hour early and thereby screwed up the whole operation.

I was separated from the others when one goon after the other came in to look at my uniform. Finally *Hauptmann* Pieber also arrived and couldn't believe his eyes.

'Where did you get that uniform?' he asked.

And when I said, 'Take a good look', they all started feeling and closely examining the fake material and unfinished inside of the tunic.

I had to undress and was given new clothes. All my equipment, compass, maps, and papers were lost except for one thing. I had managed to curl up my paper money in a tight little roll, which I could keep in my hand while changing clothes. When all the excitement had died down, the entire group was marched to the cooler. The others were put in the bigger cells, in twos and fours, but I had to go into solitary confinement.

The German camp doctor and *Feldwebel* Glemnitz came to me in the cell and once again expressed their amazement about the uniform. When they saw the butt of the Luger pistol they first took it for a real gun. But when they removed it from the leather holster, seeing that it was only a butt, they couldn't believe it. They made me undress again and again the doctor examined me. He looked in my mouth, between my buttocks, under my arms, and between my toes. But they never found my German money, which now was under the blanket on my bunk.

The cell was only about eight feet by twelve feet. The only furnishings were a double bunk with one mattress, a blanket, and a pillow. The heavy wooden door had the familiar square hole in it. In the opposite wall was a small window with iron bars, with a piece of plywood about one foot outside the window, so that there was no view.

Twice a day, they brought in a big pot of the standard soup with an enamel bowl and spoon. We could take as much as we wanted and even call for a second helping if there was enough left. In the mornings we could wash and use the toilet, during which time we could freely talk with each other. It made no sense to pass secret little notes or knock out messages on the walls, because escaping from the cooler was totally impossible – unless someone simply tried to run, which no doubt would result in shooting.

The twenty-one officers who were caught with me were sent back to the camp after fourteen days of disciplinary action in the cooler. But I had to stay. For a week, I was the only one in the cell block so I had nobody to talk to except the Germans. It was obvious that I could not execute any escape attempts, so after a while I was not considered a very dangerous prisoner. Some of the guards engaged in long conversations to break the endless hours when they had nothing to do, but still had to be alert for one single prisoner. It helped me, in a way, because it was difficult to get through the day in a cell with nothing but a wooden bunk. Even week-old newspapers didn't help much. I tried to exercise but that became boring.

Another cooler customer was brought in, and the next morning while shaving I found out it was our hot-headed Irishman, who had insulted the commandant. Colonel von Lindeiner had entered the camp with some dignitaries, all in fancy uniforms. The commandant was in spotless white and had introduced his guests to our Group Captain Massey and Colonel 'Red' Clark, the senior American officer at the time.

Our little Irishman had jumped forward and yelled, 'Ice cream, ice cream', as if Colonel von Lindeiner looked like a street vendor.

The commandant did not appreciate the poor joke, pointed his finger at the stupid boy, and said, 'cooler'. *Feldwebel* Glemnitz and a ferret grabbed him, and five minutes later Mac was in the cell next to mine.

One of the guards in the cell block, Wilhelm, was a young lad from Hamburg. The day after the bombing of his hometown he talked to me while we were washing and shaving. He could not understand why the Allied bombers had dropped so many bombs and incendiaries over the city, killing thousands of innocent people. His family came out alive, but they had lost their house and everything in it.

I tried to explain, 'Willie, don't you know what the Luftwaffe did to Warsaw, Rotterdam, London, Coventry, and a hundred other cities?'

'Oh, yes,' Willie answered. 'But *Krieg ist Krieg*, war is war. That was necessary.'

'Willie,' I said, 'we are also fighting a war, remember?'

Young Wilhelm wanted to wash his face and hung his tunic on a nail on the wall. When he turned to me to continue our conversation, our Irishman swiftly pulled Willie's soldier's book from a pocket of his tunic, threw it in the toilet and flushed it.

I looked at him in disgust and shouted, 'You idiot! Why the hell did you do that?'

'All Huns are my enemies,' he answered.

There was no point in saying anything else. *Kriegies* can go berserk. The shouting brought other guards to the washroom and the Irishman was roughly returned to his cell. Later, Willie told me that he had retrieved his soldier's book from the sewer and was given a new one.

Willie became depressed after realizing that the phrase, 'War is War', also applied to German cities. In their victorious days of 1940, the Germans simply couldn't see it that way. But now, since their own cities were bombed, in spite of Hitler's promises, they saw that they were not immune to the realities of war. One morning, Willie started a conversation again and, like so many Germans, echoed the loud propaganda talk of Germany's leaders – Hitler, Goebbels, Himmler, and the others.

Finally he said, 'It's the Jews, those goddamn Jews. We should put them all in the camps and get rid of them!'

'So you know about the concentration camps?' I said. 'How would you like it if we did the same with all our enemies, after the war is over? You say the Jews are your enemies. Don't we have the right to call all Germans our enemies?'

Wilhelm had already felt for some time that a German victory was not very probable anymore.

He started to cry like a small child, 'What will happen to us if the Allies win the war?'

In a fatherly tone I tried to calm him, saying, 'I don't think you should fear anything. Just be sure that you're not on a list of war criminals. Don't kill unarmed prisoners!'

By now, I had already spent four weeks in the cooler and I felt the strain of my uncertain future. Suddenly, I received two letters from my mother. We were allowed to write and receive one letter a month.

Obviously, the Germans had held one of her letters for a month, which had been censored as well. Several portions were blacked out.

My mother wrote that Hans, my younger brother, was now officially engaged to his long-time Swedish girlfriend, and that she and Père, my father, had gone to Hilda's place. She had not seen my older brother, Felix, for two months but he was still in the same job with Uncle Bart. I immediately understood my mother's words, as only a son can.

Hans never had a Swedish girlfriend, but I knew he had tried to find an escape route through Sweden. Hans had arrived in Sweden. My parents had moved to my cousin Hilda's, in the town of Hattem. There was no other possibility than that they had had to evacuate from their home in The Hague. We had no Uncle Bart, so my mother meant something else. No doubt Felix had continued his underground work and had had to dive under now. Hans in Sweden, Felix in hiding, and my parents kicked out of their house; it all spelled unpleasant developments.

In her second letter she wrote that she had sent me a parcel with candy, watercolours, and vegetable seeds, because food was getting scarce and flowers were planted everywhere to cheer up the oppressed Dutch in the face of the worsening general situation. With a friend, she had planted marigold seeds in the park opposite the 'White House', in the north-end street in The Hague. Thousands of others throughout the country had done the same, and she included a package of the seeds in the parcel.

My mother would never write so elaborately about marigold flowers, so there was a special meaning behind the seeds. I knew immediately what it was. The 'White House' at that address was the Queen's Palace. The marigold is an orange flower, and our Royal Family was the House of Orange. Millions of the Dutch planted orange flowers in parks, on the grounds of government buildings, and along roads as silent tokens of their bond with Queen Wilhelmina.

It was now seven weeks that I had been in the cooler. All the others had been returned to the compound, but my case was blown up to more serious proportions – escaping in a German uniform, threatening with a pistol, and so on. From the guards I learned that the Gestapo had demanded that I be transferred to a Gestapo prison. Group Captain Massey and Wings Day had talked to von Lindeiner, explaining that according to the rules of the Geneva Convention I had my rights and my duties. My duty was to try to escape and my right was to be treated as an officer. The uniform was not a German uniform, it was a homemade imitation to fool the guards, not to threaten them. I had had no gun, merely a wooden handle that looked like a gun. Massey and Day insisted that I had simply done my duty – nothing else, nothing criminal.

For several days the ferrets, assisted by a team of Gestapo members, searched the camp. But Big X had suspended all operations and they found absolutely nothing. They knew we were digging, they knew that we made civilian clothes and false papers; but the evidence remained elusive.

When I was in my eighth week of cooler punishment, a guard opened the door of my cell and said I had to see the commandant. Escorted by two guards, I was walked to Colonel von Lindeiner's office. Inside, I noticed that the German camp doctor also was in the room.

'Good morning, Captain Vanderstok. Sit down please. I have something to discuss with you. Do you want to speak in English, or German, or in Dutch, if you like?'

I saluted and sat down on the chair in front of him. I knew the commandant spoke Dutch, since he was married to a Dutch wife, but what about the doctor?

'I would prefer Dutch, *Herr Colonel*. But is that OK with the doctor?'

Von Lindeiner looked at the young physician, saying, 'You understand Dutch, don't you?'

'Yes, yes. Of course, *Herr Colonel*,' was the doctor's reply.

Although I didn't know what the commandant had in mind at the time, I felt I'd made a good move. Working frequently in the camp hospital, I had got to know the doctor quite well and I knew that he would not understand a single word of Dutch.

Von Lindeiner continued in fluent Dutch. First he elaborated on the fact that I had done my duty but that now it was all over for me. There was nothing I could do to change the outcome of the war and the Luftwaffe had decided to offer the following proposition. I had to remember, of course, that he and the Luftwaffe High Command had gone through considerable trouble to keep me out of the hands of the Gestapo.

The proposition was that I could return to Holland, go back to medical school and graduate – all of which would be paid for by the German government. In return, I would have to offer my services to the cause of the German Reich.

The doctor just sat there, with a blank expression on his face, and I knew that the whole conversation had meant absolutely nothing to him. But von Lindeiner handed me a paper to sign. I noticed a slight tremor in his hand.

I was tired and utterly fed up with my solitary confinement in the cooler. On the soup diet and with practically no exercise, I was physically worn out, so the proposal to go home and finish my medical education sounded sweet for a moment. But I recovered very quickly from this instant of weakness and the words, 'offer my services to the cause of the German Reich', sounded like a sledgehammer in my head. My God, a traitor – in return for my freedom and medical degree?

Von Lindeiner was nervous and the doctor stared at his fingers, obviously embarrassed and ill at ease. Suddenly, I felt myself in control again.

After several minutes of thought, I said, 'Colonel von Lindeiner, if I were your son, what would you advise me?'

The German commandant rose and extended his hand. I felt a slight tremble when he said in Dutch, 'Thank you, my boy. I was ordered to offer you the proposal. It wasn't my idea.'

'I knew that all the time, Colonel,' I said. 'And I also know that our medical friend here didn't understand a word of what was said between us.'

Von Lindeiner put the unsigned document in a large, brown envelope and pressed a buzzer. The two guards came in and escorted me back to the cooler. Somehow I felt an awful lot better, in spite of the rotten prison cell.

Exactly what happened after the interview with the camp commandant, I never learned until after the war. There was, as we all knew, much animosity between the German military forces and the armed political forces, the SA, the SS, and the Gestapo. The Luftwaffe said the Vanderstok case was strictly a Luftwaffe responsibility, and the Gestapo said that 'undesirables' like Vanderstok should be eliminated. Very fortunately for me, the Luftwaffe won the argument.

Two weeks later, as unexpected as the interview with the commandant, a guard opened my cell door and said, '*Raus,* you are going back to the compound.'

I couldn't possibly just walk out at that very moment. My German money was hidden in the casing of the door and I needed a few minutes – alone.

'Oh, *Herr Feldwebel,* that *ist fantastisch!* I'll be ready in a minute. May I use the toilet first?'

'*Ja, ja,*' the guard said. And then, to his friend, '*er ist so verstummt das er scheissen muss.*'

'*Kommen Sie hier wenn Sie fertig sind.*'

'*Jawohl,*' I said and stalled enough to get the little roll of money. Then I faked a visit to the toilet and went to the guardroom, all ready to be returned to the North Compound.

When I walked through the gate there was a true reception committee waiting for me, including *Feldwebel* Glemnitz, who still talked about the incredible uniform the Tobolski department had produced. Roger Bushell came toward me with outstretched hands. Our handshake lasted just long enough for him to realize that he felt something in his palm, and when he looked he saw sixty German marks in paper money.

My old roommates organized a party, with lots of booze, and there was a parcel from Holland in my room. It was the package my mother had written about, but when I opened it I realized what the people in Holland went through. The food was a can of tomato soup and a can of black rye bread. There was a cardboard box with watercolours and three brushes. A pair of woollen socks and a box of seeds completed the contents of the parcel. Holland had no food; the shops were empty and the Dutch were suffering shortages of everything.

Except for a generous amount of 'vodka', the party didn't include a big meal. I learned that the Red Cross parcels had not come through for the last month. Living on German food was no pleasure, Germany was experiencing shortages itself. The tide of war was not one *Blitz* victory after the other at all, anymore. *Kriegies* were hungry and stole food from each other. This could not be tolerated and records were made for later reference. All in all, morale was not at its best, which proved the old principle of, 'keep your soldiers happy by keeping their stomachs happy'.

That evening I talked to Roger and Bob Tuck.

Roger said, 'You know what, Van? Tom, Dick, and Harry are intact.'

The parcel situation had been corrected and we were getting the desirable supplies regularly again. Morale improved, activities resumed, and within a week Big X and all its departments were in full swing.

Although it was a little early in the season, I planted the seeds my mother had sent at the end of our building, in double rows under the windows. The Germans, in an effort to improve on the food situation when our parcels didn't come through, also had distributed seeds, mostly of vegetables. I prepared an area next to our room for an extensive vegetable garden. Freshly dug-up earth, most of which was sand, also would be a good place to hide some sand from the tunnels, which were under construction again.

One day when I was digging in my future garden, a large tank wagon came by and started to pump the sewage from the latrine shack next to our hut. On his way back, I asked the driver to deposit some of his watery manure on my garden, which he did. The stink was tremendous, even after I covered the entire area with almost a foot of dirt. The next few days I ploughed and shovelled my newly fertilized garden. There were considerable objections from roommates and neighbours, but there was little I could do about the shit that was already well-mixed in my future agricultural enterprise.

I had a long talk with Roger Bushell and Bob Tuck. They told me how the lack of Red Cross materials had affected all of the Big X operations. Not only had the lack of food lowered morale, but there were insufficient KLIM cans for the air tubes in the tunnels, and insufficient uniforms and blankets for Tobolski's tailors. One tunnel was found and destroyed by the ferrets, but fortunately, it was one that would have had little chance of completion anyway. The Germans already were clearing an area for additional barracks, just where the exit of the tunnel had been planned.

They told me the sad story of MacIntosh, the wild little Irish potato millionaire who had pulled the stupid trick with the soldier's book while he was in the cooler. The food shortage and the depressed atmosphere hadn't helped the Irishman at all, and his behaviour became increasingly irrational. He thought he could make himself invisible.

Mac filled his pockets with packages of candy and other edibles and announced that he could climb the fence without being seen by the guards. His roommates and several other *Kriegies* tried to bring him to his senses, but Mac went on. He walked to the warning wire and crossed it.

We shouted to him, 'Mac, come back. Come back!' And to the tower guard, *'Nicht schiesen! Bitte, nicht schiesen!'*

Mac walked to the fence and we heard the first warning shot. He simply continued to climb the barbed wire and reached the inner fence. A second warning shot cracked through the air. While his friends shouted, 'Stop, Mac, Stop!' he simply walked on and started to climb the inner fence. A third warning shot was fired but Mac didn't stop.

When he reached the top, he jumped over to the upper barbed wires of the outer fence. The machine gun rattled and Mac was shot, in full view of a hundred of his comrades. His lifeless, bloody body had folded over the barbs of the fence.

I looked at Bushell and said, 'That is bad news, perhaps not entirely unexpected. Mac is dead but Tom, Dick, and Harry are alive.'

When the flow of parcels resumed, the warehouse in the *Vorlager* couldn't hold the quantities that came in. Each of us received three parcels and many of us were given new battledress uniforms. Supplies for Big X and its departments were replenished instantly. The distillers had to work overtime to fill orders for 'Sunmaid raisin vodka'. Tobolski received blankets for his 'civilian clothing plant', and all *Kriegies* suddenly had an abundance of coffee, soap, cigarettes, chocolate, butter, and all of those luxuries the Germans had not seen for years. They were officially not allowed to accept anything, because 'The Führer took care of all the needs of his soldiers.'

Of course we gave the Germans all those goodies anyway. That we were doing well and had psychological superiority were strongly emphasized. The German military disasters on the Eastern Front were blown up and rumours were spread that mean guards would be punished after the war, while cooperative guards would be pardoned.

Big X was an escape organization and also caused as much damage to the enemy as possible in every other way. German morale sank, and we were able to use more guards than ever before. We still were fighting a war!

A familiar signal brought us to the hall, where we heard, 'This is the BBC news, as read to you by Harry Hopkins. The Russians have scored another victory at …'

An episode of thaw and rain followed the snow. The ground was wet, and under our windows the first marigolds came up.

I told Heye Schaper, 'There'll be orange flowers everywhere.'

With our pride in Holland's Royal House of Orange, we exchanged a knowing smile.

Tunnels of Freedom
Tom, Dick, and Harry

Stalag Luft III filled at an incredible rate. The British air raids at night and the American daylight raids hammered at the German home front in increasing numbers. At first, the heavy industry in the Ruhr area received the brunt of these raids, but now any place in the German Reich felt the might of the Allied bombs. The oil fields and refineries at Ploesti were attacked and, for all practical purposes, destroyed.

The German war machine could not produce enough to supply its armies and replace its heavy losses. The Reich had plundered the occupied countries to the point where they could not supply anymore. Germany had mobilized so many of its men that factories were filled with forced-labour from occupied countries. These foreigners would not perform like Germans, who worked for their Fatherland.

As a result of the enormous air offensive by the Allies, many of our planes were shot down and many prisoners of war were taken. By now there were more than two thousand American officers in our camp. With this increase of *Kriegies,* our pool of talent also increased.

Tobolski's clothing department was split into two major sections; one did the actual tailoring and another provided the materials by shaving and dying army blankets into civilian-looking fabrics.

With that many men available, security was doubled in strength so the long and boring watch times could be shortened. On two occasions a security man had fallen asleep, resulting in Rubberneck finding a radio and a pair of wire-clippers. The radio was an old one, kept only for parts, and the hardened steel wire-clippers were no great loss. But it could have been so much worse. From now on, watches were only two hours.

The big map in the library, with its red front line, was updated constantly. Every day, the Germans nervously visited the room and compared our information with their own from newspapers they brought along. The ferret Rubberneck called it wishful predicting, but officers like Pieber understood that our information was too accurate to be anything but from foreign radios. The BBC broadcast from London could not be received directly because of the German electronic jamming, but there were at least thirty shortwave stations that repeated the BBC news, in that many languages, and we were not short of linguistic talent. The news came from Stockholm, Moscow, Switzerland, and possibly from ships.

Our elusive radio boys sometimes apologized for bad reception and blamed it on Herman Goering who, with all his medals, had screened off the radio waves. The radio department was a psychological plus for the *Kriegies* and remained the most secret outfit in the camp. Not knowing anything about their operation, I told the Germans our RAF and American experts could make radios out of empty cans and salt crystals. That statement may have been somewhat optimistic, but the fact remained that we received the Allied news every day.

New talent showed up in our scrounging department and an American bombardier, probably a psychologist by profession, managed to smuggle a complete radio into the camp. I am sure the poker-faced Yankee could have converted a Catholic into a Jew. In some cases, guards offered totally useless items in exchange for cigarettes or coffee. Some of us got wristwatches for two packs of cigarettes, and sometimes we returned such items with an extra pack of cigarettes to maintain our psychological advantage.

Tobolski and his tailors were ordered to make two hundred sets of civilian clothing, in a variety of styles. We in the false-paper department were instructed to produce papers for two hundred persons. This was quite a tall order, because drawing counterfeit papers was a very slow process, so we had priorities. Fifty *Kriegies* of high-priority would be equipped with three papers each. Another fifty would get two papers, and the remaining hundred would get one travel permit each. We had enlarged our group to twenty-four artists and everybody in the entire camp was to collect German money. With more than four thousand willing bodies, it was not too difficult.

These four thousand also received Red Cross food parcels every week, which made the Sunmaid raisin supply a constant flow of raw material for the vodka-brewing chemists.

The technical department became much bigger and was divided into three sections – engineers, diggers, and dispersers. Because of the strain on our eyes, the false-paper artists would draw only about two hours a day, so I had time to do other things and tried digging. Three times I went down in 'Harry', but then told Wally Floody that digging was not my bag and asked for a transfer to sand dispersing. He smiled when I told him what I thought about the diggers. It was, no doubt, the most difficult and most dangerous work in the entire Big X organization.

Often, the only light the diggers had was an oil lamp, which burned up the precious little oxygen available. There had been tunnel collapses and one Australian digger was almost buried alive. The job also was dangerous because the entrance of the tunnel would be sealed off whenever the diggers went down, so the ferrets would not find this most secret and important part of the tunnel. They would stay down for two hours, during which they were cut off from the world above.

I suggested that these incredible heroes automatically should receive the Victoria Cross. A sense of claustrophobia was unavoidable in the small working space of these tunnels, where there was no light, no air, and a constant danger of collapse. It was because of my unsuccessful trial as a digger that I became acquainted with the general plan called 'Tom, Dick, and Harry'.

Three tunnels were to be constructed at the same time, in preparation of a mass-escape. This would do more harm to the German war effort than an occasional, individual escape. If one tunnel was found, two others would instantly be available to continue the action. Earlier tunnels had always been started from a point not too far from the fence, but that principle was abandoned, and tunnel entrances were to be constructed where they had the least chance of being discovered. This meant the tunnels would have to be much longer, but they would start in huts that were considered unlikely to be chosen for tunnel construction.

The tunnels had to be shored up all the way, not only for the safety of our diggers, but to withstand the traffic of a mass-escape. There was to be an air-conditioning system and electric light in each tunnel. The dispersing of sand was a big problem, which was assigned to Hornblower and his force of four hundred men.

Wally and Czech engineers designed and constructed the three entrances. 'Tom' started in the washroom of a barrack about three hundred feet from the fence. The floor of each washroom was made of concrete and sloped slightly to a drain in the middle, which was covered by a square grid of 18 by 18 inches. Underneath the grid, there was a box-like collecting basin from which the actual drain pipe started.

The engineering team moved the pipe to the side and carefully chiselled the bottom of the collecting basin loose from its sides. This concrete bottom became the entrance of 'Tom'. The trap could be opened by lifting the slab, and when closed, a small amount of water would be poured on top of it, making it look like a drain again. It was a masterpiece.

The entrance to 'Dick' was in the kitchen of another hut. Every building had a small room especially constructed as a community kitchen, with a stove and large sink. The floors of these kitchens were made of wood, except for concrete slabs under the stoves and sinks. Again some plumbing changes were accomplished, and the slab under the sink was chiselled free. The entire wall of the room next door was loosened so that it could be lifted six inches.

With the wall up, the slab could slide far enough into the room to make way for a very solid and well-protected tunnel entrance. A special team was assigned to open and close 'Dick', which could be done in less than three minutes. When closed, even the dust in the cracks was replaced to make the floor look like an ordinary kitchen floor, including the dirt.

'Harry's' entrance was as ingenious as the other two. It was made in an ordinary room of a hut at the side of the *Vorlager*. Any tunnel from here had to be dug all the way under the 150-foot-wide area, and then run another 150 feet in order to reach the woods outside the fences. It was a very unlikely place to start a tunnel.

Every room had a stove, standing on a square brick platform of about four by four feet. This base stood on a concrete box of sand which was, like the slabs in the kitchens and washrooms, not accessible from the space under the huts. The engineers removed the stove, including the chimney pipe, chiselled the entire brick floor under the stove loose from its base, and remounted it on wooden planks. Now they could lift the brick base and replace it within a matter of minutes. The entrance to 'Harry' was underneath.

Every time the diggers went into action, the stove was removed, the slab lifted, and the trapdoor opened to let the workers down. After this procedure the trap, the brick platform, and the burning stove were replaced. To get the diggers out, the same procedure was done in reverse. Here again, cracks between the floor and the brick slab had to be filled with dust to make the stove corner look as if it received normal use.

The special teams to open and close the secret entrances became extremely proficient in this procedure. For every digging team sent to work underground, it had to be repeated four times – first to open and let the diggers in, then to close the entrance after them, and the same for letting them come out again. All of this had to be done between the morning *appel* and the evening *appel,* when we all had to parade on the sports field to be counted. Tunnel opening and closing also could only be done when security gave the 'all clear' sign for the area.

When diggers emerged above the ground, they had a lot of sand to get rid of. In the earlier days, we simply had spread it out under the barracks. But the ferrets quickly recognized freshly dug-up sand, which told them there was digging in process. The dispersing of sand became a major problem until one genius came up with a workable plan.

The tailors made long, thin sacks which were filled with sand. With a strap around the neck, our stooges could carry two of the sausage-like sacks inside their pants. With a great-coat on, the 'sand sausages' weren't visible at all. With this cargo a prisoner could walk almost anywhere and, when the time was right, pull a string which opened the bottom of the sack to let the sand trickle out of his pants. Another stooge walking behind him would drag his feet a little, walking the new sand into the surrounding soil. We had an army of four hundred men to perform this healthy bit of exercise and we got rid of tons of sand.

It was still a slow procedure, because the filling of the narrow sacks was a tedious process which had to be done in a special underground chamber. The sacks could hold only a relatively small amount of sand, and had to be hauled out of the tunnel during the very short time that the trapdoor was open. Additional methods had to be invented.

The design of the tunnels was a masterpiece of its own. After the entrance trapdoor was made, each of the three tunnels started with a vertical shaft, two by two feet in width and lined with wooden boards. About ten feet down, another trapdoor was made. To one side of this, a room three by six feet wide and four feet high was dug out. This was a storage room for sand. Through the second trapdoor, the vertical shaft continued down another fifteen feet. The entire shaft was lined and there was a ladder running down one side.

At the bottom of the vertical shaft, three rooms were created. On the fourth side of the square, the actual horizontal part of the tunnel started. The direction had to be established exactly; this was done when the entrance was open and a crossbar was wedged in the desired direction. This was checked frequently by compass. The three rooms were workrooms – the one opposite the tunnel was for transportation equipment, a second was for filling the sacks with sand, and the third was for construction materials.

I asked Wally why the tunnels were so deep, because it seemed such a waste of energy and equipment. But there were good reasons for the great depths of the shafts. First, the trapdoor, or the false bottom ten feet down, might fool the Germans if they found the entrance and destroyed it. Access to the lower part, the real tunnel, still would be possible from another place close by. Second, the sand was packed harder at this depth and there was less chance of collapse, although the whole tunnel would be shored anyway. Third, the Germans had microphones in the ground under the barbed wire fence.

These mikes were supposed to record scratching sounds, but through bribery we learned they were placed at four-foot depths and would not register sounds at twenty-five feet. It was believed that the Germans thought we would only dig at night, not during the day, when the German personnel was present inside the camp. At night, the ferrets crawled under the barracks to see and listen, but every hut had its security men who knew the whereabouts of every ferret.

Tunnels were dark and our original lights were small oil lamps. They produced little light and used an awful lot of precious oxygen. When the tunnels grew to a length of fifty feet or more, the oxygen problem became acute and something had to be done. I tried to produce oxygen bottles by filling them with oxygen, which I could make by mixing permanganate and hydrogen peroxide tablets, stolen from the hospital. The oxygen in my bottles was good for about one deep breath, no more, and we had to abandon that approach.

First, the light was fixed. Using the endless supplies of wire from earlier days, the engineers installed electric lights in all three tunnels. Fortunately, the electricity was on day and night, perhaps the same electricity that provided light along the fence, and energy for the searchlights in the towers. Next the air problem was resolved.

Group Captain Massey issued an order that all KLIM cans had to be saved and the engineers performed one miracle after the other. An American invented a way to solder and the Czechs built an air pump from an old accordion. This was used in tunnel 'Tom'. For the other two tunnels, they made air pumps of much greater capacity. The KLIM cans were soldered together in units about three feet long, and inside the tunnel these were assembled into a pipe which ran all the way to the end, where the actual digging was in progress. One of the three rooms at the bottom of the vertical shaft became the air-conditioning room, and whenever a crew worked down below, a special crew would operate the air pump.

Now we had three major tunnels, with electric light and air-conditioning, under construction. The dispersal of sand was, in spite of the ingenious sausage-like sacks, still one of the biggest problems. It was almost certain that the Germans knew we were digging. This was confirmed by one of the ferrets, who even revealed that the hut where 'Tom' had its entrance was suspected.

After a few days, we were instructed to save our Red Cross food parcel boxes, and at an *appel* more than a thousand *Kriegies* stood in line with a cardboard box under one arm. *Hauptmann* Pieber became nervous and more guards were called in for the daily counting procedure. Six ferrets walked between the long rows of prisoners and ordered us to open the boxes.

The boxes were empty, and after the first hundred or so, Pieber stopped the inspection and asked Wings Day, 'What is this about? Why are you carrying empty boxes?'

Wings smiled and said, 'Nothing to worry about. Just English humour.'

Hauptmann Pieber looked at him and said, while shaking his head, 'Well, you have had your "English Humour". But now you'll take your boxes to the garbage bins and get rid of them!'

English humour was a sensitive point because it was always compared to German humour. The psychologists had made it well-known that we regarded German humour as being on the level of gross, dirty jokes, far below the level of the sophisticated and more civilized English jokes. Some of the ferrets and other guards laughed at the joke of the empty boxes, to show that they understood and appreciated English humour. It all helped to confuse the German mind, at least the minds of some Germans.

The next day, during the afternoon *appel,* we again appeared with Red Cross boxes under our arms.

Pieber tried to smile at the 'very funny' joke, saying, 'OK, that's enough of that. It was very funny, but no more! Anybody with a box tomorrow will get disciplinary punishment.' Then he dismissed the roll call.

We lingered a little until the Germans marched off. Then we opened our boxes, which now were filled with sand from our tunnels, and emptied them onto the sports field. Four thousand feet shuffled the sand into the soil. We had got rid of the sand of ten days' digging!

In spite of the clever tricks and methods of dispersing the sand, the Germans knew we were digging. They became nervous and our bribers found out a bonus was offered to the guard who discovered the tunnel.

For us, the problems were not any easier. We had to get rid of enormous amounts of sand. And, since the Germans knew there was tunnel activity, we didn't care too much anymore if they found the sand. But we could not let them find out where the sand came from and we could not afford to let a guard catch someone carrying sand, so the problems were still there.

Security did a remarkable job of regulating the traffic of sand-carrying stooges to places unobserved by Germans. The boxes, bags, or sacks never seemed to come from the buildings which actually housed the tunnel entrances. Even when a guard in one of the towers spotted a suspicious box or bag with his binoculars, the carrier came from the 'wrong' hut.

An almost-fatal accident occurred in 'Harry', our best and most advanced tunnel. There was a collapse and the digger couldn't get out by himself. Floody went down with three others and, with some good luck, they dragged him out alive!

Each tunnel was now about three hundred feet long and shored with bed-boards all the way, except for the working area at the very end. Here, the sand was scooped into basins and pulled all the way to the beginning of the tunnel to fill the sacks. There was very little room and the diggers had to crawl to the end and back, a procedure which often caused a little scraping or even damage to the sides of the tunnel. At the end, where there were no struts yet, the sand was too loose to hold on its own.

The shafts and tunnels had to be strong enough to withstand the traffic of a mass-escape, not just two or three diggers at a time. The solution was to run a rail and trolley wagon the entire way, pulled by a rope from sub-stations that were big enough to work without damaging the shoring planks. It was a big job, but within a week a wooden rail and a trolley car, strong enough to carry the weight of a large person, were installed. At a distance of 150 feet, they had built the first station and named it 'Piccadilly Circus'. Station No. 2 was under construction, 'Leicester Square'.

Only the first digger had to propel himself through the tunnel to the end, while lying flat on the trolley. The others were pulled through and back by long, homemade ropes. The sand and bed-boards also were transported by trolley now. The new system was a vast improvement, a time-saver, and there were no more incidents of damage to the shoring.

'Harry' became the masterpiece of tunnel construction, and Big X decided to speed up the operation by temporarily shutting down 'Tom' and 'Dick' and concentrating all our energy on 'Harry', now almost 400 feet long. The Germans were tense; they knew something big was brewing.

One of the ferrets, Freddie, walked into the hut where 'Dick' had its entrance, under the concrete slab in the kitchen. He accidentally stepped on the slab under the sink, which moved, just slightly, under his weight. At first he seemed unconcerned. But then he realized that a concrete slab should not move at all and took a better look. Quietly, he walked to one of the watchtowers and told the guard to call Glemnitz and Rubberneck. Almost immediately, they arrived with twelve other guards and everybody was ordered out of the barrack. The tunnel 'Dick' was discovered.

Hundreds of *Kriegies* gathered around the building but were kept at a distance. A fire truck arrived, and after they exploded two hand grenades in the vertical shaft, they filled the hole with water. Rubberneck and his cohorts were jubilant, but we stood there sadly, looking at their success. Roger stood at a distance with a grim expression on his face. He had a scar over his right eye which made him look sinister and threatening when he was angry.

An American captain became almost hysterical and started to cry. With two buddies he formed a little group in front of Glemnitz, and they broke into an emotional session of grief and desperation.

'Oh, my God,' they blubbered. 'All that work! Our masterpiece, our chance to escape this life. All gone, everything destroyed!'

I found this show of emotion rather disgusting. After all, the Germans had found things before. Then I learned they were actors! Even now, in a time of disaster, Roger's organized mind was thinking. We had two other tunnels, one of which was near completion. The Germans had been nervous and determined to find the big 'thing' we were preparing and they had found it. Let them think they had discovered and destroyed our great 'thing' – emphasize their victory by reacting to our loss, with tears, masterly done by three American actors. Again our Big X, Roger Bushell, was in control.

Indeed, the tense atmosphere among the Germans was gone. They smiled and felt sympathy for our efforts. They praised our imagination and capabilities. They quickly and proudly added that it was hard to beat German efficiency. The ferrets and guards were relaxed now that they had solved their problem. We had suffered a loss, but Big X went on with more energy and determination than ever.

We had 'Tom' and 'Harry' left, but 'Tom' was not quite as far advanced as 'Harry'. On top of that, the area where 'Tom' should have had its exit now was cleared for the building of another compound (instead of at the edge of the woods). Furthermore, now that the Germans thought all digging had ceased, what would be their reaction if they found new sand? Roger decided that 'Harry' would be the one to complete, and that 'Tom' would be used for the sand that had to come out of Harry. We still needed to open and close two trap doors twice daily; but that was considered less risky than the discovery of fresh sand.

Two days from now it would be New Year's Eve, and my very long year of 1943 would be a thing of the past. We had planned a big party with lots of booze and festivities. I made preparations for the biggest banquet any *Kriegie* had ever seen, and several rooms were converted into bars, complete with decorations and dim lights. Kirby-Green, an artist and important Big X worker, had painted life-size posters of very naked girls. These attracted not only many of us, but also a number of guards.

Group Captain Massey had made a deal with the commandant to give us and the German guards more freedom that night, in return for a promise that we would not make any efforts to escape. Roger Bushell was in full agreement with this idea and gave strict orders to all potential escapees to honour the gentleman's agreement. The fraternization with the Germans would even deepen their belief that we had, at least temporarily, given up the idea of tunnelling. The ferrets and guards, now more at ease, would no doubt be a little less keen and anxious to find tunnel entrances.

New Year's Eve started much too early and some of my guests for the 'banquet supreme' could not attend. They were sick after too many visits to the various bars in every hut. Some guards lingered after the evening *appel* and, in many places, were invited to the banquet, but the ferrets did not participate. The dinner, which I had prepared, had an orange overtone to honour our loyalty to the Dutch Royal House of Orange.

The menu was elaborately drawn on orange cards, the tomato soup was orange in colour, and small bread sticks were tied together with an orange ribbon. There were carrots, a thick orange-coloured sauce with mushrooms over Wiener sausages, and orange Jello with a vanilla sauce for dessert. And, much to the annoyance of all others present, we sang Dutch patriotic songs. The Poles and Czechs also sang their songs, which nobody could understand, but the 'Roll Me Overs' and 'Waltzing Matildas' took over, not to mention the wishful varieties of 'This Is Number One'.

It wasn't long after dinner that we heard an excellent duet of 'Lili Marlene' outside our window. When I looked to see who had done us the honour, I saw that Eelco Ferwerda, one of our Dutch roommates, and a guard had performed the lovely serenade. Both were beyond the stage of normal comprehension.

An American had become an instantly ordained minister and while preaching the Gospel he crossed the warning wire and started to climb the fence under one of the watchtowers. When Heye Schaper and I saw him, the memory of Mac came back to our minds and we tried to find Colonel Clark. When we came back to the scene, he was standing in the watchtower singing 'Holy Night' with the guard, who had just as much fun as the would-be priest. The 'priest' climbed down the ladder and calmly walked to the main gate on the outside of the fence, where he asked permission to enter.

The guards at the gate were flabbergasted and didn't quite know what to do. Also, our security reported the incident instantly to Bushell, Group Captain Massey and Wings Day. Colonel Clark, who had seen the whole incident, ran to the gate and talked calmly to the guards, who asked him if he had come to bring them cigarettes and *'Ein glückliches neues Jahr'*.

They opened the gate to let him through, but the colonel ordered, 'Hey John. Come here, and that's an order!'

Our instant-priest entered the camp. Quickly, Clark said, *'Danke schön. Danke, danke'*, grabbed the young captain by the arm, and disappeared in the direction of the barracks. The guards closed the gate and continued their songs. They had been told there would be no escapes from the North Compound and they were not to shoot. Not only were the *Kriegies* of Stalag Luft III filled with booze on that famous night – 31 December 1943; the German guards were just as drunk as all of us. Nobody escaped. No word of honour was broken.

Although the tense feelings of the Germans relaxed somewhat, they knew the Big X organization was intact and that it would be silly to assume there would be no further, underground activities. They thought of other methods to break up our preparations before we could execute our plans. The Germans did this very effectively by splitting up our workforce.

Without warning, it was announced that American prisoners would be transferred to the new South Compound. This measure did far more harm to our Big X organization than they would ever know. Almost half of the *Kriegies* in the North Compound now were Americans, consequently half of our best talent was American. Tobolski's shop, the false-paper forgers, the diggers, the stooges, the engineers, and the carpenters all lost half of their best workers. It was a true disaster. We were in the middle of producing clothes and false papers for two hundred escapees. It was not the kind of work for which one could recruit new helpers in a short time. It was just a matter of, 'work harder and make the best of it'.

Suddenly the Americans were gone. We could talk to them, but between their compound and ours was the regular, double fence, and on both sides was a warning wire. The only thing we could do for them was give them the daily news until they had their own radio service working.

With renewed energy, Bushell repaired his forces and the work went on. Tunnel 'Harry' was the only one to make progress now and the sand was carefully packed into tunnel 'Tom'. According to calculations, we had another sixty feet to go to reach the edge of the forest undergrowth. The stations 'Piccadilly Circus' and 'Leicester Square' were fully operational; the lights, the trolley, and the air-conditioning worked fine but progress was slow. We didn't want to risk dispersing sand in the compound, and putting it in 'Tom' was as much trouble as getting it out of 'Harry'.

We had a spell of freezing weather and snow which made it very unpleasant for our security men. Sitting on a chair in freezing weather, with a towel as a signal, was not only a most uncomfortable position, it almost looked suspicious. Other signals were created and many watches had to be done through the windows of the barracks. In spite of the difficult circumstances, digging and construction went on, although progress was relatively slow. The tunnel was now well over four hundred feet long, leaving only sixty feet to go to reach the edge of the woods. This would take less than a month to complete at the rate we were going.

Due to the unexpected loss of the American workers, all departments automatically slowed down in their production. The original date for the escape, 10 March, had to be postponed to 20 March. But even the ten extra days hardly gave the clothing department and the false-paper department sufficient time to supply the desired equipment for two hundred escapees.

Roger and a committee of senior officers made a priority list of those who wanted to escape. Those who had contributed most to the Big X organization, and who had a much better chance to succeed, had a higher place on the list than others. Those with linguistic abilities obviously had better chances while travelling. Czechs and Poles were closest to their home countries, where they could expect help. I was placed number eighteen on the list because of my contributions to Big X, and also because of my knowledge of Dutch, German, and French. I could travel as a Dutch forced-labourer without creating suspicion due to the language.

It was impossible to provide perfect papers, money, and clothes for everybody, so the first fifty on the list were better equipped than the next hundred. For the last fifty, we had only one paper, twenty German marks, and one piece of clothing. The false papers were ready except for the date. This was not yet filled in, in case of another change in the date of the escape.

On 19 March, the engineers decided that the end of the tunnel was just under the undergrowth of the woods, about fifty feet beyond the outer fence. There was some controversy about the length – not so much about the actual length of the tunnel itself, because that could be measured, but about the length of tunnel needed to reach the woods. There was only one day to go and the tunnel was not quite ready. At the end, we needed an extra room to stow sand that would come from the vertical shaft at the exit. We needed a light trap, and there had to be more room at the end to operate the trolley and the traffic of escapees. The dates had to be filled in on all those false papers. There wasn't enough time!

The weather wasn't the best. It was a clear night, but a bit of moonlight came up too early to make it an ideal, black night. Roger Bushell, Group Captain Massey, and Wings Day had another meeting and decided to postpone until 24 March.

The four days' additional time were exactly what we needed in the paper department, the clothing department, and, not the least, the engineering department. We turned out another twelve typed papers and dated all others for 24 March. Tobolski had something for everybody. For me he had a small suitcase, in addition to a civilian suit and raincoat. Wally and his crew managed to finish the end station, putting in a large side room for sand from the yet-to-be-dug vertical shaft. A light trap was made of two blankets, which hung like curtains just in front the shaft. This way, last-minute preparations before ascending from the tunnel could be made in bright light.

The standard barracks in Stalag Luft III were built to house a hundred prisoners each. But on the night of the 24th, we would have two hundred *Kriegies* in hut No. 104 and almost none of them would be the regular occupants of that building. For this problem Big X had organized a group of sixteen marshals, all *Kriegies* who would not participate in the escape, to conduct the flow of traffic in and out of hut No. 104. The move was well-explained and would start immediately after the evening *appel*.

On the night of the 23rd, clouds obscured the last shimmer of moonlight and a gentle drizzle melted the last bit of snow. Conditions looked good and we were well prepared.

24 March 1944. This was our big day and all we had to do was wait until evening *appel*, after which the giant machine would roll into action, exactly as planned. At the morning *appel*, *Hauptmann* Pieber informed all *Kriegies* of hut No. 104 to stay out of the building until the ferrets had completed a search. Such searches were routine – but today? Hut No. 104?

Bob Tuck, standing next to me, said, 'Shit!'

I said, 'Jesus, what's going on?'

But we tried to act normal. Roger ordered all inhabitants of hut No. 104 to walk around the perimeter of the compound or play a game on the sports field; under no circumstances were they to linger around the building. It was to be a routine search and nobody should show concern.

Four ferrets searched the hut and eight guards were stationed outside to prevent anyone from going in, but nothing happened. After an hour and a half, the ferrets came out with a Red Cross box and opened it outside the door. They had found the gasoline burner which originally had been meant for the hot air balloon and later was used for soldering, but nothing else.

Roger sat in his chair, pale and tired. He felt relieved about the false alarm of the search, of course, but apparently there was more bothering him. Another survey and more calculations had made it seem almost certain that the tunnel might be a little too short. This was because there was probably a slight error in the direction, which made the needed length longer. When I came to his room he explained his worries. For a short time, he, Bob Tuck, and I just sat there, not knowing what to say. This silence didn't help things either.

I said, 'I am going to get a drink for you guys. This is no time to get depressed.'

When I came back, with three glasses of my best 'vermouth', Roger said, 'Good old Van. You never show fear, do you?'

'That's right, Roger,' I replied. 'It wouldn't help anyway.'

The stage play *Pygmalion* had been scheduled for next week and Roger had a part in it. It had been organized that way to clear him from suspicion, on the basis that people rehearsing for a play would not have time to prepare escapes.

It was the first time I saw Roger show a touch of nervousness – not fear, but nervousness about the enormous responsibility he felt as head of the more-than-dangerous operation we were about to carry out.

'You know, Van. We must realize that most of our escapees have a bloody poor chance of making it,' he said. And, staring straight ahead, 'Some may not make it at all.'

'I know that. Frankly, I think we all know that. But isn't it the same as when you flew your Spitfire for the first time in the Battle of Britain?'

'You're right,' Roger said. 'However, I'm going to Wings Day and Group Captain Massey. We'll have a decision by noon.'

'Great,' I said. 'It'll make you and all of us feel better. But I think I know Wings Day well enough that I can predict his recommendation.'

'And what will that be?' he asked.

'As if you don't know yourself!'

Roger got up and left the room with a devilish smile on his face. He walked straight to Massey's room. I was not present at the meeting that followed but I knew what they were talking about. Massey and Day agreed that most escapees would have very little chance of making it to a neutral country, and even less of a chance of reaching England. Two or three pilots in the huge organization of the Allied air forces would hardly make any difference at all, but a mass-escape from Stalag Luft III would be an event of major importance. Many German troops would have to be deployed to cope with the situation; that was important.

When Roger came back from his meeting I saw the smile on his face, a sinister smile because his right eye stared under the scar over the brow.

'Tonight,' he said, 'we go!'

The Great Escape

Friday, 24 March 1944. After the evening *appel,* the marshals held their own roll call. Each of them got his group of escapees together and once again rehearsed the procedures for that night. Clothing, papers, money, and travel plans were checked. All potential escapees had to eat a good evening meal before the move to hut No. 104 began. The regulars of 104 had made arrangements to sleep in the now-vacant beds of the escapees.

I already had put my rattan suitcase through a window of hut No. 104, and at about 6:00 p.m. my marshal signalled me to walk to the hut and enter it from the south side. Gradually the barracks filled with two hundred *Kriegies* – all with a variety of civilian clothes, hats, suitcases, gloves, eye glasses, and whatever disguises one could imagine. Roger had a trench coat, a felt hat, and a briefcase under his arm. There was little talk, no joking, and practically no walking around. Half of us pretended to sleep in the bunks. But for the others, of course, there were no bunks, so they just sat around the tables. It was now a matter of waiting until 10:00 p.m.

The team for 'Harry's' entryway opened the trapdoor under the stove and Roger went down with three diggers. The vertical shaft at the exit was finished all the way up to the roots of smaller plants, probably not more than two or three feet from the surface. On one side, a ladder was installed, except for the last two rungs. Everything from entrance to exit was ready to go.

At 9:00 p.m. the guards came by, banging on the shutters as a signal to close them while shouting, *'Licht aus'*, and we switched off the lights as we did every night. Then it was quiet, until the door opened and a German guard with a flashlight in his hand entered the room. For a moment we stiffened but when he started to whisper, we recognized Tobolski, in a perfect *Feldwebel's* uniform.

At 10:00, nothing happened, and at 10:30 p.m., still nothing seemed to move. Soon word came that there were problems down below. The fellows in the tunnel asked for a rope at least forty feet long. What for, we didn't know. The stream of escapees was to have begun at 10:00. It was now almost 11:00 and no one had gone through yet.

Soon we knew what it was all about. When they had dug the last part of the exit shaft, a stream of fresh air had blown through the tunnel and we knew we had an opening outside the fence. It was a glorious moment! But when our digger, Johnnie Marshall, carefully put his head through the hole, he noticed he was twenty feet short of the edge of the woods. As fast as he could, he let himself down, crawled through the blankets that sealed off the light in the tunnel and reported his observation to Roger.

'Sir,' he stammered, 'the tunnel is too short. It's twenty feet short of the woods. Somebody goofed!'

'What the hell are you talking about?' Roger demanded, and then he realized his earlier suspicion was true.

The tunnel exit opening was outside the camp, but not quite in the projected place. Due to a slight error in direction and a miscalculation, the opening was between the barbed wire fence and the edge of the woods – not in the woods, as planned.

Roger and his crew were near panic, but this was not a time for indecision or desperation. Something had to be done now and without hesitation. After a few minutes Marshall came up with an idea.

Roger looked the two diggers straight in the eye, said, 'We go!' and then, 'Get forty feet of rope!'

The order for forty feet of rope echoed to the tunnel entrance and up to the waiting people in hut No. 104. Somehow, forty feet of rope was sent down and transported all the way via 'Piccadilly Circus' and 'Leicester Square' to the end station, where quick action was taken. One end of the rope was attached to the uppermost part of the ladder. The first man out had to crawl to the shrubs in the woods and act as a controller. Three jerks on the rope was the signal for the next man to crawl out, follow the rope and disappear in the forest. Every fifth man would be controller for the next four. Finally, they had the rope ready.

Roger said, 'Warn everyone of the new procedure.'

Bull, the second digger who had helped Marshall, was the first one to get out and establish the lead to the brush. Carefully, he popped his head up and saw a guard walking to a nearby watchtower. At the 'Goonbox' (watchtower) he tramped his feet, said something to the sentry fifteen feet above him, again stamped his cold feet and walked back. The lights along the fence were bright and both men apparently had their eyes trained toward the camp, not on the woods behind them.

Bull gave three tugs on the rope and saw Marshall coming out of the hole. Holding the rope in one hand, he silently but quickly walked to the bushes, tapped Bull on the shoulder as a farewell sign and disappeared in the dark. Bushell was number three, Tobolski and Tim Walenn followed. The guard came back in the same manner as he had before, and now our signal man could see another guard approaching from the other side. There was a delay before he could give the 'go' signal for the next man. But despite the slow pace they got out, one after the other.

As number eighteen on the list, I climbed down the shaft in hut No. 104, with my rattan suitcase thrown after me. At the bottom, Valenta pulled the trolley back, placed himself on his belly on the little cart and gave two tugs as a signal to the man in 'Piccadilly Circus' to pull. Valenta slid into the seemingly endless square hole of space, only two feet wide and two feet high. When he arrived at 'Piccadilly', I felt the tug on the rope as the signal that I should pull the trolley back.

Now it was my turn to board the homemade subway. With the suitcase in front of me, I crawled onto the trolley, gave two tugs on the rope and off I went. But not very far. After not more than twenty feet, I got stuck. My clothing, overcoat and suitcase were too bulky to squeeze through the narrow tunnel. I had not reckoned with the height of the trolley itself. Some of the boards of the tunnel lining had moved just a little, so I told my puller at 'Piccadilly' to stop. We could not take a chance of damage, or perhaps a collapse, at this early stage of the escape. I shifted my suitcase and held it in front of me, inspected the boards of the shoring, and signalled the puller to proceed. Without further incident, I arrived at 'Piccadilly Circus'.

There was a bright light at the station where I crawled into the small side room, while number seventeen boarded the trolley to 'Leicester Square'. With one hand, I let the rope of the first cart go while it was pulled back. With the other hand, I paid out the rope of trolley number two, on its way to 'Leicester Square'.

The procedure was too slow but we couldn't discuss it or wait for orders from Roger; he was already out. So we took it upon ourselves to have two men in 'Piccadilly Circus' and 'Leicester Square', one for pulling the next escapee and one for pulling the empty cart back.

I arrived at 'Leicester Square' to change for the next stretch. My God, that tunnel was long! And thank heaven for the electric light! Fortunately, the air-conditioning wasn't necessary any more. A cold stream of fresh air had flowed through 'Harry' ever since they opened the exit.

At the end, I passed through the double curtains to enter the pitch-dark room under the opening.

Somebody grabbed my hand and said, 'Here, put your hand on the ladder. At the top, you'll find the signal rope on your left. Wait till you feel the signal and follow the rope until you are in the woods. Then go. Good luck!'

'Thanks, and good luck to you,' I whispered to whoever it was twenty-five feet below the hole of freedom.

Quickly, I climbed up to the surface and immediately found the rope, which was attached to the top rung of the ladder. I felt no signal, so it was not safe yet. Then I felt the three distinct tugs and slowly popped my head up and looked in the direction of the camp. There I saw the barbed wire fence brightly lit by the lights along the periphery. The nearest 'Goonbox' was at least two hundred feet away; but, indeed, I was twenty feet from the edge of the woods.

The ground was covered with heather and there still was a little snow left. A black path already was made, by the footsteps of those who had preceded me. Again I felt the tugs on the rope, as if saying, 'Come on, Van, come on!' But, dammit, I saw the silhouette of a German guard standing exactly between me and the fence, his feet apart, looking straight at me.

He just stood there and never said a word. Then I noticed the thin stream of urine and I realized that he was standing with his back toward me … pissing.

Again the three tugs – as if to say, 'Hurry, hurry!' – but then I saw the German move and decided to let him go a little farther before I surfaced. When he was far enough, I climbed out and silently followed the rope to the woods. There I found Scruffy, one of our boys controlling the traffic of the next five escapees. Again, a touch on the shoulder and a whispered 'good luck', and I disappeared into the woods. My direction – the railway station.

Once in the protection of the forest I followed a path. But soon the air raid sirens started howling and I slowed my pace, because one was supposed to go immediately to shelters. I decided to wait it out in the dark woods.

'*Halt! Wer sind Sie? Wohin gehen Sie?* [Stop! Who are you? Where are you going?]'

The voice came from perhaps fifteen feet behind me and made me freeze in my tracks. Slowly, I turned around and saw a German soldier with a rifle pointing at me.

'*Ah, guten Abend*,' I said. 'I am a foreign worker and I am on my way to the railway station. But, you know, the air raid sirens – we are supposed to be in a shelter but I can't find one. So I thought I'd stay here until the "all clear".'

'*Ach, Unsinn!* [Oh, nonsense!]' the German said. 'As long as you are with me, no trouble. This path will take you to the station. Go to the shelter there.'

'*Danke, danke schön*,' I said, '*Wiedersehen*.'

'*Ja, ja. Auf Wiedersehen*,' the man said.

I swiftly followed the path in the dark forest. That was a close one!

About half a mile farther on, I saw the large building of the Sagan railway station. It was very dark and only a few small blue lights showed the way to the entrance. I walked into the enormous hall where hundreds of people were standing, talking, and waiting, because trains were stopped for the duration of the air raid. I liked the mass of people and the dim light. It would only make it easier to be part of the regular crowd one always finds at railway stations.

The ticket windows were lit with blue lights, and showing my travel permit I bought a ticket to Breslau. My travel permit had worked. It was one of my best forgeries, but I realized it was only inspected by a girl at the ticket window and in very dim, blue light. Breslau was on the Polish border and East of Sagan, the opposite direction of where I had planned to go. It was only half an hour by train, but I thought it unwise to buy a ticket straight from Sagan to a town in Holland.

If I were the only traveller to buy a ticket to Holland that day, and if there was one Dutch prisoner missing from the camp in Sagan, the Germans would draw conclusions. Going in the wrong direction first and then buying a ticket at a much larger railway station would be far more difficult to trace.

I stood among the mass of people waiting for the trains to start running again. There were many foreigners, speaking many languages, and German soldiers everywhere. I saw Kirby-Green talking to one of our South African *Kriegies* in Spanish. I saw several other prison colleagues standing in the big hall, just minding their own business. I am sure they recognized me, too, but we ignored each other as if we were total strangers.

A young woman came to me and said, 'Hello, where are you going?'

I thought it was a good camouflage to be talking to a girl who, no doubt, had her 'territory' at the railway station to earn a little extra income. I asked her name and where she lived. She lived right across from the station, which convinced me even more of her professional presence.

Innocently I asked her what she did for a living and she answered, 'Excuse me a moment please.' Then she called the military railway police and said, 'Check those two over there please. They look suspicious to me.'

'*Jawohl*,' answered the soldier, and walked straight to my two Spanish-speaking friends. My heart rate doubled and I almost choked.

Then she turned to me again, and continued, 'You see, I work in a very large prisoner of war camp not far from here. I work in the censor department because I know English, and I would recognize many of those prisoners. Most of them are English or American. We take turns helping the military police here at the station in case prisoners try to escape.'

'Oh, how interesting,' I said, suddenly realizing I was not talking to a 'lady of the night' but to a camp official. 'However,' (I tried to continue in an undisturbed tone) 'I am not a military man. I work for the Siemens Bau Union as a draughtsman. But after the war I'll be an artist on my own.'

'*Ach so, ach so. Und –*'

The two policemen came back, and interrupted with '*Spanischer Arbeiter, Fräulein. Alles in ordnung.* [Spanish workers, Ma'am. Everything in order.]'

My heart stood still. And when I began to apologize for the wrong impression I had had, the 'all clear' sirens sounded and a voice over a loudspeaker said, 'All passengers to Breslau, platform five. Breslau, platform five.'

It was an enormous advantage to know German. I understood immediately what was said, I did not have to ask.

So, quickly, I said, 'Oh, that's my train. *Auf Wiedersehen, auf Wiedersehen.*'

Without delay, I mixed with the horde of people moving to platform five and took a place in the most crowded train car I could find. There were more instructions from the loudspeakers, doors slammed, and the train moved.

I could hardly believe it. I had got out of the goddamn camp and here I was, standing in the corridor of a train car, on my way to Breslau. The train was so overcrowded, checking of tickets or papers was totally impossible, much to my delight.

The train moved fast in the dark night, but when I looked out of the window I saw flashes on the horizon to the northwest. Could that be Berlin? Would they be bombing Berlin?

Breslau is a large city with a huge railway station. The only way to travel any distance in those days was by rail, because travel by car was not permitted, due to the serious fuel shortage. Consequently, the railway stations were crowded day and night. This was just right for my purposes, the more people the better.

There had been more delays in this part of Germany also, as I learned at the ticket window where I bought a ticket straight to Alkmaar in Holland. I had to wait two hours for the train to Dresden. There I would have to change to a connection to Hanover, and then to Oldendaal, Holland. I didn't like the two hours in Breslau. It was now almost 3:00 a.m. and it was possible the tunnel had been discovered. This would mean a general alarm, and Breslau was not quite far enough from Sagan.

However, nothing happened. The signs and loudspeakers gave clear instructions about the delays and re-routing of trains. And I understood, I did not have to ask; I could read the signs. I even got a stale glass of beer, without saying anything but, *'Wieviel?'* Although there was no air raid in progress at Breslau the station was dark, the waiting rooms were dark, and the only illumination – at necessary places – came from those tiny blue lights.

Platform eleven. A steam locomotive thundered and hissed in. Brakes screeched, doors opened, and seemingly thousands of people filled the platform. Confused movements – suitcases, women, children, soldiers – all talking, shouting, 'Hurry up! Hurry!'

I got a seat this time, but even in the train compartments people were standing and sitting on the floor. By God, it was almost as bad as our train trip from Dulag to Stalag. But this time I liked it. Yes, it was just right; the more people the better! Again, there were too many travellers to check tickets, just too many in the compartments and in the corridors. One couldn't walk through. The air became thick and the stink of human bodies became worse by the minute. But I liked it, I liked it!

From Breslau to Dresden took five hours, with only two stops in other towns and one stop for an air raid. But we didn't have to leave the train; they just switched out all the lights. I held my suitcase firmly between my knees and my right hand clenched my money and the vitally important papers in my pocket. The train moved again, the blue lights were turned on, and as I listened to the click-click of the wheels on the track I saw the first shimmer of dawn appear in the sky. Passengers were tired. They sat on the floor and some of them must have eaten salami. The smell of garlic and dirty bodies was awful. But when somebody tried to open a window, a stream of protests forced the man to push it shut again.

The immense railway station in Dresden was almost as crowded as that at Breslau, but it was now daylight and I would have to wait five hours for my connection to Hanover. Many of the European stations have small movie theatres which show news, cartoons, and short documentaries continuously, especially for waiting travellers. I had no trouble finding one. For one Deutschmark, I spent two and a half hours in the dark theatre where nobody could see me. In the huge waiting room I bought a glass of beer, like most other waiting travellers did, and after studying the others a little more I also ordered bread and sausage. It was very cheap but it filled my stomach and, more importantly, I did what everyone else did.

I heard trains roll in. Whistles, hissing, and the command-like instructions issued from the loudspeakers and thousands of people moved from platform to platform.

'*Hanover, Oldenzaal, Bahnsteig fünf,*' yelled the loudspeaker.

I quietly walked to platform five, where a big steam locomotive was being readied to pull a long string of passenger cars. Immediately behind the coal tender, an open freight car with a 20-mm anti-aircraft gun on a tripod reminded me of our briefings. Locomotives are preferred ground targets at all times. The last car also was open and equipped with a 20-mm. I got a seat and put my suitcase on the rack above me. A whistle, and we were moving.

There were six civilians, like me, and two soldiers in the compartment. After an hour, a military conductor came in with a Gestapo agent in a black leather overcoat. We had to show our train tickets but nothing else, and since they were legitimate there were no further questions. The two soldiers, however, were checked far more thoroughly – their passes, soldier's books, tickets, and wallets. I didn't have too much fear because my ticket was real, my travel permit had allowed me to buy the ticket. But in my suitcase I had a package of real coffee beans. Coffee was worth its weight in gold and I carried it with me as a bribing or bargaining tool. If asked how I got it, my answer would be that I had bought it on the black market as a gift for my poor family in Holland.

In Hanover we stopped for an hour, but it was the same train that continued to the Dutch border. It was a matter of common sense that there would be a check at the border. The town of Oldenzaal is in Holland, so I couldn't get off the train and try to cross the border at night on foot. I would have to go through the checkpoint. Not knowing what kind of inspection it would be, I did not want to have to explain how I got the coffee.

So I went to the toilet to see if there might be a hiding place for my valuable package. There was, and even if someone might find it, the loss of a little coffee wasn't worth the risk of suspicion. I hid the small brown paper package in a roll of newspaper, which was there instead of toilet paper. The toilet could not be used at a station; hopefully nobody would go in there.

At 6:00 a.m., the train slowed and rolled into the border town of Oldenzaal. A grey, overcast sky allowed little daylight onto the concrete platform where the train came to a stop.

'*Jederman aussteigen. Aussteigen, bitte!* [Everyone out, please!]' the conductor repeated when he walked along the row of cars. There was nothing else to do but get out like all the others.

On the same platform, they had a table and two small barricades. So all passengers had to walk through this gate, where two soldiers and a black-leather-coated Gestapo agent began checking the tickets and papers of all travellers. The train moved on about fifty yards and then stopped. A little concerned about what I would do if they found my travel permit not in order, I walked with the others. At the gate, I showed my train ticket and the forged pass.

The Gestapo agent looked at the yellow paper, turned it over and looked at the 'stamp' on the back, and then asked, '*Wohin* [Where to]?'

In heavy Dutch drawl, I said, 'Alkmaar.'

The man looked at my ticket, which said Alkmaar, turned my travel pass over and initialled the stamp on the back – the only real thing on the entire paper – and said, '*Weiter!*' He didn't have me open my suitcase.

I said, '*Bedankt* [Dutch for thanks]', and walked to the same car I had come from. The package of coffee was still there and quickly I put it back in my rattan suitcase.

The same people came back to the compartment. Nobody said anything and after an hour or so, I heard a Dutch conductor shout, '*Instappen, instappuh* [All aboard].' The train started moving. '*Godverdorie*' – I was in Holland.

Alkmaar is a town in northwestern Holland, the destination of my train trip. At least, that was what the ticket said. It was entirely possible that a smart ferret or Gestapo agent had figured out which tickets to

Holland were bought on 24 March at Sagan or some place near Sagan, such as Breslau. Then it would be quite thinkable that the Gestapo simply would wait for me at the station in Alkmaar. Therefore, I decided to get off this train before it reached its final destination, somewhere nobody could possibly know. We stopped in Utrecht. I got off, no Gestapo.

Utrecht, of course, is the city of my alma mater, and I knew many people there. The difficulty now was where to go; whom could I trust and whom should I put in jeopardy?

Harbouring political enemies or Allied soldiers was a very dangerous business. If caught, deportation to a concentration camp was certain. My own parents had been kicked out of their house in The Hague and now lived with my cousin in Hattum. It certainly was not a good place to go. More than likely, the Gestapo had the house under surveillance. I could not contact my own family or even old school friends; the Gestapo knew, of course, that I was on the loose and very probably somewhere in Holland.

There were two persons I trusted without any reservation. Both were professors at the university. Professor Koningsberg, a biologist who lived in a large house next to the botanical gardens, was my first choice. Professor Jongbloed of the physiology department, who was an old Soesterberg pilot himself, also would be safe to contact. I walked from the station to the Koningsberg house and rang the doorbell.

Their daughter opened the door and, as if she recognized me, immediately said, 'Come in quick.' When I mentioned my name she called her dad and said, 'I knew who you were right away. A friend of mine in nursing school has a picture of you in her room.'

Both the professor and his wife came to the hall and welcomed me with outstretched hands. Mrs Koningsberg said, 'You must be hungry. Let's first have something to eat and then we'll see what should be done. Do you like bananas?'

'Bananas?' I hadn't seen a banana for years, but then I realized that the big hothouses of the botanical department grew many tropical plants. I smiled and was a little overcome by so much warmth and trust at this reception, which all of us knew to be a life-threatening situation.

We talked about the war, while Mrs Koningsberg produced the most marvellous meal I had had in a very long time, including the bananas, which she fried Indonesian-style. The Koningsberg family also had ties with the Dutch East Indies and had known my grandfather in Jakarta.

The professor made a telephone call, and after an hour or so Professor Jongbloed came to the house and gave me the same welcome as the others. It was like a reunion of old friends, but all of us were very much aware of what was at stake.

We talked for several hours about my experiences in the camp, but what made a bigger impression on me was the deteriorating situation in occupied Holland. There were shortages of food, clothing, and almost all necessities for ordinary living. Transportation was all but impossible. There was no gasoline, and no fuel for heating or cooking. People burned their furniture to have at least one warm room. Bicycles were the only means of travel, other than just walking, but bicycle tyres were not available anymore.

The black market often became the only source for these essential items. The Germans, who in 1940 had tried to sympathize with the Dutch, now were vicious enemies. They knew they would never win the Dutch to their side and that the Dutch who did collaborate with them were nothing more than traitors, like the Quislings of Norway.

That afternoon I took a tub bath, with warm water and soap and a huge towel – all luxuries I had done without for a long time. I had dinner with the professor's family and spent the night at their house. The true friendliness and trust expressed during my short time with this family was so overwhelming, I felt like a lost son returning to his family.

The next morning I walked to Professor Jongbloed's house at a precisely arranged time. The very moment I reached the front door of his city block house, it opened and Mrs Jongbloed urged me to enter quickly. She said their house might not be absolutely safe, as her husband was too well known in university circles as being anti-German.

The professor came from the room in the back, and with a smile he said, 'I must apologize for this strange procedure. But, believe me, we are not safe at all. Just follow me to our backyard.'

We walked through a small garden to a wooden fence, where he had placed a chair. With a gesture of 'follow me', he jumped onto the chair and over the fence. I did the same. We walked through the backyard of the house behind his, where another person beckoned to us to come in.

Now I understood this strange system of going to a certain place; it would have been impossible to follow me and a search of the house would have been useless.

The house which I entered from the back, I left through the front. Professor Jongbloed instructed me to walk to the streetcar stop on that same street and take the tram all the way to the end, in Amersfoort, where I would see a policeman waiting for me.

I now was in the hands of the Dutch underground. I began to realize that every move I made was planned and that I was in a situation which I didn't like. But there was little I could do about it, so I stepped into the tram exactly as instructed. After an hour, we reached the terminal. I saw no policeman, but another man also stepped out of the car and approached me.

'Hendrik Beeldman?' he asked.

Hendrik Beeldman was the name on my false travel permit. Nobody knew this except the two professors, to whom I had shown my masterpiece of forgery, and nobody else knew I would arrive in Amersfoort at that hour. I felt reasonably assured he was my man. Together we walked to his house.

Officer Ottens was a policeman, who lived with his wife and seven children in a small single house. In the attic, under the steep roof, they made a guest room, with a large double bed and a washbasin in one corner. It was to be my room during the time I would be their guest. I wasn't the first guest this family had in its house. Later I learned that more than fifty Allied air crew had passed through this haven.

For the children, I was 'Uncle Bob'. But when they had English airmen in the house they were 'Frisian relatives' and could only speak Frisian. One night, I had to share the bed with a French spy. He could not speak Dutch or German and what he was doing in Holland has remained a secret to me. What he could not keep secret were his homosexual feelings while sleeping in the same double bed with me. My response was rapid and clear, and he retreated to his side of the bed with a bloody nose and a punch in the ribs.

Officer Ottens was a 100 per cent Dutchman who played an important role in the underground resistance movement. On the surface, he was the policeman who did his job, even though all police forces were subject to German orders. His job became a perfect disguise for the real work he did.

It was unsafe and undesirable to contact my family, which created a problem. I was a total stranger to the underground workers with whom I became acquainted through Officer Ottens, and some of them didn't believe my story. I couldn't blame them because my experiences were, indeed, somewhat bizarre.

A Dutch medical student who happened to become a fighter pilot, who then escaped to England, became a Spitfire pilot in the RAF, was shot down over France, made a prisoner of war and was now escaping through Holland? No, that smelled fishy; it couldn't be. Let's be a little careful with this character. The albeit-justified suspicion, however, didn't help me at all. They hesitated in providing me with any help.

They finally gave me an ID card, but it turned out to be of such an obsolete type it was useless. I was given an address in Brussels which I knew was false. It was the address on the Avenue de Waterloo where three of my friends in Stalag Luft III were caught. It was a Gestapo trap but probably not yet known to the Dutch-Paris Line. No matter how I tried to explain, they didn't believe me.

After almost three weeks in the Ottens' home, with nothing accomplished, I announced that I would go my own way. But just then they gave me the address of a farmer near Maastricht, in the southern province of Limburg, who possibly could get me over the River Maas. Here, the river is the border between Holland and Belgium.

Using the same streetcar that had brought me to my hiding place in Amersfoort, I went to the railway station and bought a ticket to Maastricht. I had the ID card in my pocket but had already decided not to use it in case of an inspection on the train. It was unnecessary anyway; there was no inspection, only a Dutch conductor who checked the train ticket. I was supposed to get off the train one stop before Maastricht, then walk along the river to a hamlet, turn right and follow the river again. The fourth farm on the right was where I would get help to cross the river.

The underground workers in Amersfoort apparently were not altogether against me. They had given me enough Dutch money to buy the train ticket to Maastricht and the information I was given was correct. Because there was no check of ID cards on the train, I forgave them for that little detail.

The description I had been given of the terrain was excellent and I found the farm on the riverbank without trouble. A woman, holding a dog, stood in the driveway. When I asked her if this was Verkerk's place, she asked me to come in. I was sure that Verkerk was not their real name but that was the 'going thing', that nobody revealed his real name. They didn't know my real name either.

In the typical living room-kitchen, a man told me we had to wait until dark – but not in his house, that was too dangerous. We walked to the yard, where he gave me an old lady's bicycle and told me to follow the river north for three kilometres. There I would see a large, white house with a white wall around it and a big, double, wrought-iron gate. He called it the castle of the Count of Harreveldt, but I didn't believe the name was real.

The description of the place was such that I couldn't miss it. The 'count and countess' received me warmly and explained there were only certain times when one could cross the River Maas, and said I could wait at their house. Someone would take me to the place where we would cross. While the lady of the house served sandwiches and white wine, we talked about the war, the Germans, and their unacceptable behaviour since the collapse of the Russian front. They told me I would have to wait until 3:00 a.m., so I had better take a nap.

A woman I hadn't seen before woke me and said, 'Come, we have to go.'

Without further talk, she got on her bicycle and I followed her on my borrowed bike. We carried no lights and the night was very dark as we pedalled down the dirt road along the river, in a southerly direction. Suddenly she turned into the driveway of a farm house, much like the one I had visited before (possibly the same one). Two men were waiting with two big German shepherds. I put the bicycle behind some bushes and we all walked through a small orchard to the thick reeds along the riverbank.

Walking on a narrow plank, I approached a black rowing-boat. The two men and one of the dogs got into the boat, and then the older of the two said, 'Get in please, and make no noise. I don't want the dog to bark.'

I shook hands with the woman, who wished me luck, and stepped into the boat. With an oar they pushed us off, into the ripples of the gently flowing river. The distance to the opposite bank was about four hundred feet; we could see the other side and a few buildings, but no lights. It took almost half an hour to cross the water. At the Belgian side, there again were reeds which engulfed us, until I felt a slight bump as the boat came to a stop.

'Walk up the hill to the brick house with the red roof. Somebody is expecting you.'

With a hasty, 'Thank you. Good luck to you', I stepped off the boat and disappeared in the reeds.

Very carefully, I worked my way to the road that went up the hill where the brick house was. It was still dark and I could easily walk without being seen. On top of the hill I saw several other houses and the terminal of a streetcar station. There were no lights. I knocked on the door of the small house and a woman immediately opened it, letting me in as if in a hurry.

She brought me a glass of milk and said I would have to wait in the room until just before 8:00 a.m., to catch the first streetcar to Hasselt. I had no choice, so I agreed, and sat it out for two and a half hours in the small living room of this Belgian house. One thing I liked, I was in Belgium.

At about 7:40, the woman came to the room and said, 'Go now. Just take a seat in the last car. Good luck and say as little as possible. You talk like a Dutchman, not like a Belgian.'

I smiled and walked straight to the little streetcar station, where I boarded the last car as the one and only passenger. The woman from the house I had just left also came to the station and I saw her talk to the conductor, who then came to me to give me a ticket. I looked up at him, about to tell him I only had Dutch money to pay him with. But he stopped me by shaking his head, saying, 'It's taken care of.' Ah, those Belgians.

Hasselt is a bigger town than Utrecht, and from here on, I had my own plans again. Obviously, I gladly accepted the help to cross the Dutch–Belgian border, but going from one place to another, not knowing what to expect, gives one an insecure feeling. I preferred to take the initiative at all times, whenever possible. Walking down the main street, I noticed a branch office of a bank just opening its doors. There were no customers when I walked in. I explained to the man that I had lost my wallet and needed enough money to buy a train ticket to Brussels. He looked at me with a big question mark on his face, and I was sure he knew there was something odd about me.

'Monsieur,' I said, 'I just want to call my uncle, who is the director of the Cockerill shipyard in Antwerp, for some money. But without my wallet, I don't have the money for a phone call. You think you could help me out? You'll be reimbursed of course.'

'*Mais oui*,' he said, 'that can be arranged. What is your uncle's name *s'il vous plaît?*'

I gave him the name and within two minutes I was talking to Uncle Charlie, my mother's brother, in Antwerp. He recognized my voice and immediately understood the situation.

'Give me the clerk again and stay in the bank,' he said. 'I'll call you back in twenty minutes.'

The clerk took the phone and I heard him answer, '*Oui monsieur, très bien. Bonjour.*'

The nice man counted out the money Uncle Charlie had authorized him to give, saying, '*Voilà*. Please sit down. Your uncle will call you back, and that was three francs for the phone call.'

Uncle Charlie called back and gave me a short instruction, 'The National Insurance Company, Avenue de Waterloo.'

Then he hung up, knowing that was all the information I needed. I knew the Avenue de Waterloo was in Brussels, and the address of the Insurance Company could be found in any telephone book. No doubt he had made some sort of an arrangement with a friend of his at that office. In those days things had to be done in such a manner; it was too dangerous to use real names. I didn't know the clerk in the bank and he never heard my name or Uncle Charlie's name. The name of my contact in Brussels was not mentioned and nobody knew when I would get there.

The train trip to Brussels was uneventful and I arrived at the big Gare du Nord at about 2:00 p.m. The waiting rooms and restaurant were full of travellers of various nationalities, which was exactly what I wanted. With plenty of Belgian money in my pocket I bought the worst lunch I'd ever tasted, which reminded me once again of the hopeless food shortages in the occupied countries.

At a news stand I bought a map of the city of Brussels, then went to a telephone booth to look up the address of the insurance company. The office on Avenue de Waterloo was the headquarters of the company and quite far from the railway station. How ironic to have my contact in Brussels on the same street as the phoney transit address of the Dutch-Paris Line. Instead of taking a streetcar, I walked between the hundreds of people on the streets to the majestic Avenue de Waterloo, where I found the insurance building without problems.

First I walked by to take a good look. But everything seemed safe, so I walked up the marble steps and through the big glass doors, into the lobby on the lower floor. I stood in front of a large directory as if I were looking for the right department, when a middle-aged man, standing halfway up the stairs, snapped his fingers. When I looked, he made a small gesture to follow him and immediately walked up the big marble stairs to a private office.

Inside the room I was the first one to speak, saying, 'I had a call from Uncle Charlie –'

But the man interrupted me, with 'That's good enough for a password. Who else has an Uncle Charlie in Belgium? You must be Bob Vanderstok.' With a sigh of relief, I confirmed who I was, but then he continued, 'This is not a safe place for you to be. Leave the building through the side door, turn right on the Avenue, go to the streetcar stop. Take number two to the very end and walk to this address, Rue Kamerdelle No. 14. My wife knows. By the way, our name is Haenecour. Go quickly now.'

Rue Kamerdelle was in Uckle, a suburb of Brussels, and when I found the house I again took the precaution of passing it, making sure there was no one following me. It was a large, three-storey modern villa, with a garden in front and a tennis court in the back. Mrs Haenecour opened the door before I rang the bell, obviously fully informed about my arrival. She had prepared a small guest room on the second floor, next to an attic space from which one could get onto the roof. It was clear that everybody foresaw the possibility of a Gestapo search at any time.

Later in the day, Haenecour came home from his office and I became acquainted with this Dutch family, for whom a statue should be built. There were five small children, and again, I was a visiting 'uncle' from Holland. Although the parents spoke Dutch to each other, the children spoke better French than Flemish, which to us Dutchmen sounds like a charming dialect. It obviously was a well-to-do family. Mr Haenecour had a high position in the insurance world.

At the same time, he was a most important figure in the Belgian resistance and underground organizations. I had my meals with the family in their dining room and even played tennis with friends and visitors as if I were part of the family. The older children knew, but never said a word about my presence in their family.

A month before, the group of Belgian underground workers in Uckle had suffered a tremendous blow. Their leader and two other members were caught by the Gestapo and taken to the notorious concentration camp, Dachau. The Germans had accused them of spying, so they were not expected to get out of Dachau. They were nervous and I ran into the same problem I had experienced in Holland. They didn't believe my story.

Again, I stayed with a family, risking their lives to help me and our country, but I couldn't get the necessary help to travel. After three weeks, as in Holland, I decided to cross the border into France on my own. I couldn't wait any longer and I didn't want to put the Haenecour family in jeopardy. They had done enough for me.

Uncle Charlie had provided me with Belgian and French money but I needed a permit to travel. Unexpectedly, Haenecour got a paper which allowed Belgian workers to work in Valenciennes and commute from their homes in Belgium. That was exactly what I needed, and after a sort of farewell dinner with the Haenecour family I was on my way to Paris. In addition to the essential permit, the Belgians had given me a contact in Paris. I was to go by metro, the Paris subway, to the station at l'Opéra, walk up to street level and meet a man in a light raincoat and a French beret on his head. The man would have a green scarf around his neck and be at the steps between 10:00 and 11:00 a.m. on 8 May.

With the travel permit, I bought a ticket to Paris. Much to my satisfaction, there were large crowds of people at the station and on the train, so there would be less chance of having checks by the Gestapo. My ID card was not actually good enough to pass a check and the travel permit did not look very impressive. It was a dark night and one could only see a little, by the glow of the familiar blue lights.

Normally, the trip from Brussels to Paris would take about eight hours, but our train stopped everywhere. I finally heard a conductor announce that the next station would be Valenciennes, where most Belgian workers would get off. It also meant we were in France. There was no border check and no check for papers or tickets. In fact, I never saw any Germans on the train, at least none in uniform. Soon enough, I saw the ominous characters in their long, black leather coats and felt hats. The Gestapo was everywhere.

At the next stop, we stayed more than an hour at the small station for no apparent reason. But when the train personnel began shunting the railway carriages, I understood. The station had been bombed the day before and the tracks were damaged. An hour or two later, after going through much shunting, we continued our journey.

Finally I saw the light of dawn appear and our train continued at a terribly slow pace. We stopped in the middle of a wooded area and everybody was ordered out.

I asked the conductor, '*Pourquoi?*'

But he shrugged his shoulders and said something like, '*Bombardement, peut être.*' I never saw any airplanes and heard no bombs, at least not that time.

Slowly, we went on. I had become rather hungry but there was nothing available on the train. We stopped again and were ordered to leave the train, this time to take cover. Now I saw the bombers and could see the bombs fall through the air, onto a target well ahead of us. First a flash, then smoke and then sound. After a while, we boarded again and the train went on to the next station, where the bomb damage was clearly visible. Our train went on anyway.

That evening at 11:00 we rolled into Paris. It had taken us more than twenty-four hours to travel from Brussels, and I had not thought of the food problem. Hungry and thirsty, I went to the filthy restaurant and bought a surprisingly good meal. But I had learned my lesson. Better carry some food on these long train trips. Being a day late, I did not have much hope of finding anybody at a metro station in the middle of Paris. I stayed in one of the large waiting rooms at the station and must have fallen asleep, because when I woke up it was daylight and a huge clock showed 8:10.

The metro in Paris is a very convenient system of subway trains and I could go to l'Opéra without changing. A little before 10:00, I walked up the stairs and suddenly recognized the Opera House, which I knew so well from visits to Paris before the war. The only difference was the presence of German army trucks and soldiers in uniforms who didn't belong there.

I walked around for almost an hour but kept the entrance of the metro station in sight. No Frenchman resembling anyone I expected showed up. In the morning drizzle everybody wore raincoats and berets.

Paris is a large city and I didn't have any means to stay in a hotel. The only places where one could stay, without looking different from others, were the waiting rooms of the large railway stations. They were always crowded and full of sleeping people who had to wait for train connections.

I went back to the station, where I crossed out 'Paris' in my travel permit and wrote 'Toulouse' above it. Hoping that the French personnel at the ticket windows would not care about the alteration, I asked for a ticket to Toulouse, in the south of France. The girl said I had to go to the St Lazare station for all trains to the south.

After a meal of bread and cheese, I put an extra roll in a paper napkin in my pocket and went down to the metro again. The St Lazare station had its own metro station. With only one change, I navigated to this large railway complex, where I discovered it was a checkpoint for entering what used to be the 'Free French' part of the country. The so-called Vichy French were no longer a reality and that part of France was just as occupied as any other part of France. However, the checking stations on the platforms were still there. In the great hall I bought my ticket to Toulouse, but the man at the window kept my travel permit.

Armed only with my train ticket, I walked to the platform of the train to the south. I had to pass a gate where a German soldier checked everybody who passed. When I showed my ticket, he asked, '*Ausweiss, bitte* [Permit, please].'

'They kept my permit at the ticket office. How else could I have bought this ticket?' I said in German.

The man shrugged his shoulders and said, '*Ach so, natürlich. Weiter, bitte* [Oh, of course. Go on please].'

Without further discussion I walked on and found a seat in a third-class compartment on the train to Lyon. The train departed on time, and after leaving the suburbs of Paris I looked out on the beautiful countryside. One could not see a sign of this country being at war. A French conductor came by and said I would have to change in Lyon and Rodez. I had no objections; I was in France, on my way to Toulouse in the south and another step closer to my destination, Spain.

At Lyon and Rodez, there was plenty of time to eat in the restaurants at the railway stations. Uncle Charlie had given me enough French money, so that part of the journey was in relative luxury. With every meal I had a glass of wine.

So far the journey through France had been easier than I had expected, except for the very tricky moment at the St Lazare station in Paris. The way I passed through the gate, with the German probably half-asleep, was a bit of good luck. The Belgian underground worker, who had given me the travel permit in Brussels, also had given me the name of a café on a square in the middle of St Gaudens, a small town just beyond Toulouse.

The name was easy to remember for a Dutchman, but I was so exuberant at the time that the 'easy to remember' name had gone in one ear and out the other. No matter how I racked my brain, I could not remember the goddamn name of the café. St Gaudens, a typical French provincial town, would have hundreds of cafés, of course. But which one? Which one, dammit!

On 10 May 1944, I arrived in St Gaudens at 2:00 p.m. It was a sunny day – just like the day four years ago when Hitler's hordes invaded Holland, bombed our cities, and overwhelmed the country with their war machine. It was a different story now, with the Americans on our side and the Russians on the offensive in the East.

The railway station was half a mile outside town and I walked like a real Frenchman, complete with light-coloured raincoat, black beret over my left ear, and a small rucksack (a gift from the Haenecours) on my back. The road led directly to the centre of the town, which had to be the square we had talked about. And indeed, every other house was a sidewalk cafe along the cobblestones of the pavement. The thought of my stupidity in forgetting the name irritated me when I walked around the large town square. But then, like a flash of lightning, it happened.

In front of me was a cafe named 'l'Orangerie'. That was the place! How could a Dutchman, a soldier of Orange, ever forget the obvious name that reminded us of our Royal House of Orange? It was the right place.

When I walked in, a woman in the back beckoned with her finger to come to a room behind the taproom.

'*Bonjour madame, je suis un aviateur anglais*,' I said.

I didn't try to hide the fact that I was a fugitive. The woman had already seen that the moment I walked in. Very soon, the conversation became friendly and she insisted that I change my appearance a little. The beret in those parts was worn over to the right side, not to the left as I was wearing it. Nobody wore a white raincoat, either. With a motherly smile, she said I didn't look like a Frenchman at all; everybody would recognize me *tout de suite* as a foreigner.

They exchanged my shoes for a heavy pair of boots and gave me an extra sweater because, as the lady said, I would need them. The family who owned the cafe were *maquis,* members of the armed, underground resistance active in southern France.

They never introduced themselves but acted like old friends. There was plenty of good food and wine, and apparently they did not have that fear of the Gestapo I had seen everywhere else in occupied Europe. One of the younger men carried a pistol in his belt, just barely covered by a loose jacket. Now, with my beret properly slanted, wearing a heavy sweater and mountaineer's boots and carrying my rucksack, I could pass for a local as long as I kept my mouth shut. My French was good enough for conversation, but the local slang was almost like a foreign language.

They took me to an empty apartment, where I stayed two days, and then by streetcar to a farm house twenty miles outside St Gaudens. There I saw a number of people sitting on the ground or leaning against the walls of the courtyard. Soon I discovered that the group consisted of thirteen German Jews, an American captain, a Canadian sergeant and two other Dutchmen. We each were given a large piece of bread, and the water was cool and fresh.

Several Frenchmen walked around with tommy guns and pistols in their hands. One of them, first in French, then in broken English, briefed us about the plans. One of the Jews spoke French and translated the orders into German. I explained it to the American and Canadian; the other two Dutchmen also spoke the language.

The armed Frenchmen were *maquis*, guerrilla fighters who still controlled the hills and mountains of the Pyrenees to the Spanish border, in spite of German efforts to wipe them out. In this rugged terrain, the RAF dropped arms and ammunition to the famous *maquis*. They were the only resistance fighters who openly battled the Germans with guns and hand grenades.

Their briefing was more like issuing orders: we would walk single-file behind the guide, there would be no smoking, there would be no talking, and anybody side-stepping or trying to run would be shot. The *maquis* were to be regarded as a military unit, they would take no chances. Furthermore, the *maquis* could not do all this and survive on nothing, so all French money the fugitives carried with them had to be surrendered.

The American, the Canadian, the two Dutchmen and myself had no objections – I even gave up the rest of the Belgian money I still had – but some of the Jews did not like the idea. Some of them apparently carried all they had in money or jewels and were able to make some sort of a *mazzel*.

Our guide was a stocky Frenchman by the name of Pierre. He carried a cane in his hand and, of course, wore a beret on his head. We started walking in a long file, an armed *maquisard* in the middle of the column and two at each end. Silently, in the dark, we walked for hours – sometimes through forests, sometimes through fields, sometimes jumping across little streams and sometimes climbing over fences. Occasionally, Pierre let us sit down and allowed us to talk.

The American was Captain Bill McPherson, a Thunderbolt pilot shot down over France. The two-hundred-pound Canadian was a gunner, shot down over Paris. His name was Joe Barrel, according to my new American friend. They had travelled together for two weeks before they finally linked up with the *maquis,* who brought them to the farm in St Gaudens.

The two Dutchmen were spies, who first didn't want to talk, but softened up after the physical exhaustion of many hours of walking. One was a worker for the Philips Electrical Company in Eindhoven. His name was Rudy and he claimed he had a government assignment. I didn't ask any questions. After all, that was similar to my first escape to England. The other one was a Roman Catholic priest, who also claimed he was on assignment for an underground group from Limburg, in Holland.

All night we walked, until finally we reached a desolate farm. Far in the distance, we could see the foothills of the Pyrenees. Our guide Pierre said this would be our last chance to rest; there was a four-day mountain climb ahead of us. Today he would get bread for the group and he needed two volunteers to carry it. McPherson and I decided to take the job because Joe Barrel was ill with a fever. We did not quite trust the other two Dutchmen, and the Jews with their wives and children should have all the rest they could get.

With Pierre we walked over the hills, along the edges of woods and across small streams. Finally we reached a bluff, overlooking a small hamlet at the crossing of two country roads. There were a few farm houses and a sidewalk cafe with some tables and chairs. Pierre told us he would go to the cafe by himself, pick up three gunnysacks of bread and then return. He did not want us to follow him down the hill. With a short, 'A bientôt', he left us, skidding down the steep slope.

We could watch him all the way, until he entered the back door of the cafe. At the same time we saw a German patrol car, with four soldiers, coming from the north. When they were some fifty yards from the cafe, we saw smoke and heard gunshots. The patrol car suddenly turned and stopped, while the Germans returned fire. A machine gun rattled and two soldiers obviously were hit; the others took cover behind their vehicle. Another patrol car and a larger truck now came from the same direction and sped to the cafe. They immediately opened fire, engulfing the cafe in smoke and dust. Then everything was quiet.

McPherson and I realized that the situation at the cafe was bad and decided we had better go back to the farm to report to the other two *maquis* what had happened. We walked back, without the food supply we were supposed to be bringing.

The *maquis* at the farm already knew about the disaster and informed us that Pierre had been shot and we would need a new guide. Another *maquis* apparently had already informed our group. Food became a problem, so the *maquis* decided they would requisition a sheep. The farmer, under protest, gave up one of the many sheep that were grazing in the pastures surrounding his farm.

One of the Jewish men came forward and said he would have to slaughter the sheep in the ritual, kosher manner before the others would be allowed to eat the meat. The man was no amateur and soon we had the meat of a whole sheep boiling in an enormous pot over a wood fire. Cooked meat of a freshly slaughtered sheep is not the greatest culinary treat, but it filled our stomachs and there was nothing else to eat.

That night, the three *maquis* took us to the ruins of an old castle which was used as a regular stronghold of their forces. They gave each of us water and a big round loaf of sourdough bread.

Joe Barrel was sick and in pain but Mac and I insisted on bringing him along. There were a number of female *maquis* in the castle and we managed to get a bottle of aspirin from a girl who appeared to be a nurse. They also introduced us to our new guide, whose name was Felix, a small thin man of about forty.

Dressed in a simple suit, wearing heavy mountaineer's boots (and, of course, a beret) and carrying a thin stick as a walking cane, he came in front of our group and said, 'Everybody carry one loaf. *Eh bien, nous alons!*'

We knew the rules – no smoking, no talking and keep in a single line – but this time there were no armed *maquis*. There was just Felix, the guide, and eighteen quiet followers.

We walked all night, hours and hours of walking in the dark. None of us had any idea of direction anymore, but in the early morning hours we reached another farm, where we took a long rest. Felix went to the farmer and came back with a bucket of milk and a ladle. He told us to take a bite of our bread and some milk, but not too much; we had a long way to go. The terrain was rough, we were at a much higher altitude, and it was cold. Some of the Jews took their shoes and socks off and put their feet in the ice-cold water of a little stream. Others rested their feet up on tree trunks. We stayed at the farm most of the day. About 4:00 p.m., the farmer's wife brought another bucket of milk, just before Felix announced we would march again.

'*Alons, enfants,*' he said with a smile, showing a row of pearly white teeth.

He said goodbye to the farmer and his wife and we again started walking. The path now was much more difficult, much steeper, and in many places there was no path at all. We climbed over boulders and walked through the bed of a mountain stream, jumping from one rock to another. The night was cold and because of that, Felix made our stops short. After perhaps four or five hours we reached patches of snow and one of the younger Jewish boys, about fourteen, wanted to give up and go back. His father tried to explain but the boy could not be convinced. He had the choice of going back alone or coming along with us.

I got tears in my eyes when I heard his father's decision in his Jewish dilemma. It was, 'The family goes ... even if it means that we will go without our son.'

We spent another night above the treeline. Felix had led us to a cave, which was easily large enough to shelter all of us. It was ice-cold and patches of permanent snow surrounded us. The cave was like a beautiful picture postcard, with the snow that melted during the day freezing into icicles at night. Although it protected us from the icy wind, it was still so cold that the entire group of Jews huddled together in a heap to preserve at least some of their body warmth.

Felix took a parka from his rucksack and sat down outside the cave. I joined him, asking, 'Felix, aren't you affected by the cold?'

'Well,' he said, 'I have lived in these mountains all my life. I'm used to it. I stay here because very occasionally the Germans patrol here. But I will know if they do. They have to pass that slope, over there.'

Felix told me we would have to go again in about an hour. The going would be rough and it would still be dark. As before, he said, '*Alons, mes amis, marchez encore une fois.*'

The group got up but Joe did not think he could go any farther. The Jewish man who had acted as the butcher came to me and said his wife had started menstruating and was close to fainting. We had problems; I called McPherson, Joe, Rudy, and the priest together and explained the situation. I suggested that we should take care of Joe, and that I would talk to the Jews and tell them their men would have to take care of the woman and the boy who didn't want to walk any farther. They agreed. The Jews also promised to take turns and carry them if needed.

We climbed over icy patches, tramped through knee-deep snow and had to make rest stops every twenty minutes. The Jewish woman was pale, but managed to smile when I gave her a piece of Joe Barrel's bread.

'Here,' I said, 'compliments of Joe. He says he's too fat anyway.'

The girl smiled and tried to walk by herself. She knew that Joe was carried between two of us most of the time. During our rest periods we took off our shoes and socks to treat the painful blisters in cold water or snow. For another three hours we inched along the barren rocks. Now it was even ice-cold when the sun was shining; the wind-chill factor became impossible to tolerate for more than ten minutes at a time.

On top of the mountain, where the harsh temperature was at its worst, Felix said, *'Plus facile,* from now on.'

It became a little easier going as we headed down hill on the southern slope of the mountain, but the carrying of our disabled buddies was not any easier. For another hour, the ordeal went on. Suddenly Felix stopped.

Pointing a finger, he said, 'Do you see that grassy mountain pass? On the other side is Spain. It is easy going from now on. You're on your own now. So, good luck and *bon jour.'*

With that he turned around and happily walked back, away from us. I guessed the distance to be about two miles which, we realized, was very, very close to freedom. Nothing was going to louse it up at this final hour. We again had a short meeting and decided to split into two groups. One group would be the military bunch which included McPherson, Joe Barrel, myself, and the two Dutch spies; and the other group would be the civilian refugees. If we ran into a German patrol at least one group might get through, rather than all being caught together. Everybody agreed to the plan.

We had to carry Joe Barrel all the time now; he just moved his feet over the ground but could no longer bear his weight. The Jewish group carried the woman, who made an heroic effort to walk, but the unwilling boy simply was told to walk by himself.

The terrain was easier now, just wet alpine meadows. At the lower altitude, there were pine trees again and we sought some cover by walking along the woods, first downhill and then a long stretch uphill. I constantly scanned the land – left, right, and behind us.

'Come on Joe, just a little further. Hold on, Joe!'

At the highest point of the grassy pass, between two rugged rocky peaks, I could see the other side and looked down into a long, green valley.

I took a big step and stamped my foot on the wet grass, saying, 'Hey, fellows! We're in Spain! Joe, Mac, Rudy, and your holiness, we are in Spain!'

'Soldiers of Orange'
322 Squadron, RAF

The fact of standing on Spanish soil gave Joe an uplift, and with a choking voice he said, 'Thank you fellows. I know I would not have made it without you.'

I urged them to go down the valley another mile or so, to make sure we were in neutral territory and no German could still pop at us. About half a mile farther, a soldier in a ridiculous uniform stopped us, pointing a rifle at the priest. Our holy man spoke Spanish and explained that we had a sick person with us, and that a second sick person was on the way down from the pass.

The Spanish soldier blew a whistle and soon one of his compadres arrived. He told the other soldier something we didn't understand and then ordered us to sit down and wait for the group of Jews, which now had entered Spain also. While we were waiting, I studied the man's uniform. His hat was one of those black, cardboard Napoleon-style triangles. He wore a green tunic, green knickerbockers, puttees, and open sandals without socks. His rifle was an antique, but he had two modern bullet belts crossed over his chest. His friend came back with a push-cart for our two patients and the whole group moved to a dirt road leading to a village.

The village was Canejan. There was only one policeman, and he pronounced us prisoners to be interned. We were put in a bus, which took us to the village of Les where they gave us a meal of bread, butter, cheese, and wine. The bus then took us to Bosost, where we spent the night. The next day it was Veilla, a much larger town with a real mayor and other officials. The mayor spoke a little English and our priest, who spoke some

Spanish, immediately asked to see a priest. When the Spanish priest came they simply conversed in Latin, as if it were their mother tongue.

The mayor and chief of police had decided to transfer the entire group to a detention camp, as was done with all foreigners who illegally entered Spain. But when we heard that, Mac and I jumped up and protested.

'Just a minute, Mister Mayor,' I said. 'We are Allied soldiers. This is Captain McPherson, of the United States Air Force. This is Sergeant Joe Barrel, of the Canadian Air Force. I am Captain Vanderstok, of the Royal Air Force. And these two gentlemen are officers of the Royal Dutch Army. You will send us immediately to our respective embassies or consulates, or I will see to it that you will be in great trouble. Furthermore, I demand that you provide medical care for this Canadian soldier immediately. I hope you remember our international rights and the Geneva Convention!'

My loud speech apparently impressed the officials because we were immediately separated and taken to a school building, where we spent the night. Much later, I learned that the Jews were taken to detention camps, where most of them stayed until the end of the war.

From Veilla, we went by bus to Sort, an old health spa with marble baths and ponds full of trout, reminiscent of the old glory days, but now a closed resort. Then we travelled by train to Lerida, a large city with a big railway station. We were taken to the Hotel Fonda de Agramunt, where we were interrogated by police and military intelligence officers who were mainly interested in knowing if we were communists or not.

Spain, of course, had just freed itself from communist domination with the help of the German Air Force. No wonder they were pro-German and anti-communist. In Lerida, I was also interrogated by an Englishman from the consulate general in Madrid. He told me I would go to Madrid the next day.

In Madrid, an English consulate employee and his wife met me at the railway station. They seemed to know much about me and my escape from Stalag Luft III. But between well-meant congratulations, I noticed a tone of sadness which I couldn't quite understand. It was time for a celebration, time for a party, but the atmosphere was subdued. They took me to the consulate general, where I was introduced to the consul, his secretary, and several others. One of these officials was a high-ranking dignitary in the government, Mr Street.

First they let me tell my story and I was congratulated by all. But then the consul said, 'Vanderstok, we are extremely proud of you. A beautiful job. Well done, extremely well done, and we are so happy to have you sit with us here in this room. However, I get the impression that you haven't heard what happened after the great escape from Stalag Luft III.'

'Frankly, sir,' I said, 'I have been in hiding for more than three months and I don't know at all what happened. I hope it's not bad news.'

'It couldn't be worse,' the secretary said. 'The night you escaped through the tunnel, seventy-nine prisoners got out. The last three were immediately caught and brought back to various camps, but seventy-six really got out. Of these seventy-six, twenty-three were arrested near the camp and returned to Stalag Luft III, and three got home, including yourself and the two Norwegians, Jens Muller and Peter Rockland.'

'And what about the other fifty?' I asked, already feeling that something terrible had happened.

'They were murdered,' Mr Street said. 'Murdered in cold blood. Did you know my son in the prison camp?'

'Street ... Street. Yes, sir,' I said. 'He was security, and he was also on the list of escapees, No. 40 or so.'

'That was my son. He was one of the fifty – murdered!'

For several minutes I couldn't say a word. But then the figure 'fifty' became too much for me and I asked, 'Fifty? Oh my God! Is it known who they are? I am sure I know them all.'

'Yes, we know,' Mr Street said. 'They were caught in various places in Germany, then rounded up and simply executed on Hitler's orders.'

The shocking news was totally unexpected and left me speechless. Now I knew why the reception had been so reserved and lacked the euphoric feelings I had when I first stepped onto Spanish soil. I found it difficult to talk about anything, especially in front of Mr Street, who had lost his son by this barbaric act of Hitler and his Nazis.

Finally I had to ask, 'Who are the others?'

The secretary hesitated, but then said, 'Roger Bushell, Kirby-Green, Tobolski, Tim Walenn, Gordon Brettell, Henri Picard –'

'Henri Picard, the Belgian false-paper artist?'

'Birkland, Casey, Willy Williams, Al Hake, Chaz Hall –'

'Oh my God,' was all I could say.

'Johnny Stower, Valenta –' he continued.

'Tobolski and Valenta?' I asked. Oh my God! Just Rocky, Jens, and I had made it. And fifty had been brutally killed as revenge?

'Humphreys, Denys Street, Cookie Long, Danny Król.'

'Please stop,' I whispered. 'No more just now.'

I went to the under-secretary and shook his hand, saying, 'I am sorry about Denys, sir. By God, the bastards!'

'Thank you, Vanderstok. Let's be thankful that you are alive. My son did his duty and I am proud that he was one of you in this great escape. He didn't deserve to come to his end this way.' Street sat down on a couch, his hands covering his face. After a while he said to an aide, 'Mr Garcia, take good care of our Flight Lieutenant Vanderstok, please.'

The aide took me to a clothing store, where I equipped myself with new clothing, a watch, a tooth brush, shoes, and whatever else I needed to look like an ordinary person again. He then gave me money and drove me to a small hotel just a block from the consulate.

I needed some sleep, but Mr Garcia warned me not to go out by myself. He would pick me up and Sunday we would see a bullfight.

'Call me any time,' he said. 'Don't go out alone!'

The aide, Mr Garcia, took me to restaurants and we saw the bullfight in the famous arena in Madrid, but I was not impressed. Not only was the thought of what had happened at the prison camp constantly in my mind, but Madrid simply was crawling with Germans. In every restaurant, shop, bar, and even at the bullfight, I heard German spoken. I wished I had the power to machine-gun them down, just as they had done with our boys from Stalag Luft III.

Two days later I was on the train to Gibraltar, with a diplomatic permit to pass at La Linea. Everybody, except myself and two other passengers, had to leave the train when a platoon of British soldiers searched it before it moved on, right across a runway to the terminal. It was another milestone. Literally. I was on British soil.

An Air Force sergeant greeted me with, 'Welcome to "the Rock", sir. Don't forget you are on British soil now and a flight lieutenant-pilot of the Royal Air Force. Observe security regulations, sir!'

'You're kidding, Sarge. Where do you think I've been the last three and a half months?' I wasn't much in the mood for clicking heels and smart saluting while I was still in civilian clothes.

'Of course I'm kidding, sir. I know all about you. It's been in all the papers, about the shooting and the tunnels you people have made. I'll show you around. Let's get you a uniform first, and then you should go to the paymaster and then the officers' mess. You won't be here long.'

The sergeant was OK. He knew that I would be briefed about the security at Gibraltar and about my escape route. Apparently I wasn't the first one who had come through here. The uniform was battledress, which was good enough, and at the paymaster's office I received a temporary ID card and printed instructions about security. I should talk to nobody about my escape until fully de-briefed in London. I had a lot of money coming, a year and a half of salary, of which I naturally drew only a little.

At headquarters, they informed me I would fly back to Bristol the day after tomorrow. So I had some time to look around this famous fortress. The monkeys were kept in cages during wartime but a squadron leader gave me a tour of the fortifications and tunnels in a jeep. In uniform and with an authorized officer, there were no restricted areas and I got a first-hand view of the inside of the 'Rock'.

When we returned to the officers' mess, my guide asked, 'Remember what the sergeant said about security, when you first arrived here?'

With a smile, I said, 'My lips are sealed, of course!'

I asked the officer if I could send a postcard and have it mailed in Spain. He said that was done all the time, as Spain was a neutral country with fewer postal restrictions than England or Germany. I bought two picture-postcards, with nonspecific scenery on one side, and on the other I wrote my mother's name and address. On the other card, I wrote the name Heye Schaper, with Stalag Luft III as the address. On both cards I wrote in Spanish that the ice cream cones were terrific here, and signed them 'Roberto del Baston'.

Both postcards arrived at the proper places and both were recognized as a message that I had arrived in Spain. The name 'del Baston' is a liberal translation of Vanderstok, obvious to a Dutchman but not readily clear to others.

The next day at 5:00 a.m., I boarded the DC-3 which flew me to Bristol in six hours. At takeoff, I thought of the train that could simply cross in the middle of the runway. But every airport had to have something special, I guessed.

The big airport at Bristol was busy, not only with RAF personnel, but with literally thousands of Americans. The airfield itself was cluttered with big and small aircraft, marked with the familiar American star.

A small Hillman van took me to headquarters, where I presented the big yellow envelope they had given me in Gibraltar.

But the wing commander at the desk, without even opening the envelope, said, 'Congratulations, Flight Lieutenant Vanderstok! I have heard about your experiences and we also read about the shootings; that was terrible. I have orders to transfer you to HQ Fleet Street, in London, and you should also report to the Dutch Air Force Directorate. Fleet Street first, please. And remember the security rules. Well, so long, Van. And again, well done, old chap.'

Downstairs in the hall there was a desk, where they arranged a first-class ticket to London for me. During the two hours of waiting time I treated myself to an elaborate lunch in the officers' mess. At 1:00, I entered a first-class compartment on the express train to London and let myself sink into the red, plush pillows of luxury. It was a four-hour trip and I looked at the fields and gentle slopes of the countryside.

It took a little while before I realized that the endless rows of equipment under enormous camouflage nets were trucks, jeeps, field artillery, buses, and thousands of crates, stretching mile after mile. It was obvious that something big was being prepared, something really big. Near every village and town I saw these masses of materials.

It was 5:00 p.m. when I arrived in London, too late to go to Fleet Street. So I went straight to my 'old faithful', the Cumberland Hotel at Hyde

Park Corner. The place was crowded with Americans but I got a room; nothing much had changed.

At the RAF headquarters on Fleet Street, it was a different story. There was a reception committee of group captains, wing commanders, and – to my delight – Prince Bernhard, who all wanted to hear the story. There were sandwiches, coffee, sherry, and handshakes left and right. I had lunch in the Grosvenor Hotel with Prince Bernhard and Berdenis, the chief of the Dutch Air Force Directorate, who now was a major. We talked about the developments of the war but the Prince did not say much about the old subject, our contacts and secret agents in occupied Holland.

In the afternoon I had to go back to the Fleet Street headquarters to get my physical examination, because I had made it clear that I wanted to fly again. Everything went well, but the doctor rechecked my left ear.

With the familiar, 'Hmmm', he said, 'There is quite a hearing loss on the left.'

'Well, doc,' I said. 'That's from the explosion when I was shot down. It doesn't bother me at all.'

'I'll see what I can do,' was his answer.

At the Directorate I had another tremendous reception and that evening it was Oddeninos, the Chinese restaurant, and the big hall in the Cumberland Hotel again. That night, I heard the V-1 buzz bombs for the first time in my life.

The distinct sound of the V-1, the buzz bomb, could not be mistaken for anything else. You only had to hear it once and you would know what it was and what to do. As long as you could hear the sound there was no immediate danger. But when the sound cut off, it meant the bomb was coming down. On the street, we would run to a bomb shelter or the nearest tube station, but in a hotel room it was different. In case of a direct hit, there was nothing to be concerned about. But those near-misses were the bad ones.

I opened the windows, to at least minimize glass splinters flying through the room, and put my head under the two pillows on the bed. The waiting time between the cessation of the sound and the bang of the explosion was quite unpleasant. Most of the time, you could not see the bomb and the only thing you knew was that the blasted thing was close enough to blow you up. Once the bomb hit with its loud bang, it was all clear again.

I rented a small apartment, close to the Directorate and our daily meeting places around Piccadilly. During this unwanted, idle episode, I visited the offices of the Queen and the headquarters of Dutch Intelligence almost every day. The news about the contacts with the Dutch underground was not good. I learned that my brother Hans had indeed escaped from Holland to England via Sweden.

In London, he immediately offered his services for any job, including returning to Holland as a secret agent. I was told that he had received a short training course in parachuting and photography. They already had sent him back, together with a radio operator, but so far they had not heard from them. When I asked the major in charge of the secret service when they had dropped him, he first tried to evade the answer.

But when he saw my face as I repeated 'When?' he hesitatingly said, 'Two months ago.'

Because of my nearly two years in Stalag Luft III, during which time I had no contact with Dutch officials in London, I obviously had little idea of what had happened regarding my original plans (which I had brought along the first time I arrived in London, in 1941). I talked to Eric Hazelhoff, Peter Tazelaar, and Prince Bernhard about our mission and plans of contact with the Dutch resistance. An awful lot had happened.

The number of men and women who had escaped occupied Holland and offered their services to the Dutch leaders in London now had reached almost a thousand. Many of them offered to go back and organize communications; many of them did. There was incompetence, treason, pure stupidity, and a very capable German counter-espionage service to deal with.

At least fifty-four Dutch agents were expected and fell into Germany's open arms when they came down with their black parachutes in so-called, pre-arranged drop zones. The Germans – who knew the radio codes and the operators – called their clever plot against the organization of Dutch secret agents in London their '*England Spiel*'.

The *England Spiel* had infiltrated the entire Dutch operation of sending secret agents back to Holland. It took more than three years of bungling, incompetence, and arrogant stupidity before these dabblers finally sensed there was something wrong. One man, Major Somers, had suspected that the organization was playing into German hands and repeatedly had warned that our agents were achieving nothing – and that almost all of them were being caught by the Germans.

More *Engelandvaarders* came from Holland, confirming the same disastrous stories, before finally the leadership was replaced by new and more competent workers. Prince Bernhard had played a big role in the changes and my plan of landing agents on the beach at Scheveningen had been executed successfully, but not through the Dutch Intelligence Section in London. It was done secretly with the help of the English.

Prince Bernhard, in his difficult situation of being a German himself, hated Hitler and his Nazis almost more than we did. He openly demonstrated an unflinching desire to fight these barbarians until their last man was eliminated. The Prince developed into a true military leader on the side of the House of Orange and, therefore, on the Allied side. It was the influence of Bernhard that changed our secret service from a hopeless disaster into a functional unit.

He also established a Dutch Army Unit, the 'Princess Irene Brigade', which played a role in the invasion of Normandy, and later in the liberation of Belgium and Holland. It was Prince Bernhard, a competent pilot himself, who arranged the purchase of Spitfires to establish a Dutch fighter squadron in the RAF. He was so interested and gave so much support to all, that he was given the well-deserved title, 'the father of all Dutch War Pilots'. His involvement as a leader earned him a promotion to the rank of general. For the Dutch, he was the true General of Orange.

The bad news about Hans, who had been dropped over Holland by the old bunglers, was not the only disastrous news. A letter from the Air Ministry arrived at the Directorate that I was medically unfit for combat duty, but that they would allow me to fly as an instructor.

'Hell no!' I told myself.

Within an hour, I was at the Queen's office and asked for Prince Bernhard, to whom I showed the letter from the Air Ministry.

'Your Highness,' I said almost demandingly, 'that little hearing loss in my left ear is not related to flying as a fighter pilot. And I wanted to fly Spitfires again.'

The Prince was clearly upset by the Air Ministry's advice, not only because of the disappointment for me, but – as I later found out – because he had other plans for me.

After reading the letter again, he said, 'Let me handle this.' He ordered two glasses of sherry, saying, '*Proost*, Bob. I'll handle it!'

I spent two miserable days in my apartment, but then a letter arrived at the Directorate: 'Fl/Lt VANDERSTOK, B.. Report OTU 67 on 24 July 1944. SQ/LDR Watkins'.

The order changed the entire situation. Obviously, Prince Bernhard had used his influence to convince the officials at the Air Ministry that a minimal hearing loss in one ear should not end the use of one of his most-experienced fighter pilots. The men at the Air Ministry had made such decisions before and, in one case, even allowed a pilot who'd lost both of his legs to continue combat flying, Squadron Leader Douglas Bader.

There were four days left in London before I had to report at Hulavington airfield. At the Directorate, I found out that all so-called German pay to British prisoners of war had been refused. Therefore, my salary had been deposited in my account at Barclay's Bank since the day I was shot down over France. I re-equipped myself at Austin Reed, spent a few glorious evenings around Piccadilly Circus, and early in the morning on the 24th, I stepped onto the train to Operational Training Unit No. 67.

At Hulavington, a sergeant with a small Hillman van took me and two other foreign RAF officers to the airfield. There we were received by Squadron Leader Watkins who, at the time, headed the Operational Training Unit (OTU). Watkins was a pilot of Battle of Britain fame. He had the nickname 'Dirty Watkins' because of his clever way of tricking German pilots into separating themselves from their main force, thus becoming an easier target for his famous Squadron No. 611. He also had a special sign, formerly at the entrance to his readiness room, but which now decorated the OTU pilots' room. It read:

> **'B' FLIGHT**
>
> All orders for the removal of
> German aircraft from the sky
> promptly executed
>
> **'SWEEPS'**
> Our speciality
> to order
> Phone: ext. 66

The officers' quarters at Hulavington consisted of a very large building and I was given a private room. True to RAF tradition, I had a 'batwoman', but had to share the 'dear lady' with three others. She was a woman in her late forties who performed all those wonderful duties such as cleaning the room, making the beds, taking care of our laundry and more. But we had to polish our own buttons and shoes. Dress uniforms were worn in the evenings and it was the custom to appear in the mess with shiny buttons, so we polished buttons just before going to dinner. An OTU was an operational training unit, not a combat unit, so rules and customs were strictly adhered to.

The conversion to our new Spitfires was a delight, but not the most difficult part of the course. The Spit Mark IX was faster, could do 408 mph, and had a ceiling of 44,000 feet. The wing was a compromise between the original, elliptical design and the clipped versions, but she still had the same sweet flying characteristics as the Mark V. She was easy to fly and extremely responsive to the stick.

We also had a few of the latest Spitfire model, the Mark XIV, which had a longer nose and a bigger engine, for a speed of 448 mph at 26,000 feet. Its power of climbing and range was slightly below that of the Mark IX, because of heavier armament and its capacity to carry three bombs or six rockets. The range could be extended with an external fuel tank, made of plywood, which could be jettisoned when empty or as needed for combat.

The biggest difference was the highly secret gunsight. This was the fabulous instrument that corrected the optical line of sight for the ballistic properties of the bullet at certain distances – as well as for the rate of turn of the flight path – and gave the angle to aim in front of the moving target. This was all accomplished by a set of gyroscopes, and an optical system which projected a lighted circle and a cross on a glass plate inside the windshield.

The radius of the circle could be changed by twisting the throttle handle. After setting the instrument for wingspan of the enemy plane, it would adjust the centre cross up or down, depending on the distance (which was calibrated by keeping the circle precisely on the wing tips). When the enemy plane engaged in a turning dogfight, the rate of turn would make the cross lag behind, so the aiming point lay in front of the target. The gunsight quadrupled the number of hits during exercises.

For my first flight, after more than a year and a half of idleness at Stalag Luft III, I flew in one of the very few Spitfire trainers, a Spit converted to a tandem two-seater. After that first flight, Watkins sent me up in a regular Mark IX. It felt good again to play with the cumulus clouds in this powerful Spitfire. Without ammunition and without bomb racks or rocket racks, the Mark IX flew at its best.

I tried a slow roll to the left, then to the right, and kept the machine upside down for a while. There was not even a sputter of the engine when I turned upright again. Why not try a horizontal flip, or a *tonneau*, as the French called it, and a regular spin? I had not realized that the fellows in the control tower were watching me and had called my boss, Dirty Watkins.

In my earphones I heard, 'That's enough for the first day, Van. Come home and pancake!'

I quickly answered, 'Roger, sir.'

But I was at 7,000 feet, angels seven, so I throttled back and made two cartwheels. This brought me down to angels two, just right for a left turn and a landing.

As in 1941, I spent extra time on the Link trainer, which now was much more sophisticated than the model we had used in 1941. Also in 1941, the training was intensive – with more practical sessions in dive-bombing and ground target attacks with the six rockets we could carry.

In the officers' mess, there was a tense atmosphere and many talked about major operations in the near future. I made a one-day trip to London to visit the Directorate and pick up a uniform from Austin Reed. London was unusually quiet and Piccadilly almost void of American and other Allied soldiers. The staff at the Directorate were outright nervous and talked about rumours of a massive German attack on London by Hitler's so-called 'wonder weapons'. General Eisenhower, now in charge of all Allied forces in Europe, was planning a major move. If we could carry out an invasion across the English Channel it would have to be at Calais, of course, which was the narrowest part.

Two days later, on 6 June, it happened. It was D-Day and the Allied invasion of France was in full swing. Not at Calais, not on the Dutch beaches, not at Dunkirk, and not in Belgium – but at the beaches and cliffs of Normandy. The secret of the actual site of attack was so well-kept that even the German High Command was confused and drew wrong conclusions. Thinking that the Normandy beaches were just a diversion for the real attack, which 'had' to come at Calais, they failed to send their first line units south to Normandy, in order to defend possible invasion sites more to the north.

There was heavy fighting, unexpected bad weather, and losses of men and material. But the overall news was thunderous and, in spite of local setbacks, jubilant and victorious. Eisenhower and the vast Allied war machine had changed the tide of the war, and the front in the west, which the Russians had long asked for, was a reality. We now were the military force with the initiative in our hands. It was not a defensive war anymore.

For myself, I was still at OTU and could not officially participate in the air operations. However, Spitfire Squadron No. 91, on the other side of our field, executed almost daily missions escorting bombers to the Normandy coast. The bombers received much flak, but there were surprisingly few German fighters during the operations on the beaches.

The escorting job was not the most dangerous mission, since the flak was aimed at the bombers and not at the fighters. As part of our operational refresher course, we participated in these escort missions. Once, we were alerted by our radar boys that there were bandits in our area, but they did not attack the squadron of Mitchells we escorted.

Looking down, I saw the awesome Mulberry harbour, the huge artificial harbour made in a matter of days by sinking ships and barges to form protected piers – to unload the stream of soldiers and war materials onto the beachheads at Normandy.

I kept a book with newspaper clippings, photos, and notes of these historic events. After many years, some of these notes remain as impressive as they were at the time.

6 June 1944: D-Day: Should have been E-Day for Eisenhower. Radar station at Guernsey Islands destroyed. About one hundred other radar stations attacked. Omaha Beach sustains heavy losses. It takes thirty hours to establish a beachhead. First bombing stuns German radar network. Rommel is in Berlin when the blow falls.

7 June 1944: Twenty thousand airborne troops behind enemy lines make contact with sea-borne troops. Rundstedt is in charge of 'Atlantic Wall' defences, from Holland to Spain and along the Riviera. Rommel, under Rundstedt, has field command of defences from Holland to River Loire and keeps nineteen divisions at Calais. This leaves only nine infantry divisions and one Panzer division at Cherbourg.

10 June 1944: Escort mission, see Mulberry harbour.

11 June 1944: Six air strips for fighters are completed. Allied ships, fifty miles along the coast.

17 June 1944: Cherbourg peninsula is cut off by Americans.

27 June 1944: Cherbourg is in American hands. In the first six days, we land: 326,000 men, 54,000 vehicles, and 104,000 tons of stores. Two Mulberry harbours are constructed, one at Arromanches and one ten miles west. A four-day gale destroys one of the harbours. Only Arromanches harbour is saved.

10 July 1944: Dutch Spitfire squadron is organized. Sixteen Dutch pilots, thirty-two Dutch ground crew, the rest still English. South African squadron leader.

15 July 1944: Thirty Allied divisions in France. Germans have lost 160,000 men by this time.

17 July 1944: Rommel is wounded in his car by RAF fighters. Allied fighters strafe all roads constantly.

25 July 1944: General Omar Bradley takes St Lô to the south. Germans are cut off. Roads are jammed by retreating Germans, routed by Allied fighters and bombers.

7 August 1944: Falaise pocket, attack on Mortain. Newspaper report says Allied air forces made 14,600 sorties on D-Day.

7–12 August 1944: Falaise–Argentan. Germans attempt to retake Mortain. Surrounded in a pocket – onslaught by artillery and Air Force in a crowded pocket. We believe we also hit our own troops.

20 August 1944: Eight German divisions – 140,000 men – are annihilated. Eisenhower orders the avoidance of battle for Paris.

26 August 1944: Patton crosses the River Seine. French General Leclerc and French resistance troops liberate Paris. March up Champs Elysées to Place de la Concorde by De Gaulle, Leclerc, and 'resistance'.

The advanced course at the OTU was completed after six weeks of practical and classroom training. During this time I made eight sorties with Squadron No. 91. When the squadron moved to Tangmere, I officially was transferred to this squadron, but the unit was still kept in reserve and executed defensive and escort missions only.

After a month of patrolling the coastal areas and seeing almost no action, I was assigned to take a staff and command course at Tangmere headquarters. This took another three weeks. In the meantime, my squadron became more active by being deployed for the defence of London against the V-1 flying bombs. By now, these bombs simply were aimed at the city in great numbers. They came from launching sites in Holland, Belgium, and northern France.

The Dutch Spitfire squadron now was manned almost entirely by Dutch pilots. Their first operational assignment was the same as for Squadron No. 91 pilots. They still were based in England and scored remarkable successes against the buzz bomb attacks. The 322 Squadron destroyed 147 V-1s, but not without losses of pilots and machines. The Spit was faster than the flying bomb, so one could catch up with the little missiles and attack them from behind. Sometimes, the bomb mechanism would become disabled, dive down, and explode in some field, doing relatively little damage.

But they also could explode when the attacking Spitfire was not more than two hundred yards behind it and flying toward the explosion. The squadron lost one pilot that way. Another technique was to fly in close formation with the flying bomb and then flip the wing with our Spitfire wing. This sudden motion offset the gyro mechanism of the bomb, causing it to dive down and explode well before it reached its target. The Germans responded almost immediately, adding a built-in gadget which triggered the explosion whenever the gyroscope mechanism was disturbed. The squadron lost another pilot when he tried to flip the wing.

My squadron, still a defensive unit, also scrambled many times for the V-1s. But Tangmere was not in the line of fire and we only scored thirty-eight buzz bomb kills. These were not accredited as combat victories, of course, because the little buzzer did not fight back.

After the fall of Paris, some of us in No. 91 were used for courier services. In this capacity I flew a daily service to Buc, one of those small metal airstrips just outside Paris. The single strip was laid down on two adjoining meadows, and was quite difficult to find in the foggy weather we encountered most of the time.

One of our bullet canisters was emptied, to make room for a very official- and secret-looking briefcase with padlocks and labels. I had to hand it over personally to the adjutant of Field Marshal Montgomery, who signed for it. The same procedure was followed back in England, after the return flight. When asked, I always answered that I just flew Monty's laundry in and out.

Although we had no real high score against the 'doodle bugs', we did score against a few German intruders in the Dover–Calais region, and on up to the Antwerp area. These encounters over the North Sea were with the Messerschmitt-110s – the twin-engine German fighters – and the Junker-88s – the light, but fast, bombers. On several occasions I saw Focke-Wulf Fw.190s, but they stayed too far away. During this period I shot two Me.110s into the sea.

I was given a two-week leave, which I spent in London, as usual. I collected more clippings and photos for my scrap book, which became so thick I needed a second album. The following is a short excerpt of that time.

30 August 1944: Germans have lost 400,000 men (with 200,000 taken POW), 1,300 tanks, 20,000 vehicles, and 1,500 field artillery guns. American 4th Division lands on the wrong beach, but it proves to be better than the right one. All our planes now had Zebra stripes for easier identification. Churchill wants to stop the invasion in southern France; Eisenhower says no.

10 September 1944: Germans are kicked out of Russia.

19 September 1944: Brest surrenders. General Patton to Orleans.

20 September 1944: Nijmegen and bridges are captured intact.

25 September 1944: Arnhem failure and disaster, due to extremely bad weather and poor judgement.

30 September 1944: Breskens and Walcheren (Holland) – 125,000 German troops are withdrawn from the island. Seaway to Antwerp is opened. Eight thousand POWs are taken. Mine-sweeping the Scheld estuary.

5–20 November 1944: Allies advance through France and Belgium too fast. All supplies come from Normandy, too far away. We strafe all roads behind the front. German coal supplies pile up. Trains cannot move. Communications have all but stopped. Our field commanders have run out of maps and gasoline. The front now runs from Switzerland to the Rhine River in Holland. One should not attack along the entire front. (This is Schopenhauer's wisdom?)

28 November 1944: Antwerp receives its first convoy. The 322 (Dutch) Spitfire Squadron is transferred to Woensdrecht in Holland. Montgomery gets the blame for the Arnhem disaster. Our fronts in France, Luxemburg, Belgium and Holland are dangerously thin. Eisenhower suspects a move of the German 6th Panzer Army.

My stay in London was highlighted by a promotion to squadron leader, but I was still attached to Squadron No. 91 and flew my regular courier service to Buc, near Paris. I also flew generals and other VIPs from place to place, in the small Auster airplanes that could land in almost any field. It was during one of these missions that I had one of my proudest encounters in my military career. I came back from Paris and had to deliver that padlocked satchel to the big, underground bunker of the Allied headquarters, just outside London.

When I checked in at the guard post, I descended the wide stairs which led to another guard station and a complex of halls, more stairs, and elevators. I had been there many times before and knew my way to Room 127, where I would deliver my satchel. In the hall, I saw a small group of officers, one of whom was General Eisenhower. I made a left turn, stood at attention and saluted.

The general came straight toward me and said, 'Good morning. Ah, I see, a Dutchman. Right?'

'Yes sir, and a good morning to you.'

Eisenhower had immediately recognized the patch with the word 'Netherland' on the sleeve of my RAF uniform.

'I have met your Queen Wilhelmina,' he continued. 'A remarkable woman. I can see why they call you "Soldiers of Orange". Carry on, Dutchman.'

I saluted again and, proud as a peacock, delivered my classified cargo.

I had to take another short course at the Air Ministry on Fleet Street, which took only ten days. I rented the same small apartment I had had before. Things happened fast in those days and during my staff course I was informed that I would be given command of the Dutch Spitfire squadron. I knew, of course, that Prince Bernhard had had a lot to do with this new assignment, as I had visited him frequently.

In London, not only did some buzz bombs get through – in spite of our intercepting fighter units – but Hitler's second 'wonder weapon', the V-2, began hitting the city. One could not hear the rocket coming. In fact, the whistling sound could be heard after the explosion because the missile travelled with a speed faster than sound.

Radar detection was possible, but the time element was so short that only a general air raid alarm was given. It could not be determined where the rocket would hit. I heard the sinister sounds of the V-2 several times – first a loud explosion and then the whistling – but by then you knew the danger was somewhere else and had passed you by.

There were rumours about our front being too thin, about the long supply lines, about the bad weather, and about the fact that the incredible Allied advance had come to a halt. The V-1s and V-2s fell more than ever. Dirt roads and the small, temporary airfields we used became mud pools. The front stopped at the Rhine River and everything seemed to have come to a halt.

My notes of that time run as follows:

16 December 1944: General Rundstedt attacks with what is thought to be all that Germany can mobilize in the west. Rundstedt attacks in the Ardennes with twenty-four divisions, ten Panzer and fourteen infantry. His obvious objective, to break through to Antwerp. The 322 Squadron at Woensdrecht is twelve miles to the north and could be cut off.

20 December 1944: Initial German success, a fifty-five-mile penetration toward the Meuse River. Eisenhower reacts speedily, redirecting sixteen divisions.

22 December 1944: Bad weather, snow and mud. Americans at St Vith and Bastogne distinguish themselves. 101st Division, 'nuts' to Hitler. Montgomery attacks from the north, Bradley attacks from the south. The weather is somewhat better. Tactical air attacks.

24 December 1944: Air attacks by fighters on front targets and bombers on supply lines, day and night.

26 December 1944: Germans are exhausted. They have suffered fantastic losses and are unable to supply their troops. Rundstedt's advance is stopped, sixty-five miles from Antwerp.

We could breathe again. Eisenhower, Bradley, Montgomery, and the Allied air forces (including the 322 Squadron) had regained their strength and again beat the Germans in the field. The Rundstedt offensive had been stopped. For the next few days there were no troop movements; each side had to take a deep breath.

On 30 December, I flew to Woensdrecht in a Dakota and visited the boys of the 322, although not yet as their commander. I spent the night in a tent, with mud all over the place, and every ten minutes a buzz bomb zipping over our heads. These were aimed at the harbour and ships of Antwerp, not at us; but the low-flying V-1s and our own anti-aircraft guns made so much noise that there was no such thing as sleeping.

The personnel of the squadron were already packing for their move to the new base at Schijndel, near Eindhoven, about thirty miles behind the front. On New Year's Eve, I flew back to London and spent a very quiet end of the year with a few friends from the Directorate.

The next morning, 1 January 1945, another explosive surprise thundered through our sleepy minds. We heard that the German Luftwaffe had attacked our forward airfields and positions, in the biggest air operation since their 1940 Blitz. It was one of the strangest and most stupidly planned air attacks in the history of the German Air Force.

It was an all-out effort to support the Rundstedt offensive, but could not be carried out when Rundstedt attacked because of the weather. But it was launched anyway, fourteen days later, after Rundstedt had been stopped. The air attack was kept so secret that even the numerous German anti-aircraft units were not informed about this New Year's Day air offensive. Furthermore, the German planes approached from Holland, in the north, at tree-top altitude. The highly capable German anti-aircraft gunners thought they were being attacked and shot down some hundred of their own pilots.

Rundstedt had made a 'bulge' in the front and history has termed that episode the 'Battle of the Bulge'. It was a succession of military blunders which proved the stupidity of war-making in the extreme. The planners of the Rundstedt offensive must have known that the operation would cost them an awful lot of men and material, and what for?

Even if the breakthrough to Antwerp had been successful, the Germans could not have hoped to win the war. Their front to the east had all but collapsed, they faced a vastly superior army to the west, and they had no functional industry left to support their army. They dealt us a blow, but that only made us more angry. The air offensive on New Year's Day was even more stupid. The entire plan broke Germany's military back, predictably.

The losses suffered on both sides were enormous, but there were many estimates of these losses by both sides. They differed considerably.

We estimated the Germans had deployed about 800 planes for the attack. Herman Goering declared that the figure was 2,300. The admitted airplane losses of the Allied forces were 150 planes lost and about 130 damaged. Germany's Adolf Galland figured 400 Allied planes had been damaged, while Feuchter and Girbig spoke of 800 Allied planes lost. Most likely, we lost 300 planes.

The estimates of German losses were even more startling. The official Allied reports spoke of ninety-three German planes shot down, while St George Saunders reported 252 destroyed. Galland said 300 German planes were lost, which was by far the lowest estimate from the German side. Most Allied planes were destroyed on the ground, without the loss of pilots. Almost all German losses consisted of both plane and pilot. At least 160 German planes were shot down by their own flak. Many of these cases were witnessed by Dutch residents who lived near the German flak positions.

Rundstedt and his ground troops had lost 120,000 men and almost all their tanks and vehicles. Their air force was broken and yet they continued the absurd fight. They continued to send young soldiers as cannon fodder to the fronts. And they continued to fly their newest plane, the jet-fighter Messerschmitt-262, against our bombers. They even scored some successes with this, the fastest of all war planes.

In spite of the setback and the high losses, especially for the Americans, our generals pushed through harder than ever. Holland was liberated only south of the rivers which cut the country more or less in half. Holland north of the Rhine River, where my parents lived, was still under German occupation. From sites near The Hague and Hook of Holland, the Germans still launched V-1s and V-2s. Why? Because Hitler had told them to do so.

Murdered and Liberated

When I was reading a newspaper at the Air Force Directorate about the historic meeting at Yalta, the mail came in and I received my orders to go to Schijndel, Holland, as commander of the 322 (Dutch) Spitfire Squadron. I was to pick up a brand new Spitfire Mark XIVe. It had a bubble canopy, clipped wings, and, at my request, no external mirror. Fully loaded with cannon and machine gun ammo, but carrying no bombs or rockets, I flew my new bird straight to Schijndel.

The base had a metal runway, running in a northeast-southwest direction and a large parking area for the three squadrons that were stationed there, under a Norwegian wing commander. We had quarters in wooden barracks, with few other comforts. The officers' mess was just another wooden barrack in a complex of about twenty buildings, not more than a hundred yards from our parked Spitfires. The planes were protected somewhat by walls of sandbags, and some of the buildings had sandbag protection as well.

There were five extremely important 'chaps' in my squadron. First the ground engineer, then the master sergeant in charge of all ground personnel, the corporal squadron clerk who handled all the paperwork, and finally my two flight commanders. The squadron was not entirely Dutch, but the planes were paid for by the Dutch government and twenty of the twenty-four pilots were true Hollanders. Of the ground crew, about 80 per cent were Dutch.

Later that day, my canvas suitcase and folding cot arrived and I felt I was among friends. We spoke Dutch only when there was no one of any other nationality around; otherwise it was English at all times. I met with the two Norwegian squadron commanders and our Norwegian wing commander, who had their readiness rooms right next to ours. We would be briefed for two seek-and-destroy missions for the following day.

I told the English flight commander to take care of those flights, so I would have a chance to get to know my pilots and the geography around our field. I arranged two flights, with a section each, just to get the feel of formation flying with my new buddies. They were pilots of all sorts of levels, some quite experienced, with pre-war flying time in the Dutch East Indies, others with no more than a hundred hours, fresh out of OTU.

The other flight commander was a Dutchman, by the name of Dekker. He had a broken nose, which had been set poorly (or not at all), and had earned the nickname 'nose'. 'Nose Dekker' was slightly unhappy with that nickname, so the boys wove a little story around the name, saying it came from counting noses after each mission, to see if all had returned. In that case, according to Dekker, they should all be called 'nose'. We couldn't argue with that, so from then on all pilots were called 'nose', followed by their name. Nose Dekker was an excellent pilot, and, with two others – Nose Harms and Nose Jantzen – I made my first flight with the 322.

We practised battle formation flying at least once a day, so I got to know my pilots and they got used to me. The actual combat missions were of the seek-and-destroy type, to disrupt all German forms of traffic in an area some twenty to thirty miles behind the front line.

General Patton took the bridge at Remagen and four divisions of the 1st United States Army crossed into Germany. Later, the Germans destroyed the bridge by artillery, but Patton's advance became a symbolic boost to the Allied forces and another blow to the German will to resist. We flew one mission to Remagen, in squadron strength, when it was thought that the bridge would be bombed by German planes, but we did not encounter the Luftwaffe.

We flew many missions without seeing much of the Luftwaffe, which apparently never recovered from its losses on that fatal first day of the year. On these flights, my pilots got used to my strict rules of battle formations. They began to like the style and I had a first-class opportunity to get to know the abilities and personalities of these special pilots of Orange.

My English flight commander, John Fletcher, had completed his operational tour of sixty missions and deserved a tour as an instructor back in England. He was replaced by Nose Pieter Cramerus, whom I knew from college days. Nose Cramerus had an analytical mind and handled every problem with a calm manner.

'Let's take a quiet look at this little matter and see how we can solve the problem,' was his stock response.

One day, he returned from a tactical ground support mission with a hole in his plane's tail as big as a bread box. When I came to look at the damaged elevator, he said, 'Well, let's take a quiet look at this little matter and see –'

Here I interrupted him, saying, 'My dear Nose Cramerus. You are not going to take a quiet look anywhere. The new XIV with the bubble canopy that just came in is now your bird.'

And then he said, 'Well, I'll take a quiet look at that little matter as well. Thanks.'

The damaged plane could be repaired, but not at our air strip at Schijndel. It was dismantled and driven to Brussels on a truck. Many of our planes received hits, but if there was no structural damage we repaired it ourselves. We were extremely fortunate to have Larry, our squadron engineer, who had to make decisions on such 'little' matters. Larry, the miracle man.

We were ordered to intensify our attacks on ground targets, especially on German communications and transports, which included anything that moved on roads, railway tracks, canals, and even open fields. We made daily sorties, mostly in sections of four Spits, armed with machine guns, cannon, and rockets. During these days the squadron scored a great number of direct hits. Nose Arts, a huge fellow from Amsterdam, came home with one of the best movies of an exploding German locomotive I had ever seen. His bullets went right through the pressure kettle, producing a huge white mushroom of steam. I sank a row of barges in a canal.

The German transportation system was all but lame behind the German front. On 24 March 1945, the combined Allied armies crossed the Rhine and staged an offensive almost as big as 'Operation Overlord', on D-Day. On 29 March, the Americans took Frankfurt and encircled the industrial city complex of the Ruhr. More than 325,000 prisoners of war were taken. Open car loads of thousands of prisoners passed by our base at Schijndel. I didn't feel sorry for them; I was in their shoes a few years back.

Our armies to the north were Canadians and Poles. It was called the Canadian sector. We made daily flights in support of the ground troops, using maps with grids, and a mobile radio station in a truck at the Canadian command post. We called the post on arrival, usually at an exact time, and reported readiness. The Canadian command post would answer with something like this:

'Juliette arrived post.'

The Canadian command post would then answer with something like this:

'Juliette Leader, this is Charlie. Target, farm house. Red tile roof and two haystacks on the north side, in Delta five.'

We did not use the word 'over'. The click of the mike and the message itself was clear enough and we had to be brief.

I would answer with, 'Charlie, this is Juliette. Stand by.'

I then would look at the grid on my map and find square D-5, still staying well on our side of the front line. When I recognized the target, I would position the three flights of my squadron so we could attack instantly.

Then I would call in, 'Charlie, this is Juliette. Target identified.'

And Charlie would come right back with, 'Go ahead boys. Hit them hard.'

Our order of attack was Red Section first, with myself as the lead plane, followed by Blue and then Yellow. I would indicate the moment of the first dive.

'This is Juliette Leader. Red Section, attack. Blue and Yellow to follow.'

At that moment, on this particular run, I made a diving turn to the right and the three others of Red Section did the same, in sequence, about three seconds later. This way, their line of approach took a slightly different angle and did not follow straight behind me. We aimed slightly short of the house until we saw the puffs of our bullets in the sand, then corrected our aim to hit directly on the target. We dived to a very low altitude and flew at tree-top level for about a mile, before pulling up and turning to the safety of the Canadian line.

This was an easy target. I saw Nose Dekker lead his attack from an angle slightly more to the west, and finally Nose Cramerus with Yellow Section followed, again from a more westerly angle.

I called in, 'This is Juliette Leader. Battle formation.'

In a matter of seconds, I saw Blue to my right and Yellow to my left.

Nose Dekker said, 'This is Juliette Blue Leader. Red and Yellow Sections intact.'

And I answered, 'Thank you, Nose. Your Blue Section also intact.'

When I had the entire group of twelve Spits together, at about 6,000 feet, I looked at the farm house and saw a number of tanks and soldiers in the grasslands, moving toward the target we had attacked.

Then came a voice over the radio, saying, 'This is Charlie to Juliette Leader. Thank you boys, well done.'

That was all, no further talk was needed. On our way back, visibility became poor and I asked for a homing. When we reached our field, we couldn't see it at all. There was a thick soup hanging over the entire area, up to about 4,000 feet.

I asked Nose Dekker, 'Juliette Blue Leader, how are you in your GCA and how much fuel do you have left?'

He answered, 'I'm OK on GCA. Plenty fuel.'

'And how about you, Yellow Leader?' I asked Cramerus.

'OK here,' was his answer.

Then I continued, 'This is Juliette Leader. Red Two and Red Three, close formation on me. Red Four, stay with Blue Section.'

'Juliette Leader, this is Yellow Three. I can take my Yellow Four down on GCA.'

I answered, 'That's OK. Nose Rudy, do you have enough fuel to be last?' He said he had.

At Schijndel, we had a top GCA officer and he immediately came into action. When my Red Two and Red Three were tight on my wings, we went down to angels two and simply did what our GCA man told us.

'Steer two-six-nine, rate of descent two. Steer two-seven-two, steady.' And, after a short while, 'Steer two-seven-zero, your altitude now 250 feet. Wheels out.'

I still couldn't see anything but my two buddies, who kept their wing tips about a foot and a half from mine.

'Flaps down, set your pitch,' was the next command.

I took a quick look at the two Spits on my left and right. Good, their wheels and flaps were down. Then the runway appeared in front of me.

'Red Two and Three, pancake on your own,' I said.

Then I opened my throttle, pulled up the flaps, took the wheels up and climbed to just above the cloud layer, where the others were waiting patiently.

'This is Juliette Leader. Red Four and Blue Four, close formation on me.'

They responded immediately and I repeated the GCA landing and landed myself. That made five of us safe.

Nose Dekker brought his numbers two and three in, followed by Nose Cramerus with his number two and three, and Nose Rudy with his number four. When all twelve Spits were neatly parked in their sandbag stalls, our Norwegian wing commander and some fifty other pilots and ground personnel gave us a round of applause, inviting us into the Norwegian readiness room to celebrate something we all were supposed to be able to do.

With a feeling of satisfaction, I remembered the many hours I spent in the Link trainers at the OTUs. I knew what the weather in Holland could be and I knew most of our pilots were not able to do a GCA all the way to a pancake. I went to our control tower (a truck) and congratulated the officer who had talked us in. Flight Lieutenant Spencer was a man in his forties, and an air traffic controller in peace time.

The German military might was broken, but large groups of Nazi-oriented soldiers and civilians continued with their absurd dreams of victory and glory. The SS and Gestapo gangs also continued their barbaric practices in concentration camps, where Jews and political enemies were murdered by the thousand each day. Troops of the 1st United States Army were the first to liberate one of the concentration camps. They could not believe their eyes when they discovered the gas chambers and ovens, where tens of thousands had been killed for no other reason than being Jewish, or just not on Hitler's side.

Our squadron flew daily missions, which now were mostly tactical support in the Canadian sector in the north. We also escorted bombers on their relentless pounding of German positions and industrial targets. On these escort missions we had to be vectored to the bomber formations, because they came from other airfields and our range was limited. Often, when we were in full squadron strength, Flight Lieutenant Spencer directed us to the bomber group through heavy cloud masses.

'Jackknife Leader, this is Olympic. Steer one-two-seven, angels ten.'

'This is Jackknife Leader. Roger. One-two-seven, angels six now.'

After a few course corrections, Olympic came on the air again, saying, 'Jackknife Leader, this is Olympic. When you get through this soup at angels nine, you will see your big friends three o'clock above.'

Almost immediately, our tight formation of twelve Spits shot through the cloud layer into the bright sunshine and blue sky. On our right, slightly above us, we saw a formation of sixteen Mitchell bombers, flying in the same direction we were. No further radio talk was necessary, because escorting was a well-known and well-practised procedure. We would fly at least a thousand feet above the bombers, in groups of two, and spread out over the entire bomber force.

Due to our limited fuel supply, we could only escort for about half an hour. Then another squadron would take over for the next stretch of thirty minutes. In our case, Olympic would call and give us a five-minute warning before another squadron would relieve us. After four minutes, we saw a squadron of Mustangs approach us from the right.

Mustangs, at a distance, looked much like Messerschmitts. So the twenty-four eyes of my boys carefully followed the approaching fighters, until we recognized the black-and-white 'zebra' stripes all our planes had worn since D-Day. When they were in position, I wiggled my wings and made a sharp turn to the left. The others followed in battle formation. There was radio silence from our side, but our ground station Olympic would have to help us get back to base because we did not know our position and could not see the ground.

After a while, I heard Olympic say, 'Jackknife, this is Olympic. Steer three-zero-five.'

That was our homing course and we were now far enough from the bomber force so we could safely use the radio again.

The weather in Holland in March often consists of heavy cloud cover, fog, sleet, occasional snow flurries – in short, pea soup. Since the disastrous failure at Arnhem, a few months ago, the front at that city remained the Rhine River. A large house was used by the German Command as headquarters, and our high command had decided to wipe it out.

Our Norwegian 'Wingco' led the flight of twelve Spits, one section of four of each squadron in his wing. I took my Red Section for the mission, which was well-briefed with actual photographs of the building, located in the town itself and surrounded by many private houses. It was pea-soup weather, with a cloud ceiling of less than 400 feet. Navigation had to be done by map-reading, so the formation flew all the way below the clouds.

When we approached the river it was raining, and visibility became considerably worse. We had to go even lower to see anything at all. Then we crossed the Maas River and the Waal, and saw a flash of the Rhine, with the houses of the city on the north side. Visibility was almost zero but we continued following our leader, in close wing-to-wing formation.

Suddenly I heard, 'Target in sight, white building. Drop bombs ... now.'

We all carried one five-hundred-pounder. I looked down and saw several explosions of bombs which had overshot the target. When I released my bomb, I looked down to see if anything had hit the white building. I saw more exploding bombs and a lot of smoke, but the rain and fog made it impossible to identify anything. Our 'Wingco' ordered us up to angels five, where we could see each other again. We then flew back on a homing to Schijndel base.

The Dutch pilots who had participated in this mission did not like it at all. The target could not be readily identified and we had just dropped twelve five-hundred-pounders on the Dutch town of Arnhem. One bomb might have hit the target, but that was not at all certain. The other eleven bombs just destroyed private houses and Lord-knows-how-many Dutch lives. The Norwegian wing commander did not gain popularity after that mission.

There were other missions, when spirits were high as we returned to base. A small hamlet, just east of the Rhine at Wesel, was heavily defended by the Germans and our command had requested we blow it up. The 322 Squadron was assigned to the job and I ordered twelve Spits to be loaded with six rockets each. We recognized the crossroads and the few red brick buildings which apparently were causing trouble for our infantry.

A small church was the centre building and we easily saw the dug-in positions of the stronghold. German machine guns and 20-mm guns were shooting at us, but we pumped seventy-two rockets and all the ammunition we had in our guns into our target. The nose count on our way home was twelve.

At Schijndel, the stories grew by the minutes. Nose van Daalen Wetters had shot the church bell out of the steeple and Nose Jantzen personally had heard the sounding bell. Nose Cramerus had seen brother Heinz flying through the air, holding on to the bell rope.

The Canadians advanced to the north, but Holland, west and north of Arnhem, remained occupied. There was no food, no transportation, and the German occupation forces were cut off from their own command. The Dutch ate tulip bulbs and burned their furniture for heat. The housing problem was immense. The Allied Air Force dropped tons of packed and canned food on fields near The Hague and Amsterdam. It helped somewhat.

With the Canadian advances, the squadron moved to the old Dutch airfield at Twente. The Germans had modified it and made it into a main fighter base with a modern control bunker. The bunker was destroyed, but the operations room could clearly be recognized. I found literally hundreds of telex pages, listing shot-down German aircraft and missing pilots, dated 1945. Possibly their New Year's Day disaster.

I made several field trips with Canadians in our sector and heard their side of the war. The Germans had booby-trapped roads by spreading piano wires across them; this killed soldiers in open jeeps by decapitating them. The Canadians ran into snipers in trees in areas already evacuated by the Germans. In spite of their impossible situation, there still were Germans who gave such orders and other Germans who carried them out.

It made the Canadians very angry and they consequently took care of things their own way. From now on, when they entered a village, they advanced house by house. If there were no people inside, they threw hand grenades first, then entered. Snipers were not ordered out of the trees; they were shot out of the branches.

We continued our almost daily missions to knock out the last German resistance nests. Unfortunately, these missions turned out to be more dangerous than the war in the air. The German anti-aircraft guns were as accurate and deadly as ever. During the last four months of the war the squadron lost nine pilots, all shot down by flak. We also lost five pilots who were not killed, but were injured and laid up in hospitals. Two of our 'noses' were shot down, but managed to make a forced landing and report back to our unit. Our heaviest losses occurred during the last four months of the war.

Prince Bernhard was now the general in command of all Dutch troops, including the sizeable forces of underground workers. Bernhard's promotion to commanding general meant that these underground groups received military status. In order to prevent a blood bath – not only of those Germans remaining in Holland but also of those accused of being traitors – the Prince issued an order that the 'Internal Army' would not bear arms until the official Dutch government returned to the Netherlands. After this development, the Germans in Holland gave up and Holland was liberated. Still, the war was not over.

I now could drive to the small town of Hattun, where my parents were staying with my niece Hilda and her husband. Telephone connections were not yet restored, so my visit was unannounced and caused an emotional mix of happiness and sadness. At least, I was a lost son who had returned.

But when I hugged my mother, she asked, 'Bob, do you know about Felix and Hans?'

I said, 'No. But it is bad, isn't it?'

My father, in a wheelchair, did not recognize me at first; he was blind.

When I said, 'Père, it is me, Bob,' he grabbed my hand and began crying.

Holding my hand all the time, he whispered, 'Felix, Hans, why? Felix and Hans, both.'

It was the only thing he could say. I, of course, began to understand what had happened before my mother told me the whole story.

Hans, after parachuting back into Holland, had tried to do the job for which he was trained. But he soon found out his partner, the radio man, was not much of a partner at all. They were no match for the German counter-espionage service and the Gestapo, so finding a hiding place became more important than finding subjects to photograph. His partner had stopped his radio transmissions because of the Germans' ability to pinpoint his location almost immediately with direction finders.

They split in disagreement and because of the need to find a safe hideout. Hans barely escaped his own hiding place, just before the house where he was staying was searched by the Gestapo. The man of the family, a father of three, was arrested and never seen again. The Germans evidently knew he was lodging a spy. Helping our agents was just as dangerous as being an agent. Hans felt bad about the arrest of the man who had given him shelter, and in desperation went home to our parents' house in The Hague.

They all knew Hans couldn't stay there, but Mother knew how to contact Felix, who now also had disappeared underground into the maze of resistance workers. At that time, Hans revealed the entire story of the Dutch secret service in London to my parents. At least fifty-four Dutch agents were dropped over Holland and fell into German hands the moment they touched the ground. The so-called radio communications of the Dutch underground fed the Germans with information, but Hans' partner would not believe this and continued his 'work'. It never dawned on him that the Germans let him continue.

With the help of other resistance workers, Hans went to Amsterdam, where Felix had rented a small attic room to operate from. They stayed there several weeks, until they discovered that an agent from England, another radio man, had a room in the attic of the house next door and was transmitting from the roof. The tall city blocks in Amsterdam, with their houses adjacent to one another, made it quite possible to walk from one house to the other via the rooftops. When the antenna and transmitter were found, the agent was not there. He had been warned in time of the Gestapo's impending visit.

Hans had spent two weeks at our home in The Hague; he could not find a safe place to go. He would not go to friends or other reliable families, because of the extreme danger for those who sheltered agents or resistance workers. The only possibility was to rent a small room, like university students used to do, and make frequent changes. During his stay at home he revealed his problems to our parents. He talked of the hopeless operation in London, which was supposed to be slightly better now that it was under the new leadership of Somers.

But the situation with his partner had deteriorated to the point that Hans did not trust him anymore. They finally got a message through to Felix, who agreed to meet Hans at a certain place and at a certain time. As brothers, they would recognize each other, of course. Hans simply would follow his older brother at a distance until they were convinced they were not being followed by either the Gestapo or Dutch collaborators.

When Felix and Hans were arrested a month later, my mother heard the story from Hans' partner. But she didn't believe him. Hans was transported to a prison in the south of Holland, and later to the concentration camp at Mauthausen. It was in this infamous camp that he was forced to work in the stone quarry and, when totally exhausted, was pushed over the edge of the stairs to meet his death – two hundred feet down – like thousands before him.

Felix first was kept at the pre-war prison in Scheveningen. In those days it was called the 'Orange Hotel', because so many Soldiers of Orange spent their first weeks of imprisonment in this building. The torture started here, during interrogations and efforts to get information out of the prisoners. At this stage, the Gestapo also bargained through personal dealings for money or other valuables such as gold, jewellery, or paintings.

My father tried to get Felix out this way, but the demands were absurd and could not be met. After a few months, Felix was transferred to a concentration camp near Hamburg. From another prisoner at the same camp, who made it out alive, my parents heard the last eyewitness report of Felix's fate. The man said he and Felix had stayed in the same barracks.

Felix had suffered from a severe case of dysentery, probably caused by an epidemic of typhoid fever, which had brought suffering to many. Death at these camps occurred not only in the gas chambers or on the execution line, but from disease and malnutrition as well. The bodies were thrown into a huge, ditch-like pit and covered with earth. In an effort to stop the spread of contagious diseases, the sick who could barely walk were marched to the mass grave and pushed in. They were too weak to climb out and were buried alive with the other bodies – hundreds a day.

When I escaped from Stalag Luft III, my father was arrested and interrogated, because the Gestapo was convinced he knew where I was. They questioned him, torturing him with bright lights in his eyes and physical exhaustion. They finally let him go home, because he truly did not know anything about my whereabouts. But the lights had blinded him. For three months, he could not see at all. Then his sight gradually came back – but only partially.

When Felix and Hans were arrested, the Gestapo again picked up Père for interrogation. Again he underwent the torture of bright lights and no food for two or three days. And again they had to let him go, because he did not have the information the Germans were after. This time, he came home blind – permanently blind. My parents had to evacuate their house in The Hague because the Germans expected an invasion and needed open spaces for their artillery. The house was to be bulldozed down. It never happened, but they had to get out. It was their loving niece Hilda who opened her home to them.

That was the news I received the morning I first saw my family. It already was certain that Felix and Hans were dead, and my father knew it. All he could do was pronounce the names, 'Felix, Hans'. Nothing more. He held my hands and I felt his hot tears on my fingers. Hilda and her husband had made coffee and we sat down for some sort of lunch. The doctor who had been treating Père came and explained that his understandable mental collapse was not the only thing wrong with my father. He was physically ill and we should not expect any recovery. This already was obvious to all of us.

In the afternoon, I had to return to my squadron and the time came to say goodbye. I felt that it was goodbye forever. But, amazingly, Père began to talk. He mentioned my name, said the war would soon be over, and told me to take care of my sister Anky and myself.

All the way back to Twente airfield, I heard his words – over and over again. And I heard the long story my mother had told me of the two boys, again and again. The roads were lined with debris – from German trucks and command cars, here and there with the wreck of an airplane, with abandoned, big, 80-mm anti-aircraft guns, and with hundreds of empty shells and rounds of live ammunition. In a canal, I saw half-sunk barges and pontoon bridges next to the rubble of blown-up bridges; and numerous houses had been half-torn open by explosions.

From Twente, we continued our missions, flying almost daily sorties to assist the Canadian infantry and tanks in their advance to Hamburg. The airfield was littered with the same debris I had seen along the roads, everywhere. My God, had we done that? Was this the result of our bullets, our bombs and rockets? Why did these Germans go on? We had capitulated in 1940, when there was no point in just losing more people. But these animals continued fighting, and their unbelievable deeds in prisons and concentration camps also continued.

Nine days after my visit with my parents, I received a telegram through the Red Cross. My father had died the day after my visit.

The squadron moved once again, this time to Varrelsbusch, a large German airfield near Hanover. To my surprise, the war wasn't over yet. The Russians were on the outskirts of Berlin; we had crossed the Elbe near Magdenburg and the American Army had met the Russians at Leipzig. We had captured more than a million German prisoners of war, and yet there were hot pockets of German resistance.

On 30 April 1945, at 3:30 p.m., Hitler allegedly shot himself and his mistress, Eva Braun, in his command bunker in Berlin. It is believed that his close friends and personal guards poured gasoline over the bodies and set them on fire to destroy the evidence. What evidence there was to be destroyed is unclear. The bodies of Hitler and Braun were never found and speculation remains to this day as to their actual fate. But there was no doubt about the guilt of this man and his responsibility for the deaths of millions of innocent people.

Herman Goering tried to flee but was captured in Austria. Borman disappeared. Himmler tried to flee, disguised as a farmer, and when caught, poisoned himself. Several Germans were found with glass cyanide capsules, which they could keep in their mouths and break simply by biting. Herman Goering did just that, when he realized he would be accused of war crimes.

Even during these last days of the war, we flew a few missions over pockets of final resistance. We even lost one of our pilots who, in his attack, came too low and smashed into the ground. What a terrible waste!

On 4 May 1945, the Germans surrendered in northwest Germany, Holland, Denmark, and Norway. On 7 May, we flew our last operational mission. On that same day came the total and unconditional surrender of all German forces, with General Jodl signing for the Germans and General Bedell Smith signing for the Allies. General Eisenhower proclaimed 8 May 1945, VE-Day.

The war was over. The 322 Dutch Spitfire Squadron had flown 4,896 missions and 6,382 combat hours. We helped win the war, but at a price; we had lost twenty-six pilots in the 322 Squadron alone. The damage to Holland and the loss of lives of Dutch relatives, friends, and citizens was uncountable – the figures ran into the hundreds of thousands.

We stayed at Varrelsbusch another six weeks as an occupation force, but the shooting was over. I made a trip to see my mother and we visited my father's grave near Ede. Here she lived in a small cottage, given to her by an old family friend.

In spite of the bad feelings and hatred toward the Germans, there was a jubilant atmosphere of victory in Holland and in all other liberated countries. There were celebrations and festivities everywhere. In full squadron strength, we flew demonstrations over The Hague, dropping a large Dutch flag on a square in the middle of the city. We attended a patriotic party where we were honoured as the liberators of our country, much like those who helped Holland win its historical liberation from the Spanish in the seventeenth century. My 'War Pilots of Orange' deserved the honour bestowed on them that day.

The contrasts at Varrelsbusch were incredible. It was one of the very large Luftwaffe bases, with officers' quarters like modern apartment buildings. Sports fields, gymnasiums and an Olympic swimming pool surrounded the lush clubs for officers and enlisted men. The airfield and runways were cleared for us to use, but the amount of war debris on and around the runways formed a lurid contrast to the grandeur of earlier days.

Trucks, tanks, and other war vehicles, all partially destroyed, were strewn around by the hundreds. On the concrete platforms, the newest rocket planes and jets – some still in factory crates – had been smashed by the Germans to render them unusable by the Allies. This was another example of the Germans blindly following obsolete, dogmatic military thinking.

We would not have used these new weapons against them; there was no need. We not only had the damaged rocket planes for examination and study, but we had the factories that had made them. But then, we had done the same thing in 1940. Just before the Germans arrived at Schiphol airfield, we had piled our remaining Fokker D-21s in a heap and set them on fire. Why, nobody really knew.

As in 1940, there was an automatic brotherhood among the fighter pilots of the 322. This probably occurs because a fighter squadron is a relatively small unit, with a combat strength of twelve to sixteen planes. The leaders are always fighter pilots themselves, leading the attacks as the first men going into action. The squadron leaders and the flight commanders were themselves 'one of the boys'. That is why combat fighter pilots feel a bond, a feeling of belonging to a very special brotherhood that will last forever.

The entire squadron marched in the Victory Parade in London, along with twenty thousand representatives of all of the Allied forces that had fought together to beat the Germans and the Japanese, after their treacherous attacks in the early days of World War II. The squadron was dismantled as an RAF unit and immediately reinstated as the first operational unit of the new Dutch Air Force.

I was promoted and sent to the general staff at The Hague, as chief of the Department of the Air Force. There, under the leadership of the Dutch chief of staff, General Kruls, and Prince Bernhard, we laid the groundwork for the independent Royal Dutch Air Force.

My mother went back to The Hague. My sister, who had come to England shortly after the liberation of Paris, worked at the Queen's office and now joined the MARVA, the women's component of the Dutch navy.

There was a lot to be built up – the new air force, the army, the navy, the KLM, and thousands of other official and private businesses; but also our own lives.

What was I to do with the rest of my life? Continue in the military? I had done my duty as a military man, even made quite a career. Circumstances had provided an opportunity for a career in the military that few people could ever have. But at heart I was a doctor and halfway through medical school. I had made a promise to my father and to myself.

The post-war situation in Holland was bad. There were shortages of everything, and damaged and ruined property plagued all the bigger towns and cities. Even worse were the losses of husbands, sons, daughters, and friends – losses that could not be replaced. Emotions and feelings were shown openly, and hatred of the Germans could not be kept hidden.

Many of those Dutch who had been collaborators, informers, and outright traitors tried to flee to Germany, where they hoped they would not be recognized. The rage of people and their desire to get even with those who were thought to be responsible got out of hand. Traitors were lynched, until the provisional government acted to provide protection, in order to prevent a blood bath and settlements of personal vendettas.

Every day I went to my office at the general staff headquarters and tried to evaluate my own thinking. I could work all day on the plans of our future air force. But I also could see myself as an honourable military man, probably of high rank, yet constantly confronted with the conviction that I should be a doctor, not a soldier.

In a military setting, I would be reminded of the tragedy of my family and my country. As a physician, I could pursue my dear wish to become an obstetrician and help new life arrive in this world – just the opposite of war and killing. As a physician, I would preserve the beauty of the living and ease the pain and suffering of humans. My ideals of years ago came back, stronger than ever. But then, would I be able to go back to the school benches and study? Had my five years of war experience made me unfit for academic study, for quietly absorbing the mountains of knowledge in medical science?

At general staff headquarters, I drafted the basic organizational plan for the new air force. With a huge blueprint on an easel, I presented the plan to a committee which included Prince Bernhard, the prime minister, the secretary of defence, Mr Plesman of the KLM, and a number of generals and other military men involved in the rebuilding of Holland's post-war military forces.

After the presentation, Mr Plesman pulled me aside and offered me a job as chief of flying services for the KLM, the Royal Dutch Airlines. At that moment my mind was made up.

I said, 'Thank you, Mr Plesman, but I will be a doctor.'

Epilogue

The book, in its first printing, was entitled, *War Pilot of Orange*. It details a sequence of events which, in the author's words, were not planned by him. When the 322 Dutch Spitfire Squadron was established in 1943, it was a regular RAF unit with a handful of Dutch pilots. By the end of the war it had earned its laurels as a complete Dutch combat unit. The squadron received its own coat of arms, true to RAF tradition, but the motto under the shield was in Dutch: *Niet praten maar doen* (Don't talk but do). Vanderstok served as the squadron's last wartime commander.

At the conclusion of the war, Vanderstok returned to the University of Utrecht. He graduated from medical school and took his Hippocratic Oath in 1951.

With his wife Lucie and three small children, he emigrated to the United States. There he continued his medical studies in Syracuse, New York. Later he moved to New Mexico to establish a private practice.

When their children grew up and reached college age, the family moved to California. But Bram accepted a position with NASA in Huntsville, Alabama. He participated in the medical programmes of the Space Lab, which was being constructed as a model at the huge Redstone Arsenal Army Base at Huntsville.

He subsequently moved to Hawaii and practised medicine for an addition twelve years. An active sailor, he volunteered for the US Coast Guard Auxiliary, performing 162 rescues and assists at sea with his thirty-foot boat, appropriately called *The Flying Dutchman*.

Vanderstok was decorated thirteen times by Queen Wilhelmina of the Netherlands and by the governments of Great Britain, Belgium, France, and the United States. He earned the Distinguished Flying Cross twice. He was awarded the British Order of the British Empire (OBE) and became a knight in the Dutch Order of Orange-Nassau.

An interesting postscript to Vanderstok's experience was a personal request by Stalag Luft III's former camp commandant Colonel Friedrich Wilhelm von Lindeiner genannt von Wildau. At the end of the war, von Lindeiner had been arrested by British authorities in relation to his role in the murder of fifty RAF officers participating in the Great Escape. The commandant, an old-school Prussian military officer, had run the POW camp in a strict but humane manner. The request was a solicitation for positive testimony in his British court martial. Many POWs did offer such testimony, but Vanderstok's experience differed in that he returned to the Netherlands to find two brothers murdered in concentration camps and his father tortured by the Gestapo. Indeed, while incarcerated in Stalag Luft III, the Gestapo, in Holland, had demanded Vanderstok's extradition, based on the fact that he was an enemy military pilot who had escaped their oversight in an occupied country and joined the RAF. Von Lindeiner refused, knowing that such demands usually resulted in a prisoner's death. Harsh correspondence between von Lindeiner and the Gestapo continued for over a year. So, although von Lindeiner had protected Vanderstok from the Gestapo, he did declare, upon discovering that Vanderstok was one of three successful escapees, 'Had I known then how Vanderstok would behave later on [referring to the escape], I might not have compromised myself so much on his behalf.' Vanderstok acknowledged an inherent decency in the former commandant, but felt that his linkage to the corrupt Nazi regime disallowed him from testifying on his behalf. However, neither would he testify against von Lindeiner.*

---

* Extracted from: Tim Carroll, *The Great Escape from Stalag Luft III*; Arthur A. Durand, *Stalag Luft III: The Secret Story*; and Marilyn Jeffers Walton and Michael C. Eberhardt, *From Commandant to Captive: The memoirs of Stalag Luft III Commandant Col. Freiderich Wilhelm von Lindeiner.*

Glossary of Air Force and *Kriegie* Jargon

appel — Roll call

battledress — Combat uniform, work uniform

Blitz — Lightning, fast military operations

cockerel — Code word for electronic IFF gadget

cooler — Prison cells in Stalag Luft III

Donner Wetter — German slang similar to 'Good Heavens'

Feldwebel — German rank, sergeant

ferret — Specially trained German prison guard

flak — Flugzeug Abwehr Kanonen, anti-aircraft guns

flieger — Pilot

Focke-Wulf — German aircraft manufacturer

geschwader — Squadron

Geus — Dutch name for patriotic freedom fighters loyal to House of Orange (plural: Geuzen)

goon — German guard in POW camp

gremlin — A nasty little bug that causes trouble in engines and everything else

Hauptmann — Captain (Air Force, Army)

Hun — A not so civilized German

Hurricane — English fighter plane

IFF — Identification Friend or Foe (electronic)

Luft — Air, sky

Luftwaffe — German Air Force

Luger Standard German Army pistol
Limey Nickname for English draftee (unfavourable)
maquis Armed Frenchmen and women, guerilla fighters, resistance fighters
Me.109 Messerschmitt-109, German fighter plane
Mof Dutch nickname for Germans (very unfriendly)
Mustang American fighter plane
OTU Operational Training Unit
Stalag Stammlager, prison camp
Staffel Part of a squadron, 3 or 6 planes (German)
stooges Workers who did general work in the secret Big X organization
Sagan Town in East Germany where Stalag Luft III was
Stuka Sturtz Kampf flugzeug. German dive-bomber
Soho Chinatown in London
scheissen defecate, shit
Tube London subway
U/S Unserviceable, Spitfires being repaired
Wings, Wingco Short for Wing/Commander
zebra stripes Black-and-white stripes on the wings of all Allied aircraft on D-Day, for easy recognition